PALGRAVE STUDIES IN CULTURAL AND INTELLECTUAL HISTORY

Series Editors

Anthony J. La Vopa, North Carolina State University

Suzanne Marchand, Louisiana State University

Javed Majeed, King's College, London

The Palgrave Studies in Cultural and Intellectual History series has three primary aims: to close divides between intellectual and cultural approaches, thus bringing them into mutually enriching interactions; to encourage interdisciplinarity in intellectual and cultural history; and to globalize the field, both in geographical scope and in subjects and methods. This series is open to work on a range of modes of intellectual inquiry, including social theory and the social sciences; the natural sciences; economic thought; literature; religion; gender and sexuality; philosophy; political and legal thought; psychology; and music and the arts. It encompasses not just North America but also Africa, Asia, Eurasia, Europe, Latin America, and the Middle East. It includes both nationally focused studies and studies of intellectual and cultural exchanges between different nations and regions of the world, and encompasses research monographs, synthetic studies, edited collections, and broad works of reinterpretation. Regardless of methodology or geography, all books in the series are historical in the fundamental sense of undertaking rigorous contextual analysis.

Published by Palgrave Macmillan

Indian Mobilities in the West, 1900–1947: Gender, Performance, Embodiment
By Shompa Lahiri

The Shelley-Byron Circle and the Idea of Europe
By Paul Stock

Culture and Hegemony in the Colonial Middle East
By Yaseen Noorani

Recovering Bishop Berkeley: Virtue and Society in the Anglo-Irish Context
By Scott Breuninger

The Reading of Russian Literature in China: A Moral Example and Manual of Practice
By Mark Gamsa

Rammohun Roy and the Making of Victorian Britain
By Lynn Zastoupil

Carl Gustav Jung: Avant-Garde Conservative
By Jay Sherry

Law and Politics in British Colonial Thought: Transpositions of Empire
Edited by Shaunnagh Dorsett and Ian Hunter

Sir John Malcolm and the Creation of British India
By Jack Harrington

The Scottish Enlightenment: Race, Gender, and the Limits of Progress
By Silvia Sebastiani

Art and Life in Modernist Prague: Karel Čapek and His Generation, 1911–1938
By Thomas Ort

Music and Empire in Britain and India: Identity, Internationalism, and Cross-Cultural Communication
By Bob van der Linden

Geographies of the Romantic North: Science, Antiquarianism, and Travel, 1790–1830
By Angela Byrne

Fandom, Authenticity, and Opera: Mad Acts and Letter Scenes in Fin-de-Siècle Russia
By Anna Fishzon

Memory and Theory in Eastern Europe
Edited by Uilleam Blacker, Alexander Etkind, and Julie Fedor

The Philosophy of Life and Death: Ludwig Klages and the Rise of a Nazi Biopolitics
By Nitzan Lebovic

The Dream of a Democratic Culture: Mortimer J. Adler and the Great Books Idea
By Tim Lacy

German Freedom and the Greek Ideal: The Cultural Legacy from Goethe to Mann
By William J. McGrath and Edited by Celia Applegate, Stephanie Frontz, and Suzanne Marchand

Beyond Catholicism: Heresy, Mysticism, and Apocalypse in Italian Culture
Edited by Fabrizio De Donno and Simon Gilson

Translations, Histories, Enlightenments: William Robertson in Germany, 1760–1795
By László Kontler

Negotiating Knowledge in Early Modern Empires: A Decentered View
Edited by László Kontler, Antonella Romano, Silvia Sebastiani, and Borbála Zsuzsanna Török

William James and the Quest for an Ethical Republic
By Trygve Throntveit

The Uses of Space in Early Modern History
Edited by Paul Stock

Genealogies of Genius
Edited by Joyce E. Chaplin and Darrin M. McMahon

Genealogies of Genius

Edited by

Joyce E. Chaplin and Darrin M. McMahon

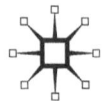
First published 2016 by
PALGRAVE MACMILLAN

The authors have asserted their rights to be identified as the authors of this work
in accordance with the Copyright, Designs and Patents Act 1988.

Palgrave Macmillan in the UK is an imprint of Macmillan Publishers Limited,
registered in England, company number 785998, of Houndmills, Basingstoke,
Hampshire, RG21 6XS.

Palgrave Macmillan in the US is a division of Nature America, Inc., One
New York Plaza, Suite 4500, New York, NY 10004-1562.

Palgrave Macmillan is the global academic imprint of the above companies and has
companies and representatives throughout the world.

ISBN: 978-1-137-49764-2
E-PDF ISBN: 978–1–137–49767–3
DOI: 10.1057/9781137497673

Distribution in the UK, Europe and the rest of the world is by Palgrave Macmillan®,
a division of Macmillan Publishers Limited, registered in England, company number
785998, of Houndmills, Basingstoke, Hampshire RG21 6XS.

Library of Congress Cataloging-in-Publication Data

Genealogies of genius / [edited by] Joyce E. Chaplin and
Darrin M. McMahon.
    pages cm.—(Palgrave studies in cultural and intellectual history)
    Includes bibliographical references and index.

    1. Genius—History. I. Chaplin, Joyce E., editor.

BF412.G385 2015
153.9'8—dc23   2015019296

A catalogue record for the book is available from the British Library.

Contents

Figures

1
Introduction

Joyce E. Chaplin and Darrin M. McMahon

"Genius" is a seductive term and slippery too—used often, and frequently abused. Motivational speakers, magazine editors, and the authors of inspirational biographies have certainly grasped its appeal, to say nothing of the hopeful parents of tiny potential Mozarts, Austens, and Einsteins. But though genius's allure helps to keep it in the public eye, popular fascination has tended to put scholars on guard. The late French philosopher Jacques Derrida acknowledged as much when he dared to broach the subject at a formal gathering among scholars in 2003. "In according the least legitimacy to the word 'genius,'" he confessed, "one is considered to sign one's resignation from all fields of knowledge...This noun 'genius,'" he added, "makes us squirm."[1] Some academic observers have doubted whether a word so commonly used can possess genuine meaning or intellectual merit. Others have worried about its associations with discredited theories of human superiority and inferiority. Social scientists and psychologists, meanwhile, respond by attempting to pin down the criteria of genius with greater rigor, hoping to detect its presence and understand its spread among populations for the benefit of humanity. As the psychologist Lewis Terman, a key architect of the IQ exam, put it in his landmark *Genetic Studies of Genius* (1925), "The origins of genius, [and] the natural laws of its development are scientific problems of almost unequaled importance for human welfare."[2]

Whatever the veracity of that claim, the impetus behind it points to a presumption that the chapters in this volume seek to question: that genius is a constant and recurring phenomenon among human populations. That presumption, in turn, highlights the fact that genius as a *historical* concept, rather than as a presumed transhistorical fact, is surprisingly underexamined. Only a handful of studies to date have attempted to explain its emergence and development as a contingent category, one shaped by the exigencies of time and place.[3] Building on this budding interest, the chapters in this volume seek to examine the uses to which concepts of genius have been put in different cultures and times. Collectively, they are designed to make two new statements. First, seen in historical and comparative perspective, genius is not a natural fact and universal human constant that has been only recently identified by modern science, but instead it is a categorical mode of assessing human ability and merit. Second, as a concept with specific definitions and resonances, genius has performed specific cultural work within each of the societies in which it has had a historical presence.

It is precisely because of the varying historical manifestations of genius that we suggest it had multiple genealogies, even as its branching lines of descent can be traced to a common ancestor. That shared ancestry is at least as complex as it is long, but its main developments occurred in three phases during the ancient, early modern, and modern eras. In the first phase, the ancient Greeks referred to *daimones* (demons)—what in Latin would be called a *genius*—to describe a type of divinity that offered protection or inspiration. Such entities could occupy hearth and household, they could accompany individuals into workshops or onto battlefields, or they could hover over families, communities, and even entire nations. *Daimones* might be "demonic" in the present and negative sense of that word, or they could be what later peoples would think of as angelic; the idea of having two guiding *daimones*, good and evil, itself comes from antiquity. For the Romans, a *genius* originally meant this kind of deity, though gradually the term began to imply not just the origin of the divine force that possessed one but also the gift that an individual possessed. In Roman times (and here we see one origin of a long-standing and insidious prejudice), only men were thought to possess a *genius*. All men had a *genius* for something, which gave shape to their individual character, but the greatest individuals could lay claim to a superior force of this kind—what Cicero, in describing the *daimonion* or "little demon" of Socrates, called the philosopher's *quiddam divinum*, his "divine something." That mysterious force was what set a man such as Socrates—said by the oracle at Delphi to have been the wisest who lived—apart from all others. It was the supernatural source that gave him superhuman, even godlike, powers.

The eventual dominance of Christianity in Europe did not dispel these associations, nor did it do away with the name or the concept of the pagan *genius*. Although Christian monotheism in its western and eastern manifestations certainly discouraged open acceptance of blessings that did not come from the Trinity, faith in interventions from angels, appeals to patron saints, and fear of demonic influence bore more than passing resemblances to the pagan beliefs that had preceded them. In short, the *daimones* and *genii* survived.[4] Well into the seventeenth century, European dictionaries bore testimony to that fact, recording, like Robert Cawdrey's *A Table Alphabeticall of Hard Usual English Words* (1604), that genius implied "the angell that waits on man, be it a good or evil angell."[5]

Genius as a notion that bore a more direct relationship to the modern understanding of individuals of superior creative or intellectual endowments began to emerge only gradually in the early modern period and rose to prominence in the eighteenth century. During the Renaissance, the elision of the word *genius* with *ingenium*, a classical Latin term for natural talent or ability, began to articulate the possibility that human beings could actually possess godlike abilities, not just borrow them or receive them via divine inspiration or bestowal.[6] "Genius," that is to say, began to imply a kind of superior human mind, an understanding that gained widespread acceptance during the eighteenth century, when illustrious individuals were celebrated as geniuses themselves, persons who embodied the force of genius.

Indeed, whatever the place of reason in the Enlightenment, and despite that era's amply noted liberationist tendencies in political philosophy and actual reform, it was precisely during this period that the genius figure achieved prominence as a member of a kind of supra-human elite with godlike capacities that seemed to surpass ordinary human reason. That may have been gratifying to the early living exemplars—almost exclusively white men of European origin—though genius, like sainthood, was most often conferred after the fact. Still, it is from contemporary descriptions that we inherit the designation of Jean-Jacques Rousseau, for example, as a genius in letters, Isaac Newton or Benjamin Franklin as geniuses in natural science, or Napoleon Bonaparte as a genius in statecraft and war. This novel meaning of genius as a human individual of original and exalted powers was also, in the eighteenth century, extended backward in time, bestowed upon the likes of Homer or William Shakespeare, neither of whom would have recognized the label in its new form, however convinced the latter may have been of his "ingenuity" and "genius" for playmaking.[7]

But it was really only during the modern period, the nineteenth century and continuing into the twentieth, that geniuses acquired the full range and complement of associations they now most commonly share. The genius became in this period a human paragon—unique, exceptional, and one of a kind—and yet somehow multiplying in ever-greater numbers and across an expanding set of domains. The proliferation was first apparent in terms of Romantic definitions of the individual, and especially the artist, as beyond human typicality. That view endorsed a strong sense of individual differentiation, indeed of individualism as essential to the human personality—any personality. But geniuses were deemed more individual than ordinary human beings, less likely to think and act by established conventions and norms, genuinely original and so often eccentric, or even mad.[8] Geniuses were imagined as lawgivers and lawmakers (at times lawbreakers) who challenged established authorities in art and thought and were believed to follow a higher law. And they were driven by powerful energies and an intense capacity for sustained concentration and labor.

As if to make genius indelible, beyond any human ability to acquire or alter it, nature was assigned a fundamental role in governing human experience (and determining human aptitude). That designation of genius as deeply natural grounded it within each person who had it, or supplied him (typically) with an intensity of knowledge from without, as in Wordsworth's "impulse from a vernal wood." And it was precisely because of their engagement with nature, with universal truths based in materiality, that many more scientists joined artists as the kinds of people thought most likely to personify genius, just as they increasingly played a role—in fields such as phrenology, craniometry, statistics, and medical psychology—in identifying its alleged presence. Whereas artists broadly conceived (poets, musicians, painters, etc.) captured truths about the human soul, scientists saw into the tiniest constituents of life and across the vast expanse of the universe. Together, they could be imagined as visionaries and prophets, revealers of wonder. At the same time, those working in the human sciences—philosophy or social theory—might lay claim to such prerogatives. Nietzsche would be hailed as a prophet, or, as Engels said of Marx, a "genius." Statesmen, finally, could be styled (or style themselves) on the model of Napoleon as visionaries and "artists," who might shape from human material works of imagination, originality, and sublime and transcendent power.

Such emerging cultural ideals helped to give genius, and geniuses, a commanding presence in nineteenth-century Europe, as well as the neo-Europes created by imperialism abroad. Even before the cults surrounding the British Lake Poets, and thereafter resounding in the reverence for cultural figures and virtuosi such as Byron, Beethoven, Goethe, Verdi, Delacroix, Darwin, Hugo, and Wagner, the ideal of the genius figure merged with that of the celebrity, who was also an eighteenth-century invention.[9] The hundreds of thousands of well-wishers and enthusiasts who attended Victor Hugo's funeral in 1885 are just one indication of the extraordinary outpouring of reverence for publicly recognized "geniuses," whose lives and deaths were followed closely in the press, encouraging a trade in "relics" and memorabilia, along with "pilgrimages" to select sites of memory.[10] Such veneration, whether among the living or the special dead, carried over into the first half of the twentieth century, when contemporaries were quick to compare the worship of genius to a "religion," replete with martyrs such as Van Gogh, saints such as Einstein, and wizards such as Edison.[11] And though, after World War II, the religious enthusiasm for great men was steadily called into question, a figure such as Picasso could still pay his restaurant bills with a sketch. Genius commanded privilege.

Arguably, it does so still—witness the adulation heaped on Stephen Hawking or Steven Jobs. Yet the gap between celebrity and genius, always close, is now closer than ever, with less and less differentiation between the two. At the same time, the field of possibility has widened well beyond the domains of high culture, science, and statecraft that once confined it. Geniuses now bask under that designation in every possible realm of human endeavor, from cooking, to sports and rock and roll, to the selling of goods on the Internet. The trend is quite obviously an aspect of a new willingness to democratize human excellence, to make exceptionalism typical, as if everyone were a genius at something. Never mind that this is paradoxical—what was once considered the prized possession of a natural human elite is now imagined to be within the grasp of all.

It is easy enough to mock the process. Already in the 1950s the philosopher Hannah Arendt was decrying what she saw as the "commercialization and vulgarization" of genius, and it is difficult today not to laugh when genius is presented in a thriving self-help literature as an aspirational goal (Learn to think like da Vinci!).[12] To be sure, the tendency to define genius broadly and democratically is laudable insofar as it has facilitated the recognition of extraordinary achievement in overlooked, maligned, or marginalized groups, especially those who have struggled against the historical exclusions of racism and sexism. Yet, to make everyone a genius would be the end of the idea. Do we face a future, to paraphrase Andy Warhol, when all might enjoy 15 minutes of genius? By that point, clearly, we would be ready for a new term.

In order to help make sense of these developments, this book aims to explore the changing fortunes of genius since its self-conscious birth in the eighteenth century. It aims to do so in new ways. For although the literature on genius is extensive, too rarely have scholars considered the subject from a position of historical awareness, let alone historical knowledge.[13] On the one hand, social and natural scientists since the nineteenth century have sought to identify the enduring properties of genius, searching (largely in vain) for its markers and traces in everything from cranial size to the intelligence quotient. Such investigations persist, as witnessed by the ongoing fascination with studying the brains of luminaries such as Einstein, while social psychologists continue to study the qualities and correlations of eminence and elite performance.[14] Scholars of literature, the arts, and aesthetics, on the other hand, though once concerned to identify genius and geniuses as the creators of timeless *chefs d'oeuvres*, have in recent decades been more interested in toppling genius as an arbiter of aesthetic distinction, unmasking its ideological character and exposing its myths.[15] Though often instructive, this literature has tended, with some exceptions, to eschew a broader historical analysis of genius in favor of exposing specific facets of its use around salient individuals or themes.[16] Finally, there persists to this day a celebratory literature that has accompanied genius since the eighteenth century. Seeking to glorify rather than to analyze or explain, such writings seldom bother to question the category they seek to promote.

The chapters of this volume, by contrast, build on recent work examining the history of genius in order to bring greater historical awareness to the complex and often contested ways the category has been deployed in the modern era.[17] The volume includes ten essays, which together span the eighteenth through the twentieth centuries, and is organized into three chronologically distinct sections that examine the changing meanings of genius over time. Collectively the essays bring to light a revealing and persistent paradox: that the conceptual category of genius, understood as a natural and privileged form of human difference constituting a new kind of human elite, emerged alongside and often in conjunction with modern democratic societies that frequently claimed legitimacy on the basis of some form of human equality. As with all historical paradoxes, this demands explanation, which the essays of the volume undertake in a series of focused, evocative case studies.

The book's first section concentrates on definitions of genius in the age of Atlantic revolutions, the period of the modern genius's birth. At that time, multiple reforming trends called into question established ways of defining human beings as different from one another in order to organize them,

accordingly, into hierarchies. Were aristocrats really superior to common-
ers by blood? Was there really such a thing as a natural slave? How could
one understand the differences between the sexes and between peoples
of different "races"? While the movements to abolish the slave trade and
emancipate slaves, and the political insurgencies that climaxed with revolutions in North America, France, the Caribbean, and "Latin" America did
not all conclude with the establishment of modern democracies, their legacies contributed to that longer history. But how large a contribution was it?
Historians have long pointed out that, beginning in the eighteenth century,
modern liberal regimes showed themselves particularly adept at defining
"liberal exclusions" to the rights and privileges accorded to others. Women
and people of color, among other disenfranchised groups, were held, on the
basis of a spurious new science and anthropology, to be less equal than others, thus calling into question the apparent self-evidence of the claim that
all were created equal. The category of genius, which sought to identify in
dramatic terms the disparity in natural human endowments, is useful in
this context as a means to further identify the extent to which revolutionary politics altered conceptions of human inequality in the American and
French republics. Joyce E. Chaplin thus considers "The Problem of Genius
in the Age of Slavery," examining how the word was applied to new world
individuals, at first as a kind of incredulous admission that they, of all people, might be extraordinary, and then withdrawn once the designation
threatened to appear as an actual compliment, least of all with respect to
slaves or former slaves, and by implication others of non-European ancestry. Nathalie Heinich, in her chapter "Genius versus Democracy: Excellence
and Singularity in Postrevolutionary France," also establishes that utilizing
the label and concept of genius was logical in postrevolutionary France. Yet
doing so clearly revealed what the revolution had not accomplished. Finally,
John Carson examines "Equality, Inequality, and Difference: Genius as
Problem and Possibility in American Political/Scientific Discourse," tracing
how deployment of "genius" within two professionalizing communities in
nineteenth-century the United States, those of politicians and scientists,
registered unease with what the concept implied about the postrevolutionary republic.

In the next section of the book, the authors analyze nineteenth-century
conceptions of genius, with particular attention to the role of science and to
the challenges of feminists. In "Genius and Obsession: Do You Have to Be
Mad to Be Smart?" Lennard J. Davis tackles the persistent efforts to link positive and negative forms of human exceptionalism, identifying the origins of
this shotgun marriage in nineteenth-century sciences of the human mind
and body. Janet Browne analyzes one particularly famous proponent of scientific definitions of genius—as themselves genealogies—in her "Inspiration to
Perspiration: Francis Galton's *Hereditary Genius* in Victorian Context," which
pays special attention to the class- and gender-specific assumptions about how
talent ran through families, though somehow unevenly, lodging with particular strength in some (including Galton, in his generous self-estimation), but

finding no purchase in others. Not everyone agreed. Lucy Delap focuses on the exclusion of women from concepts of genius and on the radical redefinitions that modern feminists accordingly insisted on to reshape the concept in her "'Genius must do the scullery work of the world': New Women, Feminists, and Genius, circa 1880–1920."

Chapters in the final section of the book concentrate on the twentieth- and twenty-first-century debates over who was or could be a genius. Julia Barbara Köhne, in "The Cult of the Genius in Germany and Austria at the Dawn of the Twentieth Century," examines genius idolatry in the German-speaking lands before and after World War I, a culturally and historically specific fascination that seems, in retrospect, ominous and prophetic. Irina Sirotkina, in her "Cultivating Genius in a Bolshevik Country," pursues the western concept of genius into the postrevolutionary Soviet Union where, no less than in postrevolutionary America or France, the idea both reinforced the status of certain heroic figures yet warred with the claims of a self-announced egalitarian state and society. David Bates traces a possibly even more radical affront to humanity. His chapter, "Insight in the Age of Automation," considers how modern definitions of that quality, as a peculiarly rapid and penetrating form of cognition, have been conditioned in large part in relation to artificial intelligence; no longer is the superhuman demonic, but instead, robotic. In the concluding chapter, Darrin M. McMahon's "Genius and Evil," the author examines the once widely disseminated contention that genius was somehow beyond good and evil. That, ultimately Nietzschean, contention existed well before Friedrich Nietzsche, and it would have a disturbing trajectory afterward, as incisively analyzed in the work of Thomas Mann.

What does this book not cover or, to put it another way, where might future research on the history of the concept of genius be fruitfully extended? It became clear in organizing and editing this volume that the concept of genius has been (and is being) much better studied in relation to the nations of the global West. On the face of it, and according to the dialectical tension between genius and democracy examined here, there is a certain logic to this pattern. Just as forms of democracy and arguments over political and social inequalities have dominated scholarship on western nations in a way that is less apparent for other parts of the world, so it would make sense that a subject like genius would have loomed less large in non-western historiographies. Certainly, the etymological history of genius, with the word's classical origins in the ancient Mediterranean, would indicate a birthplace for the concept, as well as its persistence in those societies claiming cultural descent from Greece and Rome. And it may be that the emergence of the concept of genius in the eighteenth century was related to religious and economic developments specific to the West, where it developed in tandem not only with (and as an antidote to) certain forms of disenchantment, but also with the dictates of commercial society.[18] As scholars have long recognized, genius—with its emphasis on creative originality—was a concept particularly well suited to buttressing emergent notions of intellectual copyright.[19]

And yet these same conjectures beg new questions. Future research might, for instance, draw comparisons with the understandings of divine protection (and inspiration) that extended well beyond the classical world to Africa and much of the ancient Near East, if not farther still. The old correlation between the West and modernity, moreover, of which increasing social and political equality has been a part, is itself suspicious. It may be an artifact of historiography rather than a fixed truth of history. Given that a steady and straightforward trajectory toward human equality is no longer assumed for the West (as this volume's essays themselves make clear), it is possible that nations and cultures that had even less linear histories of democracy were, nevertheless, incubators of concepts similar to that of genius. In any case, virtually all societies possess conceptions of intellectual, artistic, or inventive/creative heroism. In what ways are they comparable to the western paragon of genius, and how did they evolve in different social, religious, and economic contexts? The circulation of western ideas of genius to other parts of the world, moreover, and the subsequent patterns of cultural uptake, criticism, rejection, or modification, is a subject ripe for further exploration. It is our hope that future scholarship on the category of genius will take up some of these unexplored possibilities.

Finally, a word of thanks is due to the Huntington Library in Pasadena, California, and particularly to its successive directors of research, Robert C. Ritchie and Steve Hindle, who kindly allowed us to convene the majority of this volume's contributors for two days of fascinating discussions in the spring of 2012. It became very apparent to us there that the subject of genius has the capacity to stimulate passionate interest and exchange. We hope the essays in this volume will do the same.

Notes

1. Jacques Derrida, *Geniuses, Genealogies, Genres, & Genius: The Secrets of the Archive*, trans. Beverley Bie Brahic (New York: Columbia University Press, 2006), 3–4.
2. Lewis M. Terman, ed., *Genetic Studies of Genius*, 5 vols. (Palo Alto, CA: Stanford University Press, 1925–1959), 1: v.
3. The seminal study is Edgar Zilsel's *Die Entstehung des Geniebegriffes: Ein Beitrag zur Ideengeschichte der Antike und des Frühkapitalismus* (Tübingen: J. C. B. Mohr, 1926). See also Penelope Murray, ed., *Genius: The History of an Idea* (Oxford: Blackwell, 1989); Norbert Elias, *Mozart: Portrait of a Genius*, ed. Michael Schröter (Berkeley: University of California Press, 1993); Tia DeNora, *Beethoven and the Construction of Genius: Musical Politics in Vienna, 1792–1803* (Berkeley: University of California Press, 1995); Jochen Schmidt, *Die Geschichte des Genie-Gedankens in der deutschen Literatur, Philosophie und Politik, 1750–1945*, 2 vols. (Heidelberg: Universitätsverlag, 2004). Most recently, the two editors of this volume have published studies on the subject: Joyce E. Chaplin, *The First Scientific American: Benjamin Franklin and the Pursuit of Genius* (New York: Basic Books, 2006); Darrin M. McMahon, *Divine Fury: A History of Genius* (New York: Basic Books, 2013).
4. The story of the transmutation of the ancient *genii* into Christian and modern forms of spiritual guardians is told in McMahon, *Divine Fury*, esp. chs. 1–2. See also Jane Chance Nitzsche, *The Genius Figure in Antiquity and the Middle Ages* (New York: Columbia University Press, 1975), and Jean-Patrice Boudet, Philippe Faure, and Christian Renoux,

eds., *De Socrate à Tintin: Anges gardiens et démons familiers de l'Antiquité à nos jours* (Rennes: Presses Universitaires de Rennes, 2011).

5. Robert Cawdrey, *A Table Alphabeticall of Hard Usual English Words* (1604), a facsimile reproduction with an introduction by Robert A. Peters (Gainesville, FL: Scholars' Facsimiles and Reprints, 1966), 61.

6. On *ingenium* and the fusion of *genius* and *ingenium*, see Zilsel, *Die Enstehung des Geniebegriffes*, 265–96; Harald Weinrich, "Ingenium," in *Historisches Wörterbuch der Philosophie*, ed. Joachim Ritter, 13 vols. (Basel: Schwabe, 1971–2007), 4: 36–63, and the discussion in the text and appendix of *ingenium* in Patricia Emison's *Creating the "Divine" Artist: From Dante to Michelangelo* (Leiden: Brill, 2004).

7. See Chaplin, *First Scientific American*, 1–3, 134–36; 342; Fred Inglis, *A Short History of Celebrity* (Princeton, NJ: Princeton University Press, 2010), 37–73; McMahon, *Divine Fury*, ch. 3, and Jonathan Bates, *The Genius of Shakespeare* (New York and Oxford: Oxford University Press, 1998), esp. ch. 6 ("The Original Genius").

8. References to the extensive literature on the perceived connection between genius and madness will be found in the essays that follow. A somewhat dated, but still essential, place to begin for the modern period is George Becker, *The Mad Genius Controversy: A Study in the Sociology of Deviance* (London: Sage, 1978).

9. Antoine Lilti, *Figures publiques: Aux origines de la célébrité (1750–1850)* (Paris: Fayard, 2014), and David Higgins, *Romantic Genius and the Literary Magazine: Biography, Celebrity, and Politics* (Milton Park, UK: Routledge, 2005).

10. McMahon, *Divine Fury*, ch. 5. On the fascination with the brains of geniuses, see Michael Hagner's excellent *Geniale Gehirne: Zur Geschichte der Elitegehirnforschung* (Munich: Deutscher Taschenbuch, 2007).

11. Edgar Zilsel, *Die Geniereligion: Ein kritischer Versuch über das moderne Persönlichkeitsideal*, intro. Johann Dvorak (Frankfurt: Suhrkamp, 1990 [1917]); Nathalie Heinich, *The Glory of Van Gogh: An Anthropology of Admiration*, trans. Paul Leduc Browne (Princeton, NJ: Princeton University Press, 1996); Julia Barbara Köhne, *Geniekult in Geisteswissenschaften und Literaturen um 1900 und seine filmischen Adaptionen* (Wien: Böhlau Verlag, 2014).

12. Hannah Arendt, *The Human Condition* (Chicago: University of Chicago Press, 1958), 210–11.

13. For a broad overview of scholarly (and other) attempts to study genius, see Darrin M. McMahon, "Where Have All the Geniuses Gone?," *The Chronicle Review*, October 21, 2013.

14. See, for example, Hans Jürgen Eysenck, *Genius: The Natural History of Creativity* (Cambridge: Cambridge University Press, 1995), or the prolific body of work on genius and creativity by the psychologist Dean Keith Simonton.

15. A notable exception is Harold Bloom, *Genius: A Mosaic of One Hundred Exemplary Creative Minds* (New York: Warner Books, 2002).

16. Noteworthy examples of this literature include Christine Battersby, *Gender and Genius: Towards a Feminist Aesthetics* (Bloomington: Indiana University Press, 1989); Andrew Elfenbein, *Romantic Genius: The Prehistory of a Homosexual Role* (New York: Columbia University Press, 1999); Barbara Will, *Gertrude Stein and the Problem of "Genius"* (Edinburgh: University of Edinburgh Press, 2000); Peter Kivy, *The Possessor and the Possessed: Handel, Mozart, Beethoven, and the Idea of Musical Genius* (New Haven, CT: Yale University Press, 2001).

17. In addition to the historical works already cited, see Kathleen Kete, *Making Way for Genius: The Aspiring Self in France from the Old Regime to the New* (New Haven, CT: Yale University Press, 2012); Eliyahu Stern, *The Genius: Elijah of Vilna and the Making of Modern Judaism* (New Haven, CT: Yale University Press, 2013); Patricia Fara, *Newton: The Making of a Genius* (New York: Columbia University Press, 2002).

18. For a discussion of the role of commerce, see John Hope Mason, *The Value of Creativity: The Origins and Emergence of a Modern Belief* (Burlington, VT: Ashgate, 2003), esp. chs. 4–6. On commerce and religion, see McMahon, *Divine Fury*, esp. 5–6, 71–75.

19. See, for example, Mark Rose, *Authors and Owners: The Invention of Copyright* (Cambridge, MA: Harvard University Press, 1983); Martha Woodmansee, "The Genius and

the Copyright: Economic and Legal Conditions of the Emergence of the 'Author,'" *Eighteenth-Century Studies* 17 (1984): 425–48; Zeynep Tenger and Paul Trolander, "Genius versus Capital: Eighteenth-Century Theories of Genius and Adam Smith's Wealth of Nations," *Modern Language Quarterly* 55 (1994): 169–89; Carla Hesse, "The Rise of Intellectual Property, 700 B.C.–A.D. 2000: An Idea in the Balance," *Daedalus* 131 (2002): 26–45.

2
The Problem of Genius in the Age of Slavery

Joyce E. Chaplin

In a private letter written in 1778, Ignatius Sancho, famous black British man of letters, deplored the persistence of racial prejudice, yet he did so in terms that proposed another kind of human inequality, and this has been the problem of genius ever since. Sancho reported (in order to denounce) an ongoing debate among white colonists and Britons over whether the African captive who had been taken to Boston as a child, sold as a slave, and named by her owners Phillis Wheatley, had herself actually written the *Poems on Various Subjects* published under her name in 1773. Sancho observed that Wheatley's poems had been preceded by a list of worthies who swore to her authorship, yet these testifiers made no comment on her status as chattel, let alone offered any criticism that she (or anyone else) might not deserve that degraded status:

> The list of splendid—titled—learned names, in confirmation of her being the real authoress—alas! shows how very poor the acquisition of wealth and knowledge is—without generosity—feeling—and humanity.—These good great folks—all know—and perhaps admired—nay, praised Genius in bondage—and then, like the Priests and the Levites in sacred writ, passed by—not one good Samaritan amongst them.[1]

Within the ongoing recovery of black authorship as a serious subject for those who study eighteenth-century literature, Sancho's letters to the great and the good have earned a particular place of merit. His evocative phrase, "Genius in bondage," has been quoted multiple times and often used as a title or subtitle for books written by those who work within the field. And yet Sancho's triad of words has never been fully contextualized within the history of the concept of genius. The phrase has instead tended to incite debate over whether Sancho was right: was Wheatley in fact a genius? That question accepts present-day definitions of genius, as a talent, or person possessing a talent, so far above the average that she or he is qualified to enter a pantheon, a short list of extraordinary worthies and their amazing works. In those terms, one is supposed to ask, does Wheatley deserve to be placed alongside Sappho, Dante, Shakespeare, Byron, Dickinson, and so on? Or was Sancho, in his well-meaning and protective rage about her, instead exaggerating her talents?[2]

One difficulty with this level of debate is that it does not bother to recover what Sancho, or any of his contemporaries, might have meant by using the word "genius," which did not carry the same meaning for him as it might for whoever would, today, confidently call Shakespeare a genius. What cultural work, exactly, did the word "genius" perform, in English, during the late eighteenth century, when it was used to describe a person of sub-Saharan African descent, a person who either was in or had only recently been released from bondage?

I interrogate the significance of Sancho and others in the late eighteenth century who put "genius" in proximity not only to slavery but, more specifically, to the chattel slavery that existed in the new world. And I do so to argue that, in the second half of the eighteenth century, chattel bondage based on racism and genius as an extraordinary human condition invoked statuses that were strangely similar. Each state was irresistible and involuntary; each also delivered its human subjects into a hierarchy. Both "race" and "genius" implied that people became what they were despite their willed intentions, and each suggested a kind of inequality. That was a problem. If someone disapproved of slavery because it used racist criteria to reduce human beings to a state of dependence that was corrupt, if not sinful, how then could they applaud instances of genius, which similarly supposed that unequal abilities might be implanted in humans from their birth within places or circumstances more or less conducive to genius, or perhaps even descend through certain lineages? If superior merit could be thus fixed within specific places or lineages, why not inferior statuses?

Although it had always had its critics, racially defined chattel slavery was only beginning in the eighteenth century to be publicly contested as unjust, and therefore defined as an injustice that would require substantial changes in law and society. Those who undertook the contestation were aware that they were up against centuries of arguments that social status (and concomitant levels of privilege and respect) could be determined by how, where, and to whom a person was born. Meanwhile, genius was beginning to signify a human capacity that sprang from some mysteriously endowed ability, which echoed the divinely instilled kind of genius that had once been conveyed by the word, yet was now thought to be something within human nature, if only among a minority of human beings.

All of this is to say that the phrase "genius in bondage" is particularly fascinating for its internal tension. Genius seems revolutionary, in the same way that contestation over the justice of fixed human statuses was revolutionary. Racially defined arguments for slavery seem to be the opposite. And yet this trio of ideas coexisted historically, as examples of how the likelihood of human equality seemed debatable, indeed, was debated. There was a similarity between genius as a human capacity unbidden and race as a marker of human biddability, convenient to the person who could command labor and service based on a naturalized theory of human inequality. Sancho himself reemphasized that odd family resemblance in the same letter quoted above, with a repeated use of the word "genius," this time in relation to rumors that Wheatley's owner had been slow to manumit the now-famous author: "It reflects nothing either to the glory or generosity of her master—if she is still his slave—except he glories in the *low vanity* of having in his wanton power a mind animated by Heaven—a genius superior to himself."[3]

It is useful to circle outward from Sancho's indignation in order to consider how genius was used to describe several new world persons, enslaved or free, black or white, with different levels of hesitation. In the cases of the black Americans, there was particular reluctance to make a full-throated claim that each had been born and destined to her or his glory, and this was true not solely of racist protests against that possibility. Rather, there was broader unease over the possibility that description of blacks as geniuses might imply an acceptance that individuals were born and destined to predetermined places in society, which, after all, followed the logic that supported chattel slavery in the Atlantic world. In this way, as in my chapter's title, I refer to David Brion Davis's canonical work, *The Problem of Slavery in the Age of Revolution* (1975), to point out that the tensions between old and new ways of classifying humanity continued beyond the age of revolution, the start of an era in which democracy began to be the default political condition. The newest, highest form of praise for human achievement—genius—was, in the end, problematically unrevolutionary and deeply undemocratic. Ever since, "genius" has carried traces of its awkward birth in the age of slavery, when it did as much to reinforce as to challenge long-standing belief in human inequality.

Race, place, and genius

It is by now standard scholarly practice to regard the eighteenth century as a watershed in the history of racism, as a time when racial categories were hardening and when the conviction that those categories could predict a definite and ethically justified place for everyone within the social hierarchy was becoming more difficult to assail, at least in any way that resulted in legal and political change. The longer history of racialized human categories, which extends back at least as far as the middle ages, makes this claim somewhat tenuous. So does the fact that antislavery gained ground precisely when racism was supposed to be doing so. These contrasting trends are not, on the surface of things, easy to reconcile, though they do indicate that, as skepticism over inherited status may have been growing over the course of the long eighteenth century, certain extreme categories of it were becoming flash points of debate, whether those extreme conditions were monarchy and aristocracy at the top end of society, or peasantry and chattel slavery toward the bottom.[4]

Certainly, ancestry and slavery were becoming coterminous, as the societies of the Atlantic gradually discarded exceptions, such as convict labor in parts of British America and galley slavery in the Mediterranean. Anyone who criticized the Atlantic slave trade, or (more boldly) slavery itself, therefore had to counter long-standing and hardening opinions among whites that people of African ancestry lacked the mental capacity to govern themselves, yet possessed bodies capable of performing hard labor under harsh circumstances when governed by others who would profit from the labor, directly or indirectly.[5]

These conclusions had been fundamental to the adoption of slavery throughout the Atlantic world, and they were eventually embellished with the talismanic prestige of the new science that was beginning to redefine natural phenomena. Eighteenth-century science did not invent these negative opinions, nor did it refute them. Rather, the new science's systematic observation and classification tended to reinforce the hierarchy of human differences that valorized Europeans, and, above all, European men. The often deliberate implication was that European civilization (including the development of science) was not historically contingent but instead the natural product of a certain kind of embodied intellect. After Linnaeus classified humans within the animal Creation, some theorists blurred still further the boundary between non-Europeans and animals, questioning whether Africans, for example, were really different from nonhuman primates. More casually, if no less damagingly, some men of science endorsed racial interpretations of humanity's physical characteristics. One of the founders of the Royal Society, William Petty, claimed of Africans that "the Mould of their skulls" showed how "they differ also in their Naturall Manners, and in the internall Qualities of their Minds."[6]

Meanwhile, people in eighteenth-century Europe and its overseas territories were rethinking the concept of genius. This was not a simple matter of redefining the word from one dominant meaning to another, however. What occurred was instead a multiplication of its meanings. The term and concept had originally described tutelary or household gods that protected certain people. Even when it began to describe humans, "genius" in earlier eras had typically meant a specific disposition or aptitude, often divinely instilled; a person so blessed had a genius for something or other. In the eighteenth century, the term also signified human intelligence, functioning as a near-synonym for intellect. According to these terms, an individual might possess genius in one of two ways: as someone with notable intelligence overall, or else as someone with a particular intellectual gift. Certain people might embody both.[7]

The term "genius" was also used to describe corporate capacities, most obviously in descriptions of national characters. This would be a lasting use of the idea of genius, as found in the ancient "airs, waters, places" tradition associated with Hippocrates, reinterpreted in Montesquieu's *Spirit of Laws* (1748) and in the blood-and-soil assessments of human character that ran from the romantic period and into the National Socialism of Hitler's Germany, if not beyond. This last usage is particularly relevant for the history of racism. Although definitions of human races as constituted through lineage may have attached racial characteristics to people in an inescapable way, a corresponding idea that different human races resulted from long adaptation to particular places made it seem that the consequences of such physical molding could not be undone, except over many if not dozens of generations. The ostensible slowness of that process was hardly likely to imply that the national genius of anyone would be altered on a time-scale of significance to workaday political and legal regimes.[8]

Finally, "genius" was becoming a noun applied to individual humans. In this way, it acquired the common definition still used today, with various atypical people being described as geniuses, usually positively. The newer definition by no means replaced the older ones—at first, it simply augmented them. That trend probably explains why the Google Ngram for the word "genius," in English, shows an impressive eighteenth-century spike, with use of the word trending upward beginning around 1750, peaking in the 1770s, and commencing a decline around 1800. It would be hard to argue that one comprehension of genius was suddenly generating all of these "hits"; it is more credible that multiple iterations of them were doing that together, and that once the meaning of the word narrowed, use of it dwindled.[9]

That this was an ongoing and productively incomplete transition during the long eighteenth century, and of particular relevance to the Atlantic societies built upon slavery, may also be seen in a keyword search of the Early American Imprints database of printed material from colonial British America and then the independent early American republic. Plug the word "genius" into the database and you generate 101 hits; put in the phrase "a genius," and you see only two results, and these direct you to two different editions of the same work. This is of course a rough measure, and yet that 101 to 2 ratio at least hints that, however much genius was beginning to indicate an extraordinary kind of person, it was still mostly used as a modifier in order to designate something characteristic of a nation or an individual. But these verbal proportions beg a question: how was the older meaning of genius being transformed by the newer one in order to designate a personal characteristic perhaps only found in certain exceptional individuals?[10]

Tracing that shift would indicate the extent to which the ingenuity that might have been present in many kinds of people—high born or low born; male or female; enslaved or free; European or not—was turning into something reserved only to a particular sort of person. That paragon existed among a minority or even among an elite. He (but maybe sometimes she) was a leader who should not be made to follow others.

In English, descriptions of genius as existing within some state of bondage had at first described white people, especially Europeans who found themselves subjected to political or confessional tyranny. Thus the dedication to Samuel Pufendorf's 1698 work, *Of the Nature and Qualification of Religion in Reference to Civil Society*, asked, in relation to religious intolerance, "How much more in-supportable must the Slavery of the Mind be to a sublime Genius, elevated above the common Sphere of bigotted Zealots Ignorance"? In 1755, Edward Kimber quoted a criticism of King James VI and I, which concluded that the monarch had "by his superstitious and arbitrary notions, endeavoured to fetter genius." In 1780, John Richard similarly remarked, in relation to Denmark, that "arbitrary governments ever fetter genius and damp inquiries."[11]

These comments described the fate of Europeans and, by doing so, took for granted that western European society, and its constituent ethnic groups, was perfectly able to foster manifestations of genius. In this regard, it is notable that many people within Europe itself were convinced that physical environment affected mental ability. They assumed that higher intelligence was embodied and therefore found only in certain bodies, especially in those likely to be found within Europe. Although this hemispheric prejudice would in the end be most powerfully expressed against non-Europeans, Creole settlers of European descent were in the meantime likewise stigmatized (which irked them). Doubts over their intellectual capacity reflected environmentalist prejudice against the new world, especially the suspicion that the Americas were too hot, too cold, too wet, or too arid to let any living creatures flourish there. In contrast to their European counterparts, it was widely maintained, American animals remained small and weak, and its humans were rendered timid and intellectually dim. There would also have been a not entirely unfounded sense that the American colonies were undersupplied with institutions of higher learning and had scarcer supplies of printed material.[12]

For all these reasons, there was a history of publications authored by colonial peoples having to be supported by affidavits that they were actually written by their stated authors—Wheatley's volume of poetry was not the first example of this. After having several of his essays rejected by the *Philosophical Transactions* of the Royal Society of London, for instance, Benjamin Franklin was careful to publish his *Experiments and Observations on Electricity* (1751) in London, with a preface written by John Fothergill, a fellow of the Royal Society, who vouched for Franklin as the "ingenious author" of the letters describing the electrical experiments that followed. Both Fothergill and one of the addressees of Franklin's letters, English merchant Peter Collinson, who agreed to have his name printed in the book, were testifying to a metropolitan audience that Franklin was who he claimed to be: the author of the work. Franklin summarized the situation precisely that way in his subsequent *Autobiography*, by saying that his French Cartesian critic, the abbé Nollet, had initially refused to believe that the *Experiments and Observations* could have come "from America," and thought it had instead been written by his (Nollet's) detractors. Only gradually was Nollet persuaded "that there really existed such a Person as Franklin of Philadelphia," as if Franklin's existence as a colonial who could do electrical experiments and write intelligently about them had been too incredible to be believed.[13]

And yet it was Franklin's categorical unlikelihood as a genius that seemed to make him convincing as one. In sharp contrast to the early incredulity over his work in science, he thereafter constituted an early example of the word "genius" being used as a noun to describe an individual, and it is important to remember the hemispheric prejudice against the new world and its human products as one context, if not a prompt, for this new usage. How else would someone from a benighted part of the world end up being so enlightened, unless he had within him some extraordinary ability that must erupt into public view, whatever the unlikely circumstances around him? We can trace the transformation of "genius" from modifier to noun over the rest of Franklin's life. For example, a 1753 American poem wished for Franklin "those honours that are virtue's meed, / Whate'er to genius wisdom has decreed!" and another description of 1761 described Franklin's "superiour and more penetrating Genius." But Penuel Bowen in 1771 called Franklin "the distinguish'd genius of America," not merely *a* genius, but *the* genius.[14]

The praise grew thicker and more intense, and tended over time to wonder whether Franklin was fully human. In Germany especially, the idea that Franklin had a near-supernatural power—the original attribute of genius—became commonplace. In 1756, Immanuel Kant proclaimed Franklin the Prometheus of the modern age because the modern American, like the mythological figure, had defied the gods in order to draw "fire" (meaning electricity) from the heavens. A German acolyte sent Franklin some verses (composed as a dialogue between the Moon and the Earth) that celebrated how the great colonial had protected "Mankind" from lightning; what was needed next, the Earth tells the Moon, was "still one Francklin more, to secure us [from] the Power of Death."[15]

For the rest of his life, Franklin would benefit from the extraordinary nature of his status as the lightning bolt that came out of no where: the self-taught experimenter, the provincial genius who had received barely any formal schooling, and the backwoods savant. His lack of formal education and his self-driven program of improvement both supported a sense that Franklin had a peculiar genius within him, rather than having had accomplishment drilled into him by others. This was a compliment to the individual, but one that still functioned as a critique of the Americas. Franklin's accomplishment could mean everything about him while meaning nothing about his new world context. If he were a paragon, after all, America might never produce another like him. Or maybe it could. Even the eighteenth century's foremost interpreter of American climates as curbs on animal excellence admitted that physical place did not predict human ability. The 1775–1776 translation into English of the natural history of Georges Le Clerc, comte de Buffon, cautioned that because "man can defend himself better than animals from the influence of climate," it followed that "there should be men strong, and well-made, men even of genius, in all countries."[16]

Genius in bondage?

If a free white man like Benjamin Franklin had initially seemed unbelievable as a man of learning, if not a genius, it is unsurprising that attribution of learning to people of African descent would raise similar questions, particularly if they were enslaved. To seem extraordinary, their accomplishments had to express an individual genius undampened by considerable privation, or else show the capacity of their American surroundings to elicit superior achievement. The former would coincide with new abolitionist sentiment that enslaved Africans shared all human attributes with whites; the latter did not necessarily do so, and yet did not represent a lower hurdle, given that the encomia about Franklin had not accepted that America itself could foster genius.

The growing public debate over the enslavement of people from Africa or of African descent would raise the stakes on when or whether "genius" could exist in bondage. This was a new worry, focused on modern categories of race, which had not functioned in the same way in earlier phases of western history. Despite the Aristotelian category of "natural slave," people in the ancient and medieval worlds had not hesitated to say that bondmen and -women might possess particular geniuses or talents. Slaves were often prized precisely because they were talented, even to the point of being philosophically learned, or because they were thought to embody particular characteristics of their native lands, which made them good cooks or horse-tamers or bedfellows—whatever was desired by a given population of slave buyers.[17]

But for a slave to be *a* genius was a modern possibility, and a modern problem. It raised the question of whether such an individual really ought to be owned by others who might be their intellectual inferiors. And that conclusion in relation to people of African descent would be especially contested. While racism may not have been present in the ancient and medieval worlds in precisely the same form that it would take in modern centuries, prejudice against sub-Saharan Africans was virulent and long-standing. Slaveholders in the eighteenth century could mine that rich seam of prejudice very effectively in order to argue that, even as other forms of social hierarchy were being adjusted, chattel slavery for black people should not be. For that reason, use of the word "genius" to describe enslaved or formerly enslaved black people is a good litmus test of confidence—or skepticism—as to whether examples of superior intellect were found in all lineages of humanity, or only in some.[18]

This is precisely the difficulty that Edward Long exploited in his vigorously pro-slavery *History of Jamaica*, first published in 1774. Throughout his work, Long was clear and consistent in his argument for a racial hierarchy, with white Europeans and black Africans at opposing positions on the social scale. Long was well aware that he needed to address a possible exception in the person of Francis Williams, a black contemporary. Williams was the son of Jamaican free blacks, who had made sure their child had access to books and was educated. He may, with the assistance of white patrons, have received some college-level education, perhaps at Cambridge, and thereafter lived in Jamaica as a free man among his books and scientific instruments, as his surviving portrait shows him. He was especially noted for his Latin odes, only one of which survives, because Long published it in order to criticize it and its author.[19]

"I shall endeavour to do him all possible justice," Long stated of his fellow Jamaican, "and shall leave it to the reader's opinion, whether what they shall discover of his genius and intellect will be sufficient to overthrow the arguments, I have before alledged, to prove the inferiority of Negroes to the race of white men." Here Long used genius simply to designate human intellect. He undermined any possible contention that Williams had an extraordinary share of that quality by arguing that he had been "the subject of an experiment" in human education. Long insisted that members of the wealthy English Montagu family had been sponsoring his education all along, a statement that simply erased Williams's black parents from the story and replaced them with cunning, meddling white people. Their experiment, Long contended, had educated Williams in certain rote ways, as one might instill tricks in animals. This was not a demonstration of human intellect, or genius, but simply proof that any creature with intelligence could be trained. Moreover, by pointing to the Montagus as Williams's trainers, Long implied that only white people based in the metropole themselves had the ability to instill a semi-educated capacity in a black man. Long relinquished the opportunity, therefore, to promote Jamaica as a place that nourished genius, which another author might have done in order to praise his homeland. (Long had been educated at an English school and then at one of London's Inns of Court.)[20]

Even more aggressively, Long attacked the implication that "genius" might indicate a superior talent, something found only among a few, which itself would admit that humankind could be sorted into hierarchical categories. As he concluded about one of Williams's Latin odes, "if we regard it as an extraordinary production, merely because it came from a *Negroe*, we admit at once that *inequality* of genius which has been before supposed, and admire it only as a rare phenomenon." In other words, champions of racial equality could not have their cake and eat it too; either humans were fundamentally similar, or else they were not. The language used to argue for humanity's merits or rights should be consistent. This was a devastatingly clever anticipation of arguments against slavery based on intellect. Long leaned over the cradle of genius, in its modern incarnation, and he cursed it.[21]

Even those who did not favor Edward Long's defense of slavery were nevertheless careful whenever they used the term "genius" to describe a published black author. Typically, they went no further than to use the word to designate intelligence in an equal comparison to whites. That was what George Washington did in relation to Phillis Wheatley in 1775. When Wheatley sent one of her poems to him, Washington wrote a thank-you note, praising how his correspondent had been "favored by the Muses." He also explained that he would have published the poem she had sent, whose topic was himself, "had I not been apprehensive, that, while I only meant to give the world this new instance of your genius, I might have incurred the imputation of vanity." Here the use of "genius" is ambiguous, connoting either intellect or a peculiar poetic gift, though just as clearly not signifying that Wheatley *was* a genius.[22]

It is interesting, however, that Washington required no affidavits from white men to assure him that Wheatley was capable of writing the poem she sent—it was possible for a slaveholder, even, to believe that. Yet, in contrast to Washington's confidence in her, it is equally interesting to compare the number of affidavits required to launch her 1773 volume of poetry to those Franklin had needed for his volume of electrical essays: the white man had needed two worthies; the black woman needed 18. Prejudice against white creoles was relatively easy to debunk, compared to prejudice against African ancestry.

Most of the surviving positive evaluations of black authors tended to follow Washington's lead, meaning they avoided any claim that the authors were geniuses. Instead, they argued that intellect was randomly distributed across the races, evident among all peoples and sometimes rising to high levels—if someone were disciplined enough to undertake self-cultivation. The latter point mattered, because it undercut any claim that black accomplishment was the result of white experimentation. It also avoided the problem Long had identified, of trying to argue for racial equality while also maintaining the possibility of radical inequality of ability.

For some critics of slavery, demonstration of intelligence as measured by something superior to mere literacy was enough to question whether black people should be considered social inferiors, best kept under the control of others. The Reverend Robert Boucher Nickolls, a British abolitionist, in 1788 used that basic criterion to challenge the comparisons that were still being made between Africans and animals, especially African primates. "Phillis Wheatley wrote correct English poetry within a few years after her arrival in Boston from Africa," Nickolls argued, "and there is a Latin ode of considerable length written in classic language by Francis Williams... I never heard of poems by a monkey, or of Latin odes by an oran-outang."[23]

And yet it was not obvious to all that Wheatley and Williams had not been trained, like animals, to perform tricks. London and even provincial centers had, after all, featured shows with nonhumans that had been trained to exhibit behaviors associated with humans. From 1766 to 1774, a "troupe" of bees in London had, with their human owner, swarmed in patterns that resembled military maneuvers. In 1785, a "learned pig" would entertain Londoners with tasks that made it appear it could read, count, and tell time. Even those who concluded that the pig had simply been drilled (meaning tormented) into these deeds nevertheless concluded that the performances were evidence of how swine had an intelligence that resembled that of humans. Resemblance, but not identical ability. Buffon's translators, for example, conveyed to English-speaking readers the naturalist's warning that intelligence existed within all species and yet varied over them too: "the dog's genius is only borrowed, the ape has but the appearance of sagacity, and the beaver is intelligible only to himself, and those of his species."[24]

For that reason, Wheatley and her supporters had been careful to identify her as the possessor of her own, and not borrowed, talents. Her preface stated that she was the "Author" of her poetic "Products" and that she had personally struggled to overcome "Disadvantages... with Regard to Learning." John Wheatley's affidavit, which then followed, also emphasized his bond-woman's self-willed transformation. The "Family" taught her to read "without any Assistance from School Education," but, as to "her WRITING, her own curiosity led her to it." Those two statements were followed, finally, by the collective testimony from 17 other white men who attested that Wheatley, though originally "an uncultivated Barbarian from *Africa*," was now "quali-fied" to write the poetry printed under her name. The list of signers included seven college-trained ministers, meaning those colonists most familiar with learning, potential critics of Wheatley's poetry, who instead endorsed it.[25]

This then was the crucial division: debate over whether intellect alone proved blacks equal to whites, with only an occasional claim that some of those who were or had been enslaved might be examples of particular gen-ius. A review of Wheatley's book of verse in the *London Magazine* stated that "these poems display no astonishing power of genius; but when we consider them as the productions of a young untutored African, who wrote them after six months casual study of the English language and of writing, we can-not suppress our admiration of talents so vigorous and lively." But a Boston newspaper took the leap, describing Wheatley as "the extraordinary Poetical Genius, Negro Servant to Mr. John Wheatley, of this Town." (At this point, no one felt it necessary to suspect that Boston lacked a bookish culture that permitted any such outcome.)[26]

That competing set of claims was applied, as well, to Sancho. The author of the preface to his published letters, which appeared in London in 1782, explained that the writings were laid before the public to show "that an untu-tored African may possess abilities equal to an European." The introduction to the volume pointed out that Sancho's eventual patrons had "strongly rec-ommended to his mistresses the duty of cultivating a genius of such apparent fertility." Statements of the innateness of this genius were meant to offset any implication that Sancho's abilities had been instilled rather than cultivated by superiors. Another testimonial made that implication still clearer by prais-ing "the extent of intellect to which Ignatius Sancho had attained by self-education," which must show that "the perfection of the reasoning faculties does not depend on a peculiar conformation of the skull or the colour of a common integument."[27]

These patterns of praise were apparent, as well, in assessments of another black author, Benjamin Banneker, a Maryland almanac maker active in the 1790s. As with Franklin's and Wheatley's key works, all of Banneker's alma-nacs bore affidavits from prominent white men. The editors of the first alma-nac, for example, extolled Banneker's "extraordinary Effort of Genius—a complete and accurate EPHEMERIS." They rejoiced "that the Rays of Science may alike illumine the Minds of Men of every Clime" and hoped that "a philanthropic Public, in this enlightened Era, will be induced to give their Patronage and Support to this Work."[28]

These patrons were careful to stress their protégé's self-education. In the first almanac, which introduced him to the world, various prefaces explain that Banneker had acquired his facility in astronomy through solitary study, without any formal instruction; he did his first ephemeris "without the least information, or assistance, from any person." Nor did he profit from "writings of genius and discovery, for of such he had none." The result "evinces, to Demonstration, that mental Powers and Endowments are not the exclusive Excellence of white People." At this point, at the very least, there was no longer suspicion that an American setting was an improbable one for superior mental achievement.[29]

These many examples of cautious praise for American-born black authors highlight the boldness with which Sancho described his fellow author, Phillis Wheatley. Although his phrase "genius in bondage" might not necessarily have signified that he thought Wheatley herself a genius, other phrases in his letter make clear that this was exactly what he meant. Against all the painstaking emphasis on Wheatley's disciplined self-education, Sancho's letter of 1778 claims that the poet had a natural gift not explained by human artifice: "Phyllis's poems do credit to nature—and put art—merely as art—to the blush." But if genius was a free gift of nature, or of nature's Creator, on what grounds might it be bound in chains that humans forged? Sancho presented this conundrum twice, first to denounce Mr. Wheatley for his "low vanity" in holding as his personal property an example of genius, and then again to lament the hypocrisy of anyone who was generally right-thinking on the issue of slavery but unwilling to act on principle when justice demanded action.[30]

The phrasing of Sancho's latter denunciation, however, undercuts his confidence that racism could be easily supplanted by justice. By choosing the parable of the Good Samaritan, he confronted a part of scripture that itself confronted prejudice. In this case, the prejudice was that which the ancient Jews had expressed against the Samaritans who were culturally, linguistically, and religiously similar to them, but not identical, and hence the antipathy. The parable may have been intended to rebuke a lack of humanity among Jews, but it became part of anti-Semitism, against them. And so, even within Sancho's own right-thinking little outburst of support for Wheatley, there are remnants of the immense and continuing prejudice against Jews that itself constituted a part of the history of racism, whether Sancho was aware of it or not. Moreover, he did not offer a solution to the paradox that Long had proposed, that if modern slavery were based on naturally unequal human capacities, then any praise given to an extraordinary person who would otherwise have been naturally fit for bondage itself participated in a discourse of inequality.[31]

Had the paradox been solved then, with some degree of consensus that Wheatley was a human being equal to any other, and her generally despised status made all the more tragic by her competing status as a published author, then perhaps there would be no dead-end debate today over whether she was truly a genius to rival Shakespeare or Picasso, Franklin or Einstein, or any of the other figures who have been handy as examples for those people who believe that "genius," as a noun, describes something about humans because it describes only some of them. Precisely because the modern definitions of genius were evolving and circulating just as debates over race and slavery were absorbing and dividing the public, the concept was, just as Edward Long had warned it would be, tainted.

Revolution versus racism

The timing of Sancho's letter, written in 1778, at a moment during the American Revolution when the tide was turning against Great Britain, focused on slavery in a way that might have been intended to rebuke white Americans who fought for their own liberty while still holding blacks in bondage. This was not momentarily opportunistic so much as it was part of a deepening sense of unease over what European empires had created and were still creating abroad. Consider in this regard the abbé Guillaume-Thomas-François Raynal's slightly earlier contribution in his *Histoire des deux Indes* (1770). Raynal had concluded that the existence, let alone proliferation, of chattel slavery in the greater Atlantic questioned whether European colonization of the Americas had furthered human progress. (He would put the point more forcefully in 1787 when he suggested that the Academy of Lyon debate the question: "Has the discovery of America been injurious or useful to mankind?") Of course, long before imperialism troubled Raynal, it had inspired violent responses among slaves and free blacks. Historians of the enlightenments of the enslaved have therefore argued that a radical enlightenment, which stressed secular definitions of political equality, appealed most to blacks, who often suspected that they could achieve such equality only through force of arms.[32]

There were a great many white dissenters, and Thomas Jefferson has attracted much attention as an exemplar of a less radical state of enlightenment. In his *Notes on the State of Virginia*, published three years after Wheatley's death, Jefferson questioned whether Africans shared with Europeans "the faculties of reason and imagination." "Religion indeed has produced a Phillis Wheatley," he conceded, "but it could not produce a poet. The compositions published under her name are below the dignity of criticism." He held that true poets were inspired by love, which people of African descent could not genuinely experience: "Their love is ardent, but it kindles the senses only, not the imagination." In short, Jefferson rejected Wheatley's plea to be regarded as a soaring mind rather than as a sense-bound body, mocked her religious faith, and implied that her name had been attached to inferior poems she might not have written anyway.[33]

Jefferson's response indicated a new level of incredulity, and it mattered. As Benjamin Banneker prepared his first almanac, therefore, he strategically prepped a crucial member of his audience, Secretary of State Thomas Jefferson, who had a small reputation in science. On August 19, 1791, Banneker sent Jefferson a long letter introducing himself as an almanac maker, providing a manuscript copy of his almanac, and lamenting how those of African descent were considered more "brutish than human, and Scarcely capable of mental endowments." He argued that the "universal Father" had "made us all of one flesh" and had "afforded us all the Same Sensations, and endued us all with the same faculties." Eleven days later, Jefferson responded, rather astonishingly, that "no body wishes more than I do to see such proofs as you exhibit, that nature has given to our black brethren, talents equal to those of the other colors of men." He also assured Banneker that he had sent the manuscript almanac to the marquis de Condorcet, mathematician, moral philosopher, and secretary of the French Académie des Sciences, an amazing introduction into the international republic of letters.[34]

But no sooner had Jefferson put himself on record as a critic of racism than he was attacked for it—and he recanted. His political critics pointed to the contradictions between his letter to Banneker and his *Notes on the State of Virginia* (English edition 1787), which defended slavery and questioned whether black people could excel in any abstract mental art. It was indeed odd for a slaveholding Virginian to publicly declare the educability of blacks. And Jefferson was functioning in a context different from that of George Washington's moment of polite correspondence with Phillis Wheatley, which had taken place during a war against tyranny and for American liberty. Some adjustment was quite obviously taking place as slavery was becoming an established part of the southern states of a now independent United States.[35]

If Jefferson granted a spiritual equality between blacks and whites, he questioned their equal capacity for reason. Note that Jefferson's letter to Condorcet had cited Banneker's achievement as one of "moral eminence," a quality that might *eventually* prove the qualities of black "intellect," qualifications that fell short of a denunciation of racism. In a subsequent private letter, Jefferson wondered whether one of the Ellicotts had helped Banneker do his ephemeris and said that the long missive the black man had sent to him showed him "to have had a mind of very common stature indeed"—both were fundamental attacks on Banneker's claims to be self-educated to any level, let alone a high one. A British diplomat later reported that Jefferson characterized Banneker's correspondence as "very childish and trivial."[36]

Although descriptions of Wheatley and Banneker during the nineteenth century occasionally quoted earlier statements about their capacity for genius, or (more rarely) status as geniuses, new instances of such descriptions were not common. Rather, the black genius became useful as an emblematic type. This was apparent in Leigh Hunt's 1814 masque, *The Descent of Liberty*. In this allegorical play, a scene of pastoral merriment is interrupted when a "Sable Genius" arrives, "with fetter-rings at his wrists, a few of the links not broken off." He is intended, that is, to evoke the famous "Am I not a Man and a Brother" figure of the British antislavery movement, as well as the unfinished business of that movement, with only some of his bonds broken. He likewise emulates the supplicant posture of that character by laying himself at the feet of Liberty. He recounts how a similar scene of rural joy had been interrupted in his native Africa, when a slave ship arrives to tear people from their families, transport them to alien lands, and subject them to bloody torments, all in order "to glut th' accursed." It was a plea for abolition in which no actual enslaved people were involved, in which their genius functioned as a statement of their moral standing, not their achievements and intellect.[37]

Genius as inequality

No historic shift is entire. Long's and Jefferson's skepticism make clear the endurance of racism throughout the age of revolutions. And yet, even during Jefferson's lifetime, at least one other man of science was impressed with black "genius" and said so. Although Johann Friedrich Blumenbach is often vilified for championing "Caucasians" as the most beautiful of human races, he in truth criticized much scientific and casual racism and declared an opposition to slavery in the late eighteenth and early nineteenth centuries, at a time when this was still by no means the default opinion among white Europeans. Moreover, Blumenbach was careful, in his ethnographic writings, to stress the intellectual capacity of black people, including Wheatley and Banneker, whose writings he possessed and admired. He emphasized that Banneker "had acquired his astronomical knowledge without oral instruction, entirely through private study," thus validating both Banneker's self-instruction and its results as indicating an innate capacity within the man, not something instilled into him, as if into a trained animal, which would display the cleverness and determination of the trainer, but also his or her superiority to the trainee.[38]

And yet no one refuted Edward Long. It would be ahistorical to construct, from the incidence of the word "genius" in proximity to words that denote slavery and racialized status, an upward trajectory in the history of human rights and democracy. Rather than challenge racism and slavery in any revolutionary way, genius in its modern definition instead seemed uncomfortably close to what it was supposed be criticizing. Religious definitions of human equality would, in the end, prove more powerful than their secular counterparts or even, in the case of genius, its pagan ancestors. It is nevertheless significant that Wheatley, Sancho, Banneker, and others offered themselves as potential subjects of discussion within the ongoing redefinition of genius. To interpret their efforts only in relation to our present-day habit of ranking various geniuses underestimates the creative dimensions of the debate over human difference that occurred toward the end of the eighteenth century, even including that debate's dead ends.[39]

Notes

1. Vincent Carretta, ed., *Unchained Voices: An Anthology of Black Authors in the English-Speaking World of the Eighteenth Century* (Lexington: University of Kentucky Press, 1996), 83–84; Phillis Wheatley, *Poems on Various Subjects, Religious and Moral* (London, 1773).
2. S. E. Ogude, *Genius in Bondage: A Study of the Origins of African Literature in English* (Ile-Ife: University of Ife Press, 1983); Vincent Carretta and Philip Gould, eds., *Genius in Bondage: Literature of the Early Black Atlantic* (Lexington: University of Kentucky Press, 2001); Vincent Carretta, *Phillis Wheatley: Biography of a Genius in Bondage* (Athens: University of Georgia Press, 2011); Keith D. Leonard, *Fettered Genius: The African American Bardic Poet from Slavery to Civil Rights* (Charlottesville: University of Virginia Press, 2006).

3. Carretta, *Unchained Voices*, 83.
4. Roxann Wheeler, *The Complexion of Race: Categories of Difference in Eighteenth-Century British Culture* (Philadelphia: University of Pennsylvania Press, 2000); Bruce R. Dain, *A Hideous Monster of the Mind: American Race Theory in the Early Republic* (Cambridge, MA: Harvard University Press, 2002); Dror Wahrman, *The Making of the Modern Self: Identity and Culture in Eighteenth-Century England* (New Haven, CT: Yale University Press, 2004); Joyce E. Chaplin, "Race," in *The British Atlantic World, 1500–1800*, 2nd ed., ed. David Armitage and Michael J. Braddock (New York: Palgrave Macmillan, 2009), 173–90; Silvia Sebastiani, *The Scottish Enlightenment: Race, Gender, and the Limits of Progress*, trans. Jeremy Carden (New York: Palgrave Macmillan, 2013).
5. Winthrop D. Jordan, *White over Black: American Attitudes toward the Negro, 1550–1812* (Chapel Hill: University of North Carolina Press, 1968); David Brion Davis, *The Problem of Slavery in the Age of Revolution, 1770–1823* (Ithaca, NY: Cornell University Press, 1975); Larry E. Tise, *Proslavery: A History of the Defense of Slavery in America, 1701–1840* (Athens: University of Georgia Press, 1987).
6. Michael Adas, *Machines as the Measure of Men: Science, Technology, and Ideologies of Western Dominance* (Ithaca, NY: Cornell University Press, 1989); Londa Schiebinger, *Nature's Body: Gender in the Making of Modern Science* (Boston, MA: Beacon Press, 1993), 115–200; Ivan Hannaford, *Race: The History of an Idea in the West*, foreword Bernard Crick (Baltimore, MD: Johns Hopkins University Press, 1996), ch. 7; Eric Voegelin, *The History of the Race Idea: From Ray to Carus*, trans. Ruth Hein (Baton Rouge: University of Louisiana Press, 1998); Joyce E. Chaplin, *Subject Matter: Technology, the Body, and Science on the Anglo-American Frontier, 1550–1676* (Cambridge, MA: Harvard University Press, 2001); Henry W. Lansdowne, ed., *The Petty Papers: Some Unpublished Writings of Sir William Petty*, 2 vols. (London: Constable, 1927), II, 31.
7. Darrin McMahon, *Divine Fury: A History of Genius* (New York: Basic Books, 2013), esp. 1–103.
8. Jordan, *White over Black*, 3–20, 216–65; Paul H. Freedman, *Images of the Medieval Peasant* (Stanford: Stanford University Press, 1999); [Charles de Secondat, baron de Montesquieu], *De l'Esprit des loix...* (Geneva, 1748); Larry Wolff and Marco Cipolloni, eds., *The Anthropology of the Enlightenment* (Stanford: Stanford University Press, 2007); Charles Rosenberg, "*Airs, Waters, Places*: A Status Report," *Bulletin of the History of Medicine* 86 (2012): 661–70.
9. Joyce E. Chaplin, *The First Scientific American: Benjamin Franklin and the Pursuit of Genius* (New York: Basic Books, 2006), 2–3, 134–36; McMahon, *Divine Fury*, 67–149.
10. http://infoweb.newsbank.com.ezp-prod1.hul.harvard.edu/iw-search/we/Evans?p_product=EAIX&p_action=keyword&p_theme=eai&p_nbid=U74K60NVMTM4MzE1OTE2MS40NTg4NTI6MToxNDoxMjguMTAzLjE0OS41Mg&p_clear_search=yes&d_refprod=EAIX&.
11. Epistolary dedication by J. Crull, in Samuel Pufendorf, *Of the Nature and Qualification of Religion in Reference to Civil Society* (London, 1698), preface; Edward Kimber, *The Life and Adventures of James Ramble, Esq...* (London, 1755), I, 125; John Richard, *A Tour from London to Petersburgh, from Thence to Moscow, and Return to London by Way of Courland, Poland, Germany and Holland* (London, 1780), 4.
12. Gilbert Chinard, "Eighteenth Century Theories of America as a Human Habitat," *Proceedings of the American Philosophical Society* 91 (1947): 31; Antonello Gerbi, *The Dispute of the New World: The History of a Polemic, 1750–1900*, trans. Jeremy Moyle (Pittsburgh, PA: University of Pittsburgh Press, 1973); Antonello Gerbi, *Nature in the New World: From Christopher Columbus to Gonzalo Fernández de Oviedo*, trans. Jeremy Moyle (Pittsburgh, PA: University of Pittsburgh Press, 1985); Paul Semonin, *American Monster: How the Nation's First Prehistoric Creature Became a Symbol of National Identity* (New York: New York University Press, 2000); Joyce E. Chaplin, "Creoles in British America: From Denial to Acceptance," in *Creolization: History, Ethnography, Theory*, ed. Charles Stewart (Walnut Creek, CA: Left Coast Press, 2007), 46–65.
13. A. J. Leo Lemay, *The Life of Benjamin Franklin*, vol. III: *Soldier, Scientist, and Politician, 1748–1757* (Philadelphia: University of Pennsylvania Press, 2009), 96–101 (on the

multiple submissions to the Royal Society); Preface by John Fothergill, in Benjamin Franklin, *Experiments and Observations on Electricity: Made at Philadelphia in America, by Mr. Benjamin Franklin, and Communicated in Several Letters to Mr. P. Collinson, of London, F. R. S.* (London, 1751), n. p.; *Benjamin Franklin's Autobiography: A Norton Critical Edition*, ed. Joyce E. Chaplin (New York: W. W. Norton, 2012), 145; Leonard W. Labaree, et al., eds., *The Papers of Benjamin Franklin* (New Haven, CT: Yale University Press, 1959–), IV, 128 (Hereinafter *PBF*).

14. Charles Woodmason, "To Benjamin Franklin Esq.," *PBF*, V, 62; Ebenezer Kinnersley to BF, March 12, 1761, *PBF*, IX, 285; Penuel Bowen to BF, November 6, 1771, *PBF*, XVIII, 244.

15. Immanuel Kant, *Gesammelte Schriften...* (Berlin: G. Reimer, 1902), I, 472 ("Prometheus der neuern Zeiten"); Peter Hinrich Tesdorpf, "Poem in Eulogy of Franklin," *PBF*, XVI, 122.

16. *The Natural History of Animals, Vegetables, and Minerals: With the Theory of the Earth in General. Translated from the French of Count de Buffon*, 6 vols. (London, 1775–1776), I, 401.

17. Hannaford, *Race*, 17–85.

18. Jordan, *White over Black*, 44–98; Hannaford, *Race*, 115–26; James H. Sweet, "The Iberian Roots of American Racist Thought," *William and Mary Quarterly*, 3d ser., 14 (1997): 143–66; Chaplin, *Subject Matter*, 52, 122–23, 128–29.

19. Schiebinger, *Nature's Body*, 190–200; Vincent Carretta, "Who Was Francis Williams?," *Early American Literature* 38 (2003): 213–37.

20. Edward Long, *The History of Jamaica: Or, General Survey of the Antient and Modern State of That Island*, 3 vols. (London, 1774), II, 475–76.

21. Ibid., 484.

22. Washington to Wheatley, October 26, 1775, *Unchained Voices*, 70–71.

23. Carretta, *Unchained Voices*, 13.

24. Richard D. Altick, *The Shows of London* (Cambridge, MA: Harvard University Press, 1978), 40–42; Jan Bondeson, *The Feejee Mermaid and Other Essays in Natural and Unnatural History* (Ithaca, NY: Cornell University Press, 1999), 19–35; *Barr's Buffon: Buffon's Natural History, Containing a Theory of the Earth, a General History of Man, of the Brute Creation, and of Vegetables...*, 10 vols. (London, 1792), VII, 257. On contemporary debates over animal nature and intelligence (versus their human counterparts), see Jean-Luc Guichet, *Problématiques animales: Théorie de la connaissance, anthropologie, éthique et droit* (Paris: Presses universitaires de France, 2011).

25. Phillis Wheatley, *Complete Writings*, ed. Vincent Carretta (New York: Penguin, 2001), 5, 7, 8.

26. *London Magazine* (September, 1773), 456; *Boston Evening-Post* (September 20, 1773).

27. Carretta, *Unchained Voices*, 77, 100, 102.

28. Silvio Bedini, *The Life of Benjamin Banneker: The First African-American Man of Science*, 2nd ed. (Baltimore: Maryland Historical Society, 1999), 2, 3.

29. *Benjamin Banneker's Pennsylvania, Delaware, Maryland and Virginia Almanack and Ephemeris for the Year of our Lord 1792* (Baltimore, MD: William Goddard and James Angell, 1791), 2–4.

30. Carretta, *Unchained Voices*, 83.

31. On anti-Semitism, see Benzion Netanyahu, *The Origins of the Inquisition in Fifteenth-Century Spain* (New York: Random House, 1995); Benjamin Braude, "The Sons of Noah and the Construction of Ethnic and Geographical Identities in the Medieval and Early Modern Periods," *WMQ*, 3d ser., 44 (1997): 103–42; Frank Felsenstein, *Anti-Semitic Stereotypes: A Paradigm of Otherness in English Popular Culture, 1660–1830* (Baltimore, MD: Johns Hopkins University Press, 1995).

32. Guillaume-Thomas-François Raynal, *Histoire philosophique et politique des établissemens et du commerce des Européens dans les deux Indes* (Amsterdam, 1770); C. L. R. James, *The Black Jacobins: Toussaint L'Ouverture and the San Domingo Revolution*, 2nd ed., rev. (New York: Vintage Books, 1963); Laurent Dubois, "An Enslaved Enlightenment: Rethinking the Intellectual History of the French Atlantic," *Social History* 31 (2006): 1–14.

33. Thomas Jefferson, *Notes on the State of Virginia*, ed. Frank Shuffelton (New York: Penguin, 1999), 147. On Jefferson and race generally, see Peter S. Onuf, *The Mind of Thomas Jefferson* (Charlottesville: University of Virginia Press, 2007), 205–35; on Jefferson and

Banneker, see Annette Gordon-Reed, *The Hemingses of Monticello: An American Family* (New York: W. W. Norton, 2008), 474–79.

34. *Copy of a Letter from Benjamin Banneker, to the Secretary of State, with His Answer* (Philadelphia, 1792).
35. Paul Leicester Ford, ed., *The Writings of Thomas Jefferson* (New York: G. P. Putnam's, 1895), V, 379; Bedini, *Life of Banneker*, 295–96; William Andrews, "Benjamin Banneker's Revision of Thomas Jefferson: Conscience vs. Science in the Early American Antislavery Debate," *Genius in Bondage*, 218–41.
36. Bedini, *Life of Banneker*, 297–98.
37. Leigh Hunt, *The Descent of Liberty: A Mask* (London, 1815), 68–76.
38. Hannaford, *Race*, 205–13; *The Anthropological Treatises of Blumenbach*, ed. Thomas Bendyshe (London, 1865), 310.
39. Christopher Leslie Brown, *Moral Capital: Foundations of British Abolitionism* (Chapel Hill: University of North Carolina Press, 2006).

3

Genius versus Democracy: Excellence and Singularity in Postrevolutionary France

Nathalie Heinich

How can inequality be justified? This is the fundamental question of democracy.[1] During the *ancien régime*, when inequality was at the basis of social organization, aristocracy offered part of the answer, since inequality was linked to an innate greatness.[2] Religion provided the remaining explanation, justifying earthly inequality by a transcendental and temporal appeal. In the afterlife, god would reset justice ("the last shall be first and the first last"). This millennial configuration was violently subverted with the French Revolution, adding axiological factors—that is, tensions between fundamental values—to a historical and factual event.

Abolition of privileges, disenchantment of the world:[3] with these two basic grounds of the democratic regime, inequality is no longer self-evident. It needs either to be suppressed, as with egalitarianism, or justified by merit, that is according to an individual worth obtained through certain acts, as with meritocracy, and no longer according to an inherited collective worth or a status privilege, as with aristocracy. Aristocratic elitism, in which excellence requires not the singularity but the particularity of a privileged birth, was dismissed by the Revolution, and was replaced for a while by an egalitarian regime in which neither singularity nor excellence could find a place.[4] This revolutionary egalitarianism resulted in the Terror, which then gave way to a bourgeois compromise that eventually won, after long disputes over values,[5] that is, democratic elitism, as a combination of individual excellence (merit) and equalization through conformity (money and all kinds of standards), typical of what I have called the "community realm."[6]

But the democratic form of elitism opened up by the bourgeois postrevolutionary society[7] was probably not enough to satisfy all kinds of aspirations, since it was soon completed by artistic elitism. This is what will be demonstrated in this chapter through a consideration of the history and sociology of painters, writers, and musicians in the context of the sociopolitical history of nineteenth-century France. In addition, I will take into consideration two categories of literary texts: first, the sizeable corpus of nineteenth-century fiction whose main character is an artist; and second, a number of published personal testimonies of creators, such as diaries and letters.

The aristocracy of artists

"You will be our aristocracy!" says David Séchard, a young printer, to his friend and future stepbrother, Lucien, a poet, in Honoré de Balzac's *Illusions perdues* (1835).[8] We can see here how an aristocratic model shifts onto the figure of the poet: a model that is both outdated, since its reign belongs to the past, and still idealized, since this aristocracy is dreamed, turned into a metaphor—that of the poet.[9] Besides the poet, the musician and the painter also find their place in this new imaginary hierarchy: in Balzac's *Gambara* (1839), the genial but crazy composer *"showed some nobility"* in his manners; and in Jules Barbey d'Aurevilly's *A un dîner d'athées* (1874), the ancient soldier who became a painter substitutes the pride of talent for his now useless nobility and military titles.[10] The fact is that from the second-third of the nineteenth century, the romantic movement gave birth to a new social category: that of the "Artist," which, for the first time in western culture, brought together the various domains of creation, and sometimes, too, the interpreters or performers of music, theater, and dance.[11]

This trend toward aristocracy—even if merely fantasized—is of course limited by the closed nature of nobility, a well-protected category: not anyone randomly has the right to call oneself a noble. Moreover, the aristocratic identity is fundamentally collective and grounded in the past, whereas the artistic identity, according to the new vocational regime of activity, is individual and turned to the proof of posterity. Nonetheless, some aristocratic characteristics are present in modern artists: not only the prestige that surrounds them, but also the difficulty of drawing the limits of their category, which makes them hard even to count; and their valorization of disinterestedness that, for nobles as well as for artists, is considered the very opposite of bourgeois values.

This is a crucial issue: the aristocratization of creators is constructed not so much by imitating a now dethroned (even if still desirable) nobility, as by differentiating from a stigmatized bourgeoisie. The latter possesses power and money, but not prestige: a bourgeois career is something that one can try to achieve, but hardly something that everyone dreams of. There is indeed a tension between artistic heroism and mercantilism, between "the heroic creators' self-image and the impersonal commercialization of the market," as the American historian Cesar Graña has stated in his analysis of the opposition between "bohemian and bourgeois," stressing that this became a "social phenomenon."[12]

Why does this shift to aristocracy rest so massively on the opposition with the bourgeoisie? It is because the latter may represent a foil to at least three categories: first, the fallen or disappointed aristocrats who, like Alfred de Vigny's *Stello* (1832), consider art as a possible recovery of lost excellence;

second, young and aspiring bourgeois, such as the hero of Gustave Flaubert's *L'Education sentimentale* (1869) in Pierre Bourdieu's analysis,[13] who do not find in familial destiny a proper ground for their ambition; and third, those who hope to escape their popular origins through an artistic career, such as Garnotelle in the Goncourts' *Manette Salomon* (1867).[14] They all find their advantage in marginality, which blurs positions and creates improbable solidarities, and in a shared disdain toward what appears as common, average, and mediocre. Transposed onto the level of taste, this disdain turns into the avant-gardist refusal of the cliché, appreciated both by illiterate ordinary people and by the Pharisiac bourgeoisie. Thus, stereotypes, according to the Italian historian Renato Poggioli, become "the modern form of ugliness," remaining in conformity with the very elitist dimension of the avant-garde.[15]

But beyond the refusal of the bourgeoisie, the swing of the romantic generation toward vocation (no longer simply craft or profession[16]) takes the form of a retreat out of "society." Be it by transforming the ancient elite or by denying the new middle class, the aristocratization of art goes together with the renunciation of common values and established positions, that is, with an accepted—if not pursued—marginalization, practically achieved in the *vie de bohème*, and morally supported by the "singularity realm."[17] It means hatred for that "so harmful society" (these are Alfred de Musset's words in *La Confession d'un enfant du siècle*, 1836),[18] or refuge inside the famous "ivory tower" of the poet, the artist, or the scientist, as evoked by Gérard de Nerval in *Sylvie* (1853).[19]

This is why the voluntary marginalization of young heirs, be they bourgeois or aristocrats, goes together with the idealization of artistic values in place of aristocratic values. Thus, privilege turns into innate gift, name turns into signature and renown, the elite of power turns into an elite of creation and a bohemian circle of initiates, and the prohibition on manual labor turns into the dismissal of financial income and the fostering of that immaterial remuneration called glory. *"Today a great artist is a prince without titles, it means glory and fortune, the two main social advantages after virtue,"* says baron Hulot in Balzac's *La Cousine Bette* (1843).[20]

But interpreting the artists' opposition to the bourgeoisie simply as a way to react against an actual exclusion, a way to "turn necessity into virtue," as Pierre Bourdieu does, is not sufficient to explain such a massive and long lasting phenomenon.[21] Such an interpretation reduces this opposition to its reactive and agonistic dimension, and the artist to a "resentment man," in Max Scheler's words,[22] while neglecting the deep dynamics and the positive functions of this opposition. Once considered according to the sociology of values, such a way to define oneself as an opponent to bourgeois aspirations allows the construction of a genuine identity as an artist: an identity that is quite an innovation in Western culture since it is paradoxically defined both as marginal and elitist, that is, singular and excellent at the same time.

This new collective identity will be supported by a new relationship to art shared by most modern artists: that is, "art for art's sake," which claims the autonomy of art before any other requirements other than properly aesthetic ones.

For the sake of art

"It's a beautiful word: artist. As if someone said, intelligent": this is what Jules Janin wrote in "Being an Artist," an article published significantly in the first issue of the journal *L'Artiste* in 1832.[23] A year later, the same journal published an anonymous satire, epitomizing the intertwining of art for art's sake, the admiration for artists, and the various fields of creation:

> From ground level to attic, from stable to lodge, art reigns in any conversation...; even *grisettes*, when having the honour to know some bearded figure, are as wild about a word of art as of a new handkerchief...; coachmen, cooks, waiters, grooms, usherettes, chair ladies, all kinds of people, be them males or females, all pretend to particular and independent opinions on popular dramas, pictures in the Salon, illustrated novels.[24]

Not only do the lower classes consider art as a value during the 1830s, but also the upper classes, from the time of the post-Napoleon era, according to some memorialists. This is consistent with the diffusionist model of moral evolution as described by Norbert Elias:[25] "civilized" manners (here, more precisely, literate values) of the upper classes are progressively adopted by the classes immediately beneath them, then intensified by the former in order to distinguish themselves from the latter.

However, this remarkable promotion of "arts" and "artists" as one and the same category cannot be reduced to a mere ascension in the hierarchy of positions, allowing artists to be "often invited to dinners," as Flaubert ironically wrote in his *Dictionnaire des idées reçues*.[26] More generally, what is at stake is an idealization of art, now extended beyond creativity to become a moral value. Thus, the term "artist" does not designate anymore a mere activity, but a way of being, a moral quality.[27]

Of course, this introduction of artists into the elite does not occur at the same rhythm in all circles. Theater is a perfect melting pot. The intellectual bourgeoisie also fosters intermixing: in the 1870s, the *salon* of the publisher Charpentier and his wife brought together aristocrats, politicians, journalists, writers, painters, composers, actors, and singers. On the other hand, the traditional aristocracy enforced the limits of "good society" by keeping distances: artists might be invited, but would never be granted a visit.[28]

This ambivalence toward the status of creators (and especially painters, because of their previously humble origins, tracing to the medieval category of the "mechanical arts") induces a number of misunderstandings about the position of art in the nineteenth century. The first confusion consists in believing that the status of painter was unjustly despised, since bourgeois parents refused it for their children. But the accurate interpretation is the opposite: artistic vocation had been elevated to a higher status than it had been granted for centuries, so that, for the first time, the heirs of good society could wish to attain it, contrary to more ambitious or less uncertain familial aspirations. The resistance of bourgeois parents should thus be analyzed as a reaction to the attractiveness of these occupations, that is, to their new prestige. This discrepancy between a previous inferior status and a more recent prestige explains the lure of young gentlemen for an artistic career considered in opposition to bourgeois life—and, at the same time, the refusal of such a career by their families.

The ever higher social origin of artists also generates a paradoxical phenomenon, which usually induces another misunderstanding due to the spontaneous but erroneous assimilation of artistic innovation with political liberalism.[29] It is indeed difficult to admit the actual affinity between living a life of ease and pursuing avant-garde aesthetics or, symmetrically, between a conservative artistic position and low-class origin. But this phenomenon is easy to explain: in a vocational regime, the most traditionalist artists are those who owe their social position to the established system (such as the academy), especially the artists coming from a rather low class who could not benefit from familial resources, whereas innovators, whose heritage permits them to distance themselves from the rules of the game, are able to experience new possibilities, which match better with their personal abilities than with usual expectations.[30]

This is particularly clear in the case of the Impressionists: they took advantage of the general improvement in status in the hierarchy of activities, which attracted painters coming from the bourgeoisie, who could thus practice their art almost as amateurs without being obliged to make all of their living out of it. It helped them to transgress canons and to free themselves from traditions. Manet and Degas came from the upper middle class; Bazille, Sisley, Cézanne, from the middle class; Pissarro and Monet, from the lower middle class; Renoir was the only one who came from the lower class. Besides their subversion of the academic rules of figuration, they shared the same indifference toward the hierarchy of genres, as demonstrated by the near absence of any historical painting in their work (except a few attempts to be admitted to the Salon). Instead, they cultivated minor genres more suited to their interests—landscape, portrait, still life, and genre painting. Such liberty showed emancipation from the traditional modes of recognition, which has a lot to do with the fact that most of them could count on other sources of income besides income from their artistic activity, even if these sources were not always sufficient to live as comfortably as they had been used to.[31] This is a partial but plausible explanation for the emergence of a new trend in art. And the ignorance or denial of this phenomenon comes from the modern valorization of the avant-garde, which is often based on confusion between aesthetics and politics, and artistic innovation and social progress.

Elitist creators

"I hate to associate with the rabble, but I passionately desire the happiness of the common people," Stendhal wrote in his *Vie de Henry Brulard* (1835).[32] So did he beautifully explicate the ambivalence proper to the modern art world, split between a distant idealization of the lower classes rooted in a hatred of the bourgeoisie, and elitism anchored in art for art's sake. Since the time of romanticism, the world of art has swung between populism and aristocratism, both grounded in a solid disdain for the bourgeoisie. The latter is always negative, whereas art is always positive; in between, the extreme poles of the social scale swing between stigmatization and valorization, decaying or sublimated aristocracy, idealized or hated lower classes.

While populism was markedly expressed by Claude-Henri de Saint-Simon and his disciples, aesthetic aristocratism found its most typical manifestation with Edmond and Jules de Goncourt, before being strongly transmuted in Friedrich Nietzsche's philosophy. "One has to be an aristocrat to write *Germinie Lacerteux*," declare the Goncourt brothers in their diary (September 10, 1866), thus expressing both their attachment to aristocratic *ancien régime* values and their shift toward the new values of creation. This double twist is proper to the romantic status of art, to which the famous brothers give here an ideal-typical expression. Their love for the eighteenth century, as well as their fight to defend their nobiliary particle, shows their fidelity to the *ancien régime*, their class contempt toward painters as well as toward those writers who have to earn their living by depending on a publisher. Thus their aesthetic scorn for readers appears as an avowed hatred for the lower classes, while admiration for artists appears as an avowed love for aristocracy.

After having received some cousins of common birth, the Goncourt sigh: "a man of letters should use a pseudonym in order to disinherit the family of his own name" (June 23, 1856). To disinherit the family of one's name: here is a remarkable combination of aristocratic ethics, based on an obligatory transmission of one's name, and bourgeois customs, based on the voluntary transmission of material goods, which may sometimes be transmitted to others besides one's legitimate heirs. And this mixing is literally embodied in the creator, whose heritage no longer consists in an inherited name, as for the nobility, nor in material goods, as for the bourgeoisie, but in the "name" he makes by himself, in a double way: through his pseudonym if he takes one and, eventually, through his notoriety, that is his "renown." Thus can he detach himself from the familial bonds as well as from his civil name, and almost choose his descendants, who will no longer come out of heredity but out of election, through tastes and talents shared between aesthetes. One cannot express more clearly the way in which the artist—here embodied in the man of letters—can now embody a kind of compromise between aristocratic and bourgeois identities, thus forming a hybrid, mainly defined by the ambition to be neither aristocrat nor bourgeois.

The "eliticisation" of creators

Such an "eliticisation" of creators did not occur before the postrevolutionary period. *Ancien Régime* aristocrats happened to see artists only in the frame of court culture. The few writers, musicians, or even painters who were appointed there might occasionally be granted a visit, but would rarely be accepted in court society. One century later, high ranking creators were often admitted within high society, as testified by dictionaries and annuals. The 1908 edition of *Qui êtes-vous?* ("Who are you?"), a guide to high society, mentions in the preface, "artists, scientists, men of letters, teachers, civil servants, high clerics, firm directors and important tradesmen, great socialites, deputies, senators, [and] foreigners living in France, etc." It is noteworthy that creators come before aristocrats.[33] The introduction of artists into salons is a development of the nineteenth century: belonging to this category was enough to grant some prestige, allowing entry into the new elite. The criteria for inclusion in high society changed in a few generations, so that it eventually accepted not only new categories but also the very one that, since romanticism, was supposed to ignore, or even to subvert, the established order.

This "eliticisation" of artists goes together with a shift toward new values in society at large. "Time is the only capital of those who have no other fortune than their own intelligence," says David Sénard in Balzac's *Illusions perdues*: this very sentence summarizes the swing to a new axiological world.[34] To understand it, we have to take into account the polysemy of the word "fortune," which means both luck and money. Before the revolution, these two meanings were tied together by noble privilege: as soon as one was lucky enough to be born noble, one was sure to be granted some patrimony, and thus an income. In the democratic world inaugurated on the night of August 4, 1789, this privilege was not entirely suppressed, but it became possible and, moreover, legitimate to acquire a fortune and not simply to inherit it—which dramatically increased social mobility. Henceforth "fortune" (i.e., income) depended much less on native "fortune" (i.e., luck) than on work—be it the work of the previous generation for their bourgeois heirs. And work depended both on "intelligence" (i.e., competence, talent, ability, etc.) and on "time": both the time spent at work (i.e., intensity of labor) and the time one had to wait until being rewarded for one's efforts (i.e., patience). Democratic temporality is conjugated in the present and the future—encompassing effort and investment—whereas aristocratic temporality pointed toward the past—that is, ancientness.

In that respect, artists share the condition of any individual in a democratic regime, whose fortune depends only on oneself, on one's ability and capacity to last. But they also possess, like aristocrats, the "luck" of having been granted a native gift independently from their merits. As long as they are able to cultivate that gift through their work, and patiently wait for recognition, then their greatness will combine the profits of one and the other regimes. But it is not so much their person that embodies this greatness, as is the case with the noble or the dandy: it is rather their work, which became on the juridical level, it should be noted, an "emanation of the person" during the nineteenth century.[35] Moreover, this greatness no longer profits simply themselves, as in the time of privileges, but all people, since "art" is considered to be of value for the whole of society, or even as part of the wealth of humanity.

This axiological revolution was certainly not completed, as political revolutions are, in a few months or a few years, but in a few generations, and at each step it was confronted with reluctance, even from those who most benefited from it.[36] Nonetheless, after the egalitarianism of the first revolutionary years, meritocracy eventually succeeded in replacing aristocracy on the value level— which is probably, beyond political changes, the most important outcome of the revolution. And the best summary of such an upheaval is the substitution of the artist's "name," created by individual talent, for the aristocratic "name," received by birth. This is a very peculiar "capital," which owes nothing to "fortune" and all to "intelligence" and "time." Thus a new moral system arose, which was fed not by aristocratic arrogance but by the quiet pride of those who achieved greatness on their own, without harming anyone.

Life in the margins

However, the main difference between the ancient aristocracy of nobles and the new aristocracy of creators is that the latter lives in marginality, as popularized by "bohemian life."[37] Henry Murger's *Scènes de la vie de bohème* (1848) offered the first novel-like depiction, combining painters and sculptors, writers, and musicians.[38]

"*La bohème*": when trying to define it by its positive characteristics, one may notice that "bohemians" were united first of all by the sake of art and, more precisely, by the belief in "l'art pour l'art," the idea that artistic expression should not be submitted to any other end than itself.[39] But let us rather define *bohème* by that which it stands *against*, be it opposed to or deprived of: it is deprived of money and of a place in the social hierarchy, and opposed to any career or to any power.

Here lies a major symptom of the swing to the "singularity realm," which fosters abnormality, innovation, originality, and individuality in a new avant-garde ethics that becomes the very norm of artistic excellence.[40] Then isolated genius appears superior to crowds and communities of peers; eccentricity, to observance of canons; innovation, to reproduction of models; marginality, to conformity; prophetic artists, to mundane artists; and the truth of posterity, to the blindness or lies of the present. From now on, artists are no longer those who *may*, but those who *must*, be singular, in whatever way possible, because it has become a part of the normal definition of the category. This is one of the many paradoxes of the status of artists in the singularity realm: they have to be—if one may say—normally exceptional.

Van Gogh paradigmatically embodies such a phenomenon. But the novelty in Van Gogh's history is not primarily that he embodied the vocational artist: this model had already been established in history; the novelty is that, first, he embodied it as a norm and not anymore as an exception; second, that such a norm progressively extended to a wider public instead of remaining confined to an initiated circle; and third, that this new norm of what a great artist should be also included the figure of misunderstood excellence, that is, of injustice.[41]

Recognition had already been postponed to posterity in the case of writers, because of the affinity between literature and the vocational model of activity, which grounded the notion of the "cursed poet" prior to that of the "cursed artist." The ancient and the new model of success—prosperity or posterity—were both present during the nineteenth century, but the modern conception tended to dominate: first, for writers (remember Stendhal and his famous call to posterity opening the *Souvenirs d'égotisme* in 1821: "but the eyes who will read this are today hardly opened, I guess my future readers are twelve or thirteen years old"; "my one and only concern is to be reprinted in 1900"); later, with the passing of time, for painters and sculptors and for musicians. Thus the notion of success changed in the eyes of creators themselves, from the short term to the long term, on the temporal level, and from the crowd to a small circle of experts, on the spatial level.[42]

In the last third of the nineteenth century, originality and eccentricity became qualities distinguishing, and distinguished by, those who were fond of modernity—connoisseurs as well as creators. Art entered, at least for specialists, this new axiological realm where exception is normal and contestation a rule. From this point onward, the "curse" of the poet or of the artist—all the more unrecognized by his contemporaries since he transgresses established laws in order to open the way to new possibilities—became part of the normal definition.

Excellence and democracy

Split between fidelity to noble greatness and the democratic principles of equality of rights for all citizens, the nineteenth century hesitated between several criteria of worth: birth, estate property, money, knowledge, talent, and social ability.[43] What might be a democratic theory of excellence? This is the problem of nineteenth-century society, not only in its political institutions but also in its deeper axiological principles.

It is such a democratic theory of excellence that the Saint-Simonians tried to elaborate, as illustrated by Claude-Henri de Saint-Simon's parable of the bees and hornets. In *The Organizer* (1819), he advocates moving beyond a conception of traditional elites, grounded on birth and prestige, to a new type of elite, grounded on social utility, which would include "the most capable in the sciences, arts, crafts, that is the three thousand foremost scientists, artists and craftsmen in France."[44] Thus was Saint-Simon—and not by chance—the first who glorified artists for embodying both the democratic ideal, because they fight for the general interest, and aristocratic excellence, because they are legitimately superior. Such an unlikely conjunction would be embraced by avant-garde partisans from the middle of the nineteenth century to our present day.

Only artists could make possible the dream of conciliating these antagonist values—much like Victor Hugo, for example, "whose person united the aristocratic singularity of the genius with the democratic capacity to echo a whole nation," in the beautiful summary of Mona Ozouf.[45] In other words, an artist is one who, in the collective imagination, unites the democratic longing for community with the elitist longing for singularity. This is because any vocation designates both excellence and singularity, as the philosopher Judith Schlanger has accurately observed.[46] This is the ambivalence of vocational values, which are split between a universal right and a singular privilege. Vocational elitism unites with its opposite, combining the valorization of individual merit with the possibility that everyone, even if only by chance, might complete a fully achieved existence.

This combination of aristocratism (excellence is innate), democracy (everyone has a right to excellence), and meritocracy (excellence depends on nothing but individual merit) defines the modern status of artists. It is, of course, logical contradictory; but logic alone might persuade us that logics govern experience, and that a contradiction is a paradox to be reduced or dismissed by researchers. In the real world, a logical contradiction is ambivalence, that is, the copresence of heterogeneous values, which are to be explained by researchers (not explained away) and combined in practice by men and women of flesh and blood.[47] Here, this combination is performed by the very status of artists, because it unites various criteria of worth, which explains its success and power in democratic societies.

Let us summarize: what brings art closer to aristocracy is, first, that talent is innate (vocational birth), and, second, that privilege is allowed not only to one individual but to a whole category (artists, and creators in general); what brings it closer to democracy, by contrast, is, first, that greatness depends on personal merit (meritocracy) and, second, that everyone can reach it according to his/her effort or luck; and what brings art close to both aristocratic and democratic values is that excellence leans on singularity, meaning both exceptionality (excellence) and marginality (exclusion). Once ideally defined as singular, that is "out of the ordinary," art trades its renunciation of power and social inclusion for its capacity to exemplify a privilege that democracy may accept, because it is neither aristocratic (it lacks power), nor bourgeois (it resists inclusion). Hence these axiological dimensions lead to three "ideal types" (in Max Weber's vocabulary) of an artist: the mundane artist, embodying an aristocracy now belonging to the past; the engaged artist, embodying a present democracy; and the bohemian artist, embodying singularity projected in the future. Thus may be united—at least imaginarily—the three fundamental bases of greatness: privilege (aristocracy), merit (democracy), and grace (vocation).

The result is a rather odd configuration, quite new in the history of western civilization, but so familiar today that we hardly realize how strange it is. Since the first postrevolutionary generation, we have lived in a world in which part of the elite remains marginal, claiming the refusal of the very society that recognizes it: an elite that can be both excellent and democratic, with the condition that it remains singular. This is, indeed, a revolution—and no doubt it is still effective.

Conclusion: The generalization of the artist model

"Do artists have the right to do anything they want?": this was the theme of a debate organized in April 2002 at the Palais de Tokyo in Paris (a place dedicated to contemporary art) in front of an audience for which, obviously, the answer could only be positive. Artists thus appear as mandated to realize an all-powerful phantasm. But the most interesting fact is the possibility that this very question could even be raised: could it be put to any other social category without provoking stupefaction? The impunity of art would allow creators, once recognized as artists, to benefit from a moral and juridical privilege not so much as a consequence of what they *make* as of what they *are*, so that their very status would suffice to prevent them from suffering any legal proceedings in the frame of their activity. Such a privilege, however, could only be problematic in a society where the constitution has established that "no one is above the law."

Artistic elitism indexes greatness to merit, as democratic elitism, but replaces the egalitarian conformism with its contrariness, that is, the requirement of singularity, the individualization of excellence (talent). So excellence through singularity compensates for marginality and the loss of short-term gratifications (money and power). In other words, the sacrifice of an establishment is compensated by the privilege of exceptionality. It thus doubly satisfies the need for justice, but in a very paradoxical way (though familiar since it has been ours for a century and a half): the way of a marginal elite.

Since the generation of romanticism, artists have been the very best incarnation of both the valorization of singularity and the right to benefit from privilege—enjoying a moral and juridical impunity[48] fostered by the "permissive paradox" of cultural institutions[49]—but within the democratic sense of equity, since their marginality holds them apart from the advantages that ordinarily accompany one's belonging to an elite. It seems as if, today, artists are supposed to realize, for the whole community, an all-powerful fantasy, the claim for a space of absolute freedom authorized to some because they belong to a category endowed both by birth and by merit. Thus, art happens to represent the improbable conjunction of two incompatible values: the democratic value, according to which anyone has the right to be an artist, and the aristocratic value, according to which any artist is—at least ideally—above norms and laws.

This eventually raises two questions. The first is prospective: what may be the future of a society whose elite is identified with marginality? How can individuality become a common principle, singularity a norm, and transgression a model, without ruining the conditions of community, the definition of excellence, the limits of the margin, the very notion of norm, and the efficiency of transgression?

The second question is normative: how should we judge this strange phenomenon of an "artists' elite"? Should we approve or disapprove of the shift of privileges to artists? Faced with the delegation of a collective all-powerful phantasm to a certain category of native greatness, should we consider it as the remnant of an *ancien régime* nostalgia, essentially harmless, which democracy had better put up with, or else, as a victory of the Nietzschean model of the superman, to which every society should aim?

But answering these questions requires an axiological choice, taking a position about values, which is the very limit of the sociologist's competence.[50]

Notes

1. Alexis de Tocqueville, *De la démocratie en Amérique* (Paris: Gallimard, 1970 [1840]).
2. Guy Chaussinand-Nogaret, ed., *Histoire des élites en France du XVIe au XXe siècle* (Paris: Tallandier, 1991).
3. Marcel Gauchet, *Le Désenchantement du monde: Une histoire politique de la religion* (Paris: Gallimard, 1985).
4. François Furet, *Penser la révolution française* (Paris: Gallimard, 1978).
5. Arno Mayer, *La Persistance de l'Ancien Régime: L'Europe de 1848 à la Grande Guerre* (Paris: Flammarion, 1983 [1981]); Claude Nicolet, *L'Idée républicaine en France: Essai d'histoire critique* (Paris: Gallimard, 1982); Pierre Rosanvallon, *Le Modèle politique français: La société civile contre le jacobinisme de 1789 à nos jours* (Paris: Seuil, 2004).
6. Nathalie Heinich, *The Glory of Van Gogh: An Anthropology of Admiration* (Princeton, NJ: Princeton University Press, 1996 [1991]).
7. Jacques Coenen-Huther, *Sociologie des élites* (Paris: Armand Colin, 2004).
8. Honoré de Balzac, *Illusions perdues*, in *La Comédie humaine* (Paris: Bibliothèque de la Pléiade, 1981).
9. Paul Bénichou, *Le Sacre de l'écrivain, 1750–1830: Essai sur l'avènement d'un pouvoir spirituel laïque dans la France moderne* (Paris: José Corti, 1973).
10. Honoré de Balzac, *Gambara*, in *La Comédie humaine* (Paris: Bibliothèque de la Pléiade, 1981); Jules Barbey d'Aurevilly, *A un dîner d'athées*, in *Œuvres romanesques complètes* (Paris: Bibliothèque de la Pléiade, 1964); Theodore Robert Bowie, *The Painter in French Fiction: A Critical Essay* (Chapel Hill: University of North Carolina Press, 1950).
11. Nathalie Heinich, *L'Elite artiste: Excellence et singularité en régime médiatique* (Paris: Gallimard, 2005).
12. Cesar Graña, *Bohemian versus Bourgeois: French Society and the French Men of Letters in the Nineteenth Century* (New York: Basic Books, 1964), 57.
13. Alfred de Vigny, *Stello*, in *Œuvres complètes* (Paris: Bibliothèque de la Pléiade, 1986); Gustave Flaubert, *L'Education sentimentale*, in *Œuvres* (Paris: Bibliothèque de la Pléiade, 1936) ; Pierre Bourdieu, "Flaubert ou l'invention de la vie d'artiste," *Actes de la recherche en sciences sociales* 2 (1975), 67–93.
14. Edmond et Jules de Goncourt, *Manette Salomon* (Paris: Gallimard, Folio classique, 1996).
15. Renato Poggioli, *The Theory of the Avant-Garde* (Cambridge, MA: Harvard University Press, 1968), 39, 124.
16. Nathalie Heinich, *Du peintre à l'artiste: Artisans et académiciens à l'âge classique* (Paris: Minuit, 1993); Nathalie Heinich, *Etre écrivain: Création et identité* (Paris: La Découverte, 2000).
17. Heinich, *The Glory of Van Gogh*.
18. Alfred de Musset, *La Confession d'un enfant du siècle*, in *Œuvres complètes en prose* (Paris: Bibliothèque de la Pléiade, 1938).

19. Gérard de Nerval, *Sylvie*, in *Œuvres complètes* (Paris: Bibliothèque de la Pléiade, 1952).
20. Honoré de Balzac, *La Cousine Bette*, in *La Comédie humaine* (Paris: Bibliothèque de la Pléiade, 1981).
21. Pierre Bourdieu, *Les Règles de l'art: Genèse et structure du champ littéraire* (Paris: Seuil, 1992).
22. Max Scheler, *L'Homme du ressentiment* (Paris: Gallimard-Idées, 1970 [1912]).
23. Jules Janin, "Etre un artiste," *L'Artiste* 1 (1832), n. p.
24. *L'Artiste* 2 (1833).
25. Norbert Elias, *La Civilisation des mœurs* (Paris: Calmann-Lévy, 1973 [1969]).
26. Gustave Flaubert, *Dictionnaire des idées reçues*, in *Œuvres* (Paris: Bibliothèque de la Pléiade, 1936).
27. Alain Rey, "Le nom d'artiste," *Romantisme* 55 (1987), 5–22.
28. Anne Martin-Fugier, *La Vie élégante, ou la formation du Tout-Paris, 1815–1848* (Paris: Fayard, 1990).
29. Donald D. Egbert, *Social Radicalism and the Arts* (New York: A. Knopf, 1970); Maria Ivens, *Le Peuple-artiste, cet être monstrueux: La communauté des pairs face à la communauté des génies* (Paris: L'Harmattan, 2002); Jacques Rancière, *Le Partage du sensible: Esthétique et politique* (Paris: La Fabrique, 2000).
30. Bourdieu, *Les Règles de l'art*.
31. Harrison White and Cynthia White, *La Carrière des peintres au XIXe siècle: Du système académique au marché des Impressionnistes* (Paris: Flammarion, 1991 [1965]).
32. Stendhal, *Vie de Henry Brulard*, in *Œuvres romanesques complètes* (Paris: Bibliothèque de la Pléiade, 2005).
33. *Qui êtes-vous ? Annuaire des contemporains* (Paris: Delagrave, 1908); Christophe Charle, *Les Elites de la République (1880–1900)* (Paris: Fayard, 1987).
34. Pierre Barbéris, *Le Monde de Balzac* (Paris: Arthaud, 1973).
35. Bernard Edelman, *La Propriété littéraire et artistique* (Paris: PUF, 1989).
36. Mayer, *La Persistance de l'Ancien Régime*.
37. Graña, *Bohemian versus Bourgeois*; Malcolm Easton, *Artists and Writers in Paris: The Bohemian Idea, 1803–1867* (London: Arnold, 1964); Timothy J. Clark, *The Absolute Bourgeois: Artists and Politics in France, 1848–1851* (London: Thames and Hudson, 1973); Jerrold Seigel, *Bohemian Paris: Culture, Politics, and the Boundaries of Bourgeois Life, 1830–1930* (New York: Penguin Books, 1986).
38. Henry Murger, *Scènes de la vie de bohème* (Paris: Fayard, 2012).
39. Seigel, *Bohemian Paris*.
40. Poggioli, *The Theory of the Avant-Garde*.
41. Heinich, *The Glory of Van Gogh*.
42. Stendhal, *Souvenirs d'égotisme* (Paris: Gallimard, Folio classique, 1983); Alan Bowness, *The Conditions of Success: How the Modern Artist Rises to Fame* (London: Thames and Hudson, 1989).
43. Rosanvallon, *Le Modèle politique français*.
44. Claude-Henri de Saint-Simon, *Oeuvres completes* (Paris: PUF, 2012).
45. Mona Ozouf, *Les Aveux du roman: Le dix-neuvième siècle entre Ancien Régime et Révolution* (Paris: Fayard, 2001), 325.
46. Judith Schlanger, *La Vocation* (Paris: Seuil, 1997).
47. Nathalie Heinich, *Ce que l'art fait à la sociologie* (Paris: Minuit, 1998).
48. John Henry Merryman and Albert E. Elsen, *Law, Ethics and the Visual Arts* (New-York: Matthew Bender, 1979).
49. Nathalie Heinich, *Le Triple jeu de l'art contemporain: Sociologie des arts plastiques* (Paris: Minuit, 1998).
50. Many thanks to Anthony Glinoer and Ruth-Ellen St-Onge for their help in revising a previous version, and to Darrin McMahon for his excellent translation.

4
Equality, Inequality, and Difference: Genius as Problem and Possibility in American Political/Scientific Discourse

John Carson

Thomas Jefferson was a master of the succinct formulation. In his opening to the second paragraph of the *Declaration of Independence*—"We hold these truths to be self-evident: that all men are created equal..."—he fashioned perhaps the most well-known phrase in all of American political language, one that has resonated powerfully to this day. This paean to human equality, however, was not his only view on the subject. As a slaveholder, he lived out one version of the paradox of extolling equality while continuing to benefit from an extreme form of human inequality. And even from a theoretical perspective, while he might assert that all people are created equal, he was also engaged near the end of his life in an extensive correspondence with his old friend and long-time political rival John Adams, where one of the subjects they took up was the notion, as Jefferson put it, of a "natural aristocracy." Adams was rather skeptical about the notion, but Jefferson embraced it with relish: "The natural aristocracy," he proclaimed, "I consider as the most precious gift of nature for the instruction, the trusts, and government of society...May we not even say that that form of government is the best which provides the most effectually for a pure selection of these natural *aristoi* into the offices of government?"[1] All people may be equal, but in Jefferson's view some were much more qualified because of their natural "virtue and talents" to assume positions of authority in a well-ordered republican society.

Jefferson was by no means alone in the new republic in simultaneously praising equality while also suggesting that the acknowledgment of human differences and their implications was critical to establishing a viable political order. For many of the first generation of American political thinkers, the overriding question was not so much whether or not to have a republic, but how to create one that would last. Human frailty, the tendency toward corruption, and the presumed fragility of republics loomed large in their imaginations.[2] Virtue—particularly the virtue of political leaders and the small proportion of the populace that would be entrusted to choose them—was almost universally conceded to be one way to combat these tendencies and was deemed essential if a republic were to survive.[3] But virtue, while necessary, was rarely conceded to be sufficient. In theory, anyone—well, any white, adult, property-holding male—could be virtuous. But in most of the political imaginaries of the period, not anyone could rule. No one suggested choosing leaders by lot, even from the minority of the population that fit the criteria of independent and virtuous. Rather, they imagined elections where, as Jefferson suggested, those of superior talents or genius would be chosen to guide the republic. This was not accidental. Given the almost insuperable problems that establishing and maintaining a large republic were believed to present, most political writers concluded that only the most virtuous *and* talented could guide the nation successfully.[4]

This vision of rule by genius, as it were, did not come without its dangers. On the one side, as Joseph Perkins pointed out in his *An Oration upon Genius* (1797), those of genius and talent might choose other pursuits than public service, lured by the riches that seemed available to anyone in an "egalitarian republic" such as the United States, or that the electorate might be blind to its own true interests and so vote in those of lesser ability.[5] Perhaps the even greater danger lurked on the other side, where those of genius might prove themselves to be demagogues, less interested in *res publica* than in private gain and unlimited power, using their talents to turn the electorate and then the government to their own interests.[6] By the 1830s, Alexis de Tocqueville would worry about this problem explicitly when discussing the susceptibility of democratic republics to tyranny by the majority.[7] But even James Madison in the early moments of the formation of the new nation can be seen to have the problem of genius in mind when trying to fashion a structure for the republic that would insure that no single interest could dominate.[8] Genius thus seemed to bring with it both the power to make the republic and the power to destroy it.

This double nature of "genius," the sense it could be either beneficent or malevolent, has had a long history in the West, stretching at least from Goethe's *Faust* or Mary Shelley's *Frankenstein* to contemporary representations of heroic and evil scientists. This chapter will explore one aspect of that tradition, the way in which the double nature of genius figured in American social/political discourse during the late eighteenth and early nineteenth centuries, and the role that scientific/philosophical understandings of genius played in underwriting the conceptions of genius being promulgated. The chapter begins by examining the meaning of "genius" itself and the stabilities and changes in its denotations from the eighteenth century to the twentieth. There it highlights an important duality and tension in the meaning of the term and suggests how the dual nature of "genius" has remained alive in many ways right up to the present moment. The chapter then turns to the politics of "genius" and examines how "genius" was central to the development of the notion of republican meritocracy at the same time as it was seen to pose a threat to the very possibility of a republican democracy. Finally, the chapter concludes by considering how such a seemingly unstable combination as genius and democracy might have been able to persist in a kind of creative tension.

"Genius" in language and culture

In 1797, Joseph Perkins was called upon to give Harvard University's anniversary commencement address. The subject for his address was "genius," which he defined as

> significant of those variously modified intellectual powers, uncommon in kind or degree, by the possession, cultivation, and exertion of which, an individual is enabled to rise superior to the great mass of mankind, and by some extraordinary production, beneficial improvement, or difficult and important discovery, to bear away the palm of excellence from his envious or gratefully admiring cotemporaries.[9]

Perkins's characterization caught some of the key features of the term as it was commonly used at the time, mixing together almost promiscuously the sense of genius as some highly developed intellectual power, as something that raises an individual above the common run of humanity, and as something that results in (or perhaps is itself) an extraordinary accomplishment that might bring renown to its possessor. One of the tensions that would persist in the meaning of the term, right up to the present day, is whether genius refers to a kind of person ("a genius") or a specific instantiation, be it something produced or discovered ("that novel is a work of genius") or some highly developed ability ("she has a genius for research"). Giorgio Agamben, in his 2004 essay on "Genius," has highlighted another aspect of "genius," its impersonal quality, the sense that genius comes from without and remains distinct from the individual, from the "I," and indeed stands in constant tension with that "I."[10] Perkins does not directly allude to this feature of "genius," but the sense that genius might be something external to the individual is among the word's oldest associations in English, going back to notions of good or evil spirits that still persist in the plural form, "genii."[11] It contrasts with a rather different connotation, that genius is not so much a sport of nature as a product of nature, whether that be of the efforts of an individual to develop their genius or of nature itself to, in Thomas Paine's words in 1792, distribute "mental powers...as she pleases."[12] It will be worth laying out in a little detail the linguistic terrain that the word "genius" occupied in English from the eighteenth to the twentieth centuries in order to get a better sense of what kinds of possibilities, and dangers, lurked within the appropriation of the term for scientific and political speculation, as well as to understand better how its discursive field was dynamically reshaped in the course of its use.

Before examining meanings, however, we might ask a prior question, whether "genius" was a word of much social presence at all and thus worth taking the trouble to understand? One way to get some glimpse into the place of "genius" in the lexicon of the English-speaking world is to investigate its frequency of use. Figures 4.1a–4.6b were generated using Google Ngrams on the corpus of all English-language books in the Google Books data set and then on those denominated as "American English."[13] For all of the limits of Google's Ngram technology, and there are many, the sharp rise in the relative frequency of the word "virtue" and slow rise of "genius" starting in the first half of the eighteenth century are noteworthy (figures 4.1a, b), which is even more so if one were to add "talents" to "genius," as they were often used as virtual synonyms until nearly the middle of the nineteenth century (figures 4.2a, b).[14]

Figure 4.1a   English search for Genius + Virtue (1700–1940).

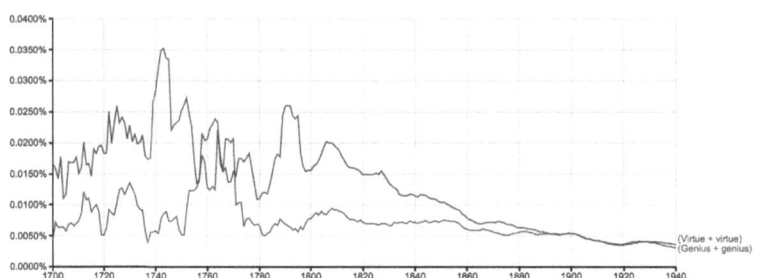

Figure 4.1b   American English search for Genius + Virtue (1700–1940).

Figure 4.2a   English search for Genius and Talents + Virtue (1700–1940).

Figure 4.2b American English search for Genius and Talents + Virtue (1700–1940).

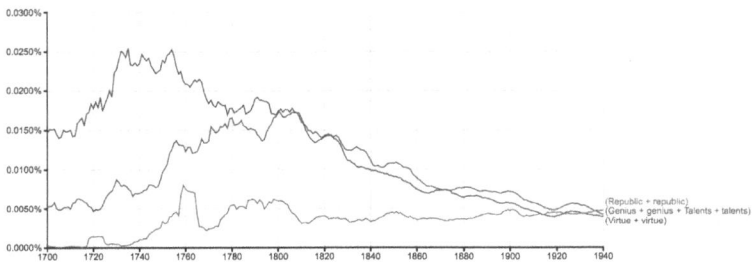

Figure 4.3a English search for Genius and Talents + Virtue + Republic (1700–1940).

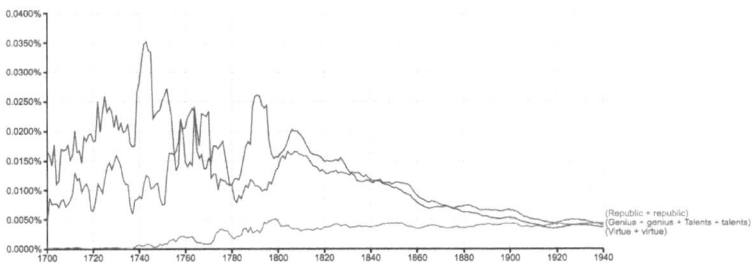

Figure 4.3b American English search for Genius and Talents + Virtue + Republic (1700–1940).

When the word "republic" is added to the analysis, we can get a sense of just how much more in play "virtue" and "genius" were even during the late eighteenth and early nineteenth centuries, a period when the concept of a republic was being debated and fought over as never before or never since (see figures 4.3a, b).

However, adding yet another keyword from the era, "fame," also reveals the limits to the language of genius, at least until the 1790s, when "fame" precipitously declined and by 1810 was completely eclipsed by "virtue" and "genius" (figures 4.4a, b).[15]

As one more point of comparison, consider the term "equality," which, like "virtue," rises to prominence during the early eighteenth century and then remains as an important term for the next 200 years (figures 4.5a, b).

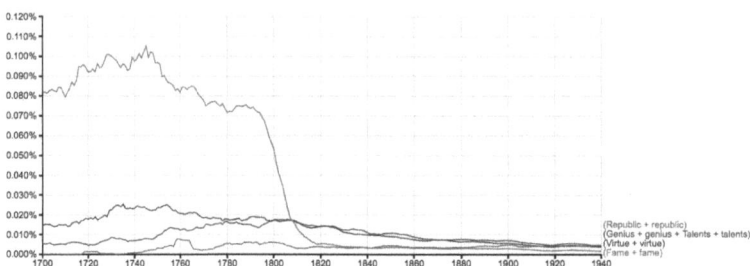

Figure 4.4a English search for Genius and Talents + Virtue + Republic + Fame (1700–1940).

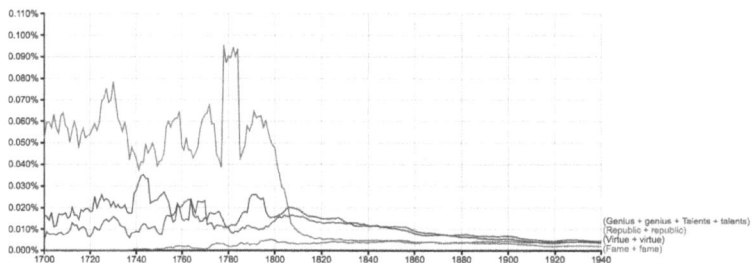

Figure 4.4b American English search for Genius and Talents + Virtue + Republic + Fame (1700–1940).

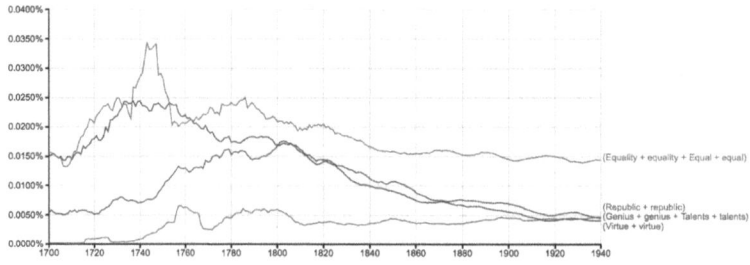

Figure 4.5a English search for Genius and Talents + Virtue + Republic + Equality (1700–1940).

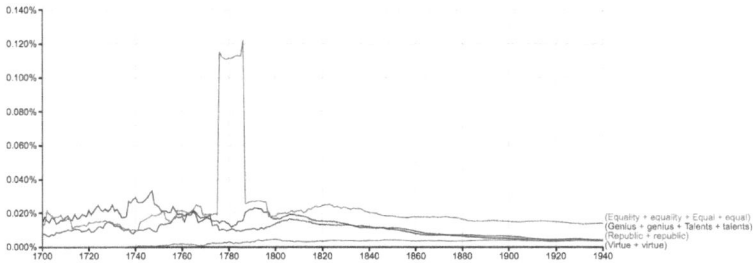

Figure 4.5b American English search for Genius and Talents + Virtue + Republic + Equality (1700–1940).

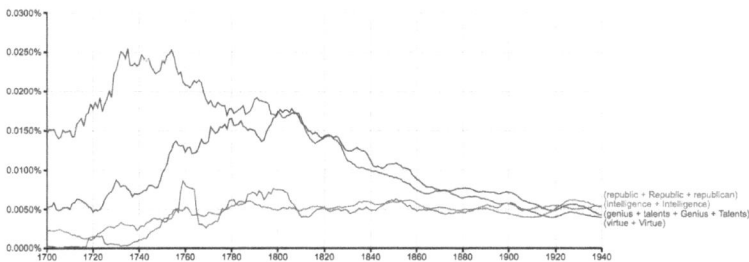

Figure 4.6a English search for Genius and Talents + Virtue + Republic + Intelligence (1700–1940).

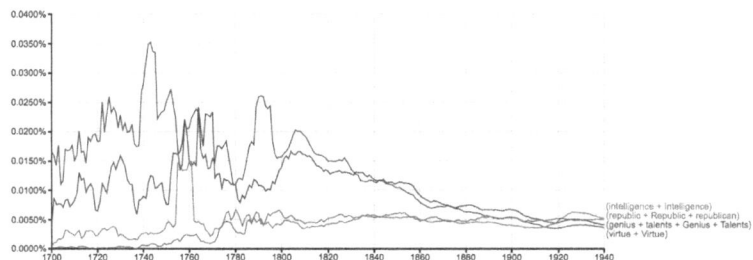

Figure 4.6b American English search for Genius and Talents + Virtue + Republic + Intelligence (1700–1940).

What the data suggest is that "genius" as a word began to rise steadily in usage in the English-language scene starting in the 1720s, peaked in the early 1800s when it matched "virtue" in frequency, and then slowly declined (along with "virtue") though still was significant until around 1920, when another word started to eclipse "genius," "intelligence" (see figures 4.6a, b).

More superficial analysis of other online databases for eighteenth- and nineteenth-century US publications confirms that the term "genius" was found everywhere, as present in African American newspapers, for example, as in elite philosophical texts.[16]

With regard to the meaning of "genius," there was a range of possibilities, as Samuel Johnson makes clear in his *Dictionary of the English Language* (1755). "Genius" could signify a spirit ("the protecting or ruling power of men, places, or things," as Johnson put it); "a man endowed with superior faculties"; "mental power or faculties" themselves; a natural disposition "for some peculiar employment"; or nature or disposition broadly understood, such as "the *genius* of the times" or, very commonly, the *genius* of a people.[17] The *Encyclopædia Britannica* of 1771 also defined "genius" first as "good or evil spirit," and then as "a natural talent or disposition to do one thing more than another," emphasizing with the latter that "art and industry add much to natural endowments, but cannot supply them where they are wanting."[18] The first American edition of the *Encyclopædia*, Thomas Dobson's published in Philadelphia in 1798, amplified this second sense, emphasizing that genius was something one was born with, but was also something very specific, such as "a genius for commanding an army."[19] In this formulation, the vision was of genius expressed in an almost unlimited variety of ways, "the diversity of genius," as the author put it, explained on the basis of the observation that nature "has made an unequal distribution of her blessings among her children; yet she has disinherited none; and a man divested of all kinds of abilities, is as great [i.e., rare] a phenomenon as an universal genius."[20] In the first edition of his *An American Dictionary of the English Language* (1828), Noah Webster provided six separate meanings for "genius," including "good or evil spirit," "a particular natural talent or aptitude of mind for a particular study or course of life," "uncommon powers of intellect," "man endowed with uncommon vigor of mind," and "peculiar character; as the *genius* of the times."[21] By the end of the century, *Webster's International Dictionary of the English Language* (1898) was still listing the same basic definitions, though now with a long explanation of how "genius" and "talent" differed: "genius" having more to do with intuition and the imagination, "talent" with mental training and command of all the faculties.[22]

What do these various definitions tell us? The notion of "genius" as "good or evil spirit," though listed by dictionaries throughout the eighteenth and nineteenth centuries as one of the principal meanings of the term, seems to have largely fallen out of fashion by the mid to late eighteenth century, at least in terms of explicit usage. Agamben's essay, however, suggests that this understanding of the term may well have shadowed some of its other meanings, a contention substantiated by the way in which a number of romantic authors characterized "genius" in their works.[23] Much more common, though, was "genius" used to refer to a highly developed but very specific mental ability, most probably present from birth. Typically, when used in this way, "genius" combined notions of inborn potential with the concentrated training or education deemed necessary to realize that potential, an emphasis on experience fully in keeping with both John Locke's associationist psychology and the faculty psychology of the Scottish Common Sense school.[24] Over the course of the eighteenth century, another meaning of "genius" began to gain traction, "genius" as suggesting overall mental superiority. In this guise, "genius" could refer not just to the power of an individual's mind but occasionally, and with increasing frequency, to a particular kind of person. The "genius," in a certain sense, began to appear as a real possibility by the early eighteenth century, a possibility perhaps already apparent in the Enlightenment's glorification of Isaac Newton. Alexander Pope's famous 1727 epitaph for Newton stands as a vivid emblem of the cult of Newton's genius. In Pope's rendering, Newton is imagined as almost a new kind of being, requiring his own special act of creation: "Nature, and Nature's Laws lay hid in Night: / GOD said, 'Let *Newton be!*' and all was Light."[25] Finally, "genius" was frequently used to refer to the peculiar character or "animating spirit" of a nation, people, religion, era, and so on. Over the course of the nineteenth century, this third sense would largely be eclipsed and "genius" as overall superiority would rise to equal and even surpass "genius" as a specific mental ability, particularly when "talents" or "abilities" or "aptitudes" came to be used much more typically to denote specific capabilities of great strength rather than overall ability.[26]

Underlying, or perhaps riding alongside, these specific denotations, "genius" has commonly embraced a second kind of distinction, one between genius as something fully naturalized and genius as in some way suggesting the uncanny. In the now classic interwar novel, *The Man without Qualities*, Austrian writer Robert Musil devoted the famous thirteenth chapter—"A Race-Horse of Genius Contributes to the Awareness of Being a Man without Qualities"—to a brilliant exploration of the tensions inherent in these two senses of genius. "If one were to analyse a powerful mind and a champion boxer from the psycho-technical point of view," Musil observes,

> it would in fact turn out that their cunning, their courage, their precision and their combinatory ability, as well as the quickness of their reactions on the territory that they have made their own, are approximately equal...In this way sport and functionalism have deservedly come into their own, displacing the out-of-date conceptions of genius and human greatness.[27]

With his reference to the "psycho-technical"—and here one might want to think about intelligence testing as the quintessential twentieth-century psycho-technics of genius—Musil suggests that genius as something out-of-the-ordinary and beyond the ken of science has been done away with. In its place is the ability to make commensurate all kinds of intellects, not just of different people but also across the whole of the animal kingdom, so that all are seen to be various degrees and manifestations of the same phenomenon, points on a series of bell-shaped curves. In this, Musil suggests, quite rightly as far as it goes, that genius was rendered via modern science into something ordinary and predictable and thus no longer a quality that could set the individual apart.[28]

However, Musil's own current standing, as one of the great writers, indeed geniuses, of twentieth-century letters, suggests that there may be another side to the story as well. Certainly the twentieth-century psychological sciences did, in a number of ways, tame genius and make it seem part of the normal order of things. At the same time, stories of the discovery of prodigies proliferated in America, particularly during the 1920s and 1930s, the heyday of intelligence testing.[29] And one of the great cultural shifts in the representation of genius, at least in America, was the displacement of Thomas Alva Edison, for whom genius was depicted as 99 percent perspiration, with Albert Einstein, whose genius seemed almost otherworldly, and who was represented more as a seer or prophet than as a tireless laborer in the vineyards of science.[30] As Marshall Missner has observed: "So, together with the view that Einstein was a great genius and a secular saint, there also developed the view that what Einstein had done would enable small groups of outsiders to use secret and mysterious methods to harness enormous power and thus control, and maybe destroy, the ordinary person's life. The reverential side became the predominant one, but the fearful side never went away, and it made a very significant contribution to the development of Einstein's fame."[31] Genius thus did not become simply psychotechnical in the modern age; rather, it retained, if in a modified form, the dual sensibility of being both part of the natural order and yet of also possibly standing in some sense outside of it, associations the word had had since it burst on the intellectual/political scene in the early eighteenth century. Indeed, these very tensions and multiplicities of meaning, as we shall see, were fundamental to making possible the political projects that saw in genius a powerful resource for articulating what a modern republic should look like. They constituted as well a fact about human nature that had to be taken into account in any serious vision of a republican polity that would be advanced.

"Genius" and the American republic

Rule by genius sounds far removed from current American politics, and even in that now mythologized moment of the "founding fathers," few would have subscribed explicitly to the notion of a republic ruled by some sort of intellectual or cognitive elite. America's revolution, as is well known, was as much about preserving a particular political and social order (and a rather stratified one, at that) as it was about trying to establish something radically new. Indeed, for all the talk of equality and universal rights as justification for revolution, most of the actual grievances were niggling at best (consider the whole second half of the *Declaration of Independence*, with its laundry list of rather minor complaints), and the underlying presumption was that stratifications in civil and political society would inevitably persist, even within the most privileged class of white, propertied males.[32] "Was there, or will there ever be," John Adams wondered in 1787, "a nation, whose individuals were all equal, in natural and acquired qualities, in virtues, talents, and riches? The answer of all mankind must be in the negative."[33] Thomas Jefferson was certainly more optimistic than Adams about the potential of education and abundant land to produce rough equality (at least for adult, white males) within a politically engaged republic of yeoman farmers. Nonetheless, the system of education he laid out in *Notes on the State of Virginia* was designed, as he so charmingly put it, so that "twenty of the best geniusses will be raked from the rubbish annually, and be instructed, at the public expence."[34] Such was the fate of young white males of the common sort; the elite would be allowed to pay for any of their children to continue on to advanced education, and women, native peoples, and African Americans simply never registered in his imaginary. Moreover, Jefferson too conceded that society would remain divided; he hoped, however, to ensure that such divisions were based on what he took to be the right criteria, the reward for an individual's virtues and talents, for their genius, rather than the legacy of family or rank.[35]

For both Adams and Jefferson, and indeed for Thomas Paine and almost anyone else touching on the subject, the nature of genius constituted one important stumbling block helping to insure that complete equality could never be achieved even in an ideal republic: some people simply were endowed from birth with particular talents, and those superior abilities, if allowed to flourish, either entitled those individuals to, or would help them to attain, positions of power in government and influence in civil society.[36] Rather than lament this "truth of nature," most political theorists sought to use it. They generally argued first that some sort of broadly available public education was necessary in order to insure that all those with natural genius would be identified and then receive training appropriate to their talents, and second that in one way or another the fact of human differences actually had the potential to help stabilize a republican form of government rather than undermine it.[37]

Although the United States never initiated any centralized plan for mass education in the manner of their French cousins after their revolution, at the local level the commitment to basic education for white males and often even white females is striking. British North America had already had a tradition of high literacy rates for both males and females well before the American Revolution, and important features of the new republican form of governance simply underscored the need for an educated citizenry.[38] Adult (white) propertied men had to be sufficiently educated so as to be able to distinguish the virtuous and able from the demagogues and self-interested when voting, and (white) women required sufficient schooling so as to be able to train properly the next generation of virtuous republican citizens.[39] Nonetheless, in addition to these rationales for broadly available comprehensive basic education, a number of writers argued that identifying those with particular genius and then training them to enhance their abilities were critical to the success of the new republic. Thus, Perkins extolled the new American republic as likely to be particularly conducive to genius, because with basic learning and education widespread, individuals from all strata of society would be able to "kindle into a flame those latent intellectual fires, which are calculated to enlighten and adorn the world."[40]

James Carter made the point even more forcefully in his *Essays upon Popular Education* (1826):

> While the best schools in the land are free, all the classes of society are blended. The rich and the poor meet and are educated together. And if educated together, nature is so even handed in the distribution of her favors that no fear need be entertained, that a monopoly of talent, of industry and consequently of acquirements will follow a monopoly of property.[41]

The value of the common school, Carter argued, lay in its ability to discover and nurture talents wherever they might arise.

This desire to find and develop the talents and genius of the populace served a number of functions for those imagining and carrying out the project of fashioning the new republic. First and foremost, of course, was its role in helping to establish a commitment to equality of opportunity, rather than equality of outcome, as a key attribute of the American republic.[42] As is well known, few of the revolutionary leaders were actually desirous of initiating fundamental changes in the social order. Their goal by and large was to place the existing hierarchy (with perhaps a few additions from among those of genius in the lower ranks) on a new, and even firmer, footing, one that would fit the dictates of reason and not just accord with the commonplaces of tradition. This meant finding ways to justify privilege and distinction that could be meshed with commitments to republican equality. A republic based on merit, one where (white, male) individuals rose or fell according to the particular set of virtues and talents that they possessed (whether through birth or education or both), for many, fit the bill admirably.[43] As even that noted champion of the common people, Andrew Jackson, declared in 1832: "Distinctions in society will always exist under every just government. Equality of talents, of education, or of wealth cannot be produced by human institutions. In the full enjoyment of the gifts of Heaven and the fruits of superior industry, economy, and virtue, every man is equally entitled to protection by law."[44]

Not that many republicans, whether radical or conservative, spoke explicitly in the language of merit. In America, direct discussions of merit would not really blossom until near the end of the nineteenth century, when the spoils system and the power of urban immigrant political machines were challenged in the name of new systems of hiring based explicitly on merit and not party loyalty. Earlier, the words "virtue," "talents," and "genius" were used almost ubiquitously to identify the kinds of characteristics that justified advanced education or election to public office. Jefferson, as has already been indicated, proposed an educational system where only the "best geniuses" among the common folk would move up the educational ladder; the purpose, as he explained, was "to avail the state of those talents which nature has sown as liberally among the poor as the rich, but which perish without use, if not sought for and cultivated."[45] James Madison discussed explicitly the interrelations of republican politics and human capacities in *Federalist* No. 58 (1788), when discussing the proper size for the House of Representatives. Those "of limited information and of weak capacities," he maintained, were most likely to be susceptible to demagogues and thus to allow a democratic republic to be transformed into an oligarchy. Republics, Madison concluded, required representatives who were knowledgeable and intellectually talented in order to survive.[46]

It is, of course, one thing to celebrate a republic of genius and another to actually create one. Or perhaps, to put it more accurately, it is one thing to celebrate talents and genius, and another literally to establish a polity where those characteristics really would supersede all others in power and influence. Clearly, that would have been the kind of social revolution for which the supporters were scarce, at least among the elite. Two related strategies emerged to contain this possibility. Jefferson's plan for education reveals one: while the poor would be sifted for those few of potential genius to gain special training, the well-off could by-pass this system and simply pay for the education necessary to make their children, if not the absolutely most talented in their areas of interest, at least skilled enough to be readily considered part of the virtuous and talented. Until the enactment of the Morrill Land-Grant Act of 1862, broad basic education for a relatively large portion of the white population was paired with higher education limited to a tiny proportion of the population, mostly white and male, and almost all requiring private support from families or a willingness to enter the ministry to attend college.[47] Thus, as the liberal arts colleges promoted their production of "virtuous, cultivated Christian gentlemen," as most of them did, they created for the social elite a direct means virtually to insure that their sons (and even some daughters) could be readily considered among the nation's talented—their genius sharpened as much as was possible.[48]

The second strategy for containing many of the radical possibilities inherent in refounding the social/political order on merit was to suggest, as so many early theorists of republican governance did, that those with genius would almost naturally rise to the top, whether in governance or any other sector of the social order. Because this was depicted as, at times, an almost natural law, the suggestion was that a corollary should follow from it: that those who had achieved positions of political and social power must be those who are among the virtuous and talented. Genius is known by its deeds, the dictionaries pointed out. Achieving a position of power or authority is a sign of success; thus, if the system is working correctly, it must have taken talent to arrive at a place of note.

Certainly not everyone accepted the most extreme form of this ideology; many of the dispossessed fought not only the authority of the elite but the very right of that elite to wield such authority.[49] Nonetheless, it is striking how often not just working-class Jacksonians but African Americans and women and others argued for their inclusion in governance or the professions on the basis of genius and talent, rather than basing such decisions on different criteria altogether. For example, Hannah Mather asserted in 1818 that "the wise Author of nature has endowed the female mind with equal powers and faculties, and given them the same right of judging and acting for themselves, as he gave to the male sex."[50] Claims about the particularly developed genius of various African Americans—including Benjamin Banneker, Thomas Fuller, and Phillis Wheatley—filled the pages of *Freedom's Journal*, the *Colored American*, and other papers in attempts to demonstrate not only that African peoples were not biologically inferior as a race, but that a system that rewarded fairly the individual talent of anyone, whatever their color, would benefit blacks as much as it did whites.[51] One need only think of W. E. B. Du Bois's celebration of the "talented tenth" at the turn of the twentieth century to see how thoroughly the language of talent and genius as justification for differential access to positions of power and influence came to seem natural in America.[52]

This undergirding and naturalizing of a language of merit around the notion of equality of opportunity was, in all likelihood, the most powerful and important political role that notions of genius played in the United States, from the founding of the republic up to the present moment. It helped establish a logic of inclusion and exclusion that continues to guide aspects of the nation's political and social debate. But it was by no means the only one. There were at least two other ways in which "genius" in its various guises proved to be a critical tool for those trying to imagine and then realize the possibility of establishing a viable republic. Both spoke directly to key problems lying at the heart of republican theory: the issue of self-interest and the fear of the passions. Without wishing to exhume or get entangled in the long and complex historiographical debate over republicanism, what it was, and who advocated which version of it, one can safely say that a concern articulated by almost every political writer who weighed in on how to organize the new republic was the worry about self-interest versus concern with the public good, along with the related issue of how to insure that the passions were kept in check by reason.[53] Typically, these were framed as the need to restrict the active citizenry—those who could vote and hold office—to those who could be deemed to be independent (i.e., property-owning adult white males), and thus able to rise above their specific interests to consider dispassionately the good of the whole of the nation, the *res publica*.[54]

By 1800, George Washington became one symbol of this figure, lionized in the American press for his self-sacrifice and, tellingly, for his genius.[55] Partly, the new nation was in search of heroes, and who better than Washington, the man who had defeated the British Empire, refused the possibility of becoming king, retired after two terms as president, and then conveniently died soon after leaving office? But encomiums to his genius as well as his virtue were signaling something else as well, that it took more than the status of being an independent yeoman farmer to actually see rightly what the needs of the nation as a whole might be. It required talents—genius—to look beyond self-interest and to overcome the ability of the passions to overwhelm reason.[56] The new nation might have foundered if a person of lesser genius had been at the helm in those crucial early moments. Independence was surely necessary, but perhaps the ability to put aside self-interest for republican virtue was not sufficient to guarantee that an individual would see rightly, guided by reason alone, what was best for the whole. From this perspective, the earnest proclamations by so many political writers that those with virtue *and* talents would almost inevitably rise to the top and be chosen by the electorate to assume positions of authority and leadership may have reflected less their confidence in the new nation than their own fears that without the ability of those with genius to see clearly and dispassionately, the republic might perish, however well intentioned the leadership.

If genius promised great things to those imagining how to create a viable new republic, it also presented certain threats. Embedded in the developing language of meritocracy, notions of genius and equality of opportunity could be used to maintain the status quo, reframing long-standing exclusions of women, the working class, African Americans, and others from significant positions of power and authority, now on the presumably rational grounds of merit rather than the arbitrary ones of privilege and custom.[57] While members of each of these groups turned repeatedly to the language of the *Declaration of Independence*, with its proclamation of the equality of all, to press for an expansion of their powers and opportunities, they faced in the nineteenth century an American republic where basic legal and citizenship rights, even when accorded, did not necessarily guarantee access to significant sites of authority. Rhetorically, anyway, they had to give evidence of their genius as well, and the structures of education plus presumptions about what kinds of talent were relevant to what kinds of authority constituted for most significant obstacles to advancement. This state of affairs was particularly clear with women, who were typically represented not so much as mentally inferior to men as mentally different (whether by nature or from education), having their own forms of genius, which suited them for domestic work and child raising, but not for politics or the professions.[58]

Genius presented a different sort of problem to those wanting not so much to change the social order as to maintain it. First, the very possibility that genius of one sort or another could flower anywhere meant that the possibility of monopolizing power and authority could never feel completely secure. New claims coming from those whose abilities were manifest might prove difficult to contain, and might include demands for much broader recognition of the talents of the social group to which the individual belonged, demands that could be readily couched in the very language of merit that was developed to help marginalize such claims. Frederick Douglass mined this possibility with great success in mid-century America, using his eloquence, intellect, and mounting fame to symbolize vividly, at least to some, the possibility that whole groups of Americans—those of African heritage—should be accorded real opportunities for intellectual development and inclusion in the polity.[59] A second kind of threat lurked in the very logic of republican theory, in the worries about the untamed passions of the multitude. That threat was the demagogue, a figure of genius but without the virtue to keep that genius working for the common good. As Francis Wayland astutely observed in 1842:

> There will always be produced native talent, vast power of influencing mankind, united with restless, aspiring and insatiate ambition. And this talent will be unfolded in greater proportion as common education is more generally diffused. The question, then, is not whether such talent shall or shall not exist. The only practical question is, whether these rare endowments shall be cultivated and disciplined and cautioned and directed by the lessons of past wisdom, or whether they shall be allowed to grow up in reckless and headstrong arrogance...It is merely a question whether the extraordinary talent bestowed upon society by our Creator, shall be a blessing or a curse to us and to our children.[60]

In this vision, the genius is able to step outside of all the careful mechanisms designed by Madison and others to keep power safely out of the hands of any single interest group. Following the logic of the tyranny of the majority that Tocqueville lays out so brilliantly in *Democracy in America*, genius linked with restless and uncontained ambition might use the very potential that a republican democracy presents to undercut the very functioning of that system.[61]

Conclusion

This chapter has sought to sketch out a picture of some of the roles that "genius" and its allied term "talents" played in the American political imaginary during the formation and early decades of the republic. Central was the way in which notions of genius and talents could create a seemingly natural and almost uncontestable language of inequality at that same time as equality could be trumpeted as a fundamental truth of politics and society. Rather than being completely at odds, there proved to be powerful ways of writing these stories together, so that the principle of equality, once rendered as equality of opportunity, could lead almost inexorably to inequality. I would like to finish, though, by returning to the tensions lurking within "genius" between the quotidian and uncanny. The sense of genius as a kind of person, a sport of nature, a conduit for truths almost independent of the genius himself, or herself, carries with it an intrinsic threat, that all attempts to domesticate genius might prove futile. Henry David Thoreau is one of the most obvious nineteenth-century examples, and perhaps Dr. Strangelove stands in well for one type of the twentieth-century version.

Notes

1. Thomas Jefferson to John Adams, October 28, 1813, in *The Adams-Jefferson Letters*, ed. Lester J. Cappon (Chapel Hill: University of North Carolina Press, 1988), 388; and John Adams to Thomas Jefferson, November 15, 1813, in *The Adams-Jefferson Letters*, 397–400.

2. See, for example, the repeated addressing of such issues by James Madison and Alexander Hamilton in *The Federalist Papers*. For some important secondary works, see Isaac Kramnick, *Republicanism or Bourgeois Radicalism: Political Ideology in Late Eighteenth-Century England and America* (Ithaca, NY: Cornell University Press, 1990); Anthony Pagden, ed., *The Languages of Political Theory in Early-Modern Europe* (Cambridge: Cambridge University Press, 1987); and J. G. A. Pocock, *The Machiavellian Moment: Florentine Political Thought and the Atlantic Republican Tradition* (Princeton, NJ: Princeton University Press, 1975).

3. For a sampling of the enormous literature on virtue, see Ruth H. Bloch, "The Gendered Meanings of Virtue in Revolutionary America," *Signs: Journal of Women in Culture and Society* 13 (1987): 37–58; James T. Kloppenberg, "The Virtues of Liberalism: Christianity, Republicanism, and Ethics in Early American Political Discourse," *Journal of American History* 74 (1987): 9–33.

4. See Gordon S. Wood, *The Radicalism of the American Revolution* (New York: Knopf, 1992), esp. 229–43, 271–86; Edmund S. Morgan, *Inventing the People: The Rise of Popular Sovereignty in England and America* (New York: W. W. Norton, 1988), 288–303; Gordon S. Wood, *The Creation of the American Republic, 1776–1787* (New York: W. W. Norton, 1969), 506–18.

5. Joseph Perkins, *An Oration upon Genius* (Boston, MA: Joseph Nancrede, 1797).

6. John Jay, in *Federalist* No. 64, argued that the age restrictions for president and senator were necessary because "it confines the electors to men of whom the people have had time to form a judgment, and with respect to whom they will not be liable to be deceived by those brilliant appearances of genius and patriotism, which, like transient meteors, sometimes mislead as well as dazzle." See John Jay, *Federalist* No. 64: "The Powers of the Senate," from *The New York Packet*, Friday, March 7, 1788 at http://thomas.loc.gov/home/histdox/fed_64.html.

7. See Alexis de Tocqueville, *Democracy in America*, 2 vols. (London: Penguin, 2003), esp. vol. 1, pt. 2, chs. 5–9, vol. 2, pt. 4, chs. 2–4.

8. In *Federalist* No. 10, Madison discusses the diversity of faculties in men and how that can mean some are much more successful in accruing property (and power) than others. James Madison, *Federalist* No. 10: "The Powers of the Senate," from *The New York Packet*, Friday, March 7, 1788 at "The Same Subject Continued: The Union as a Safeguard against Domestic Faction and Insurrection," from *The New York Packet*, Friday, November 23, 1787 at http://thomas.loc.gov/home/histdox/fed_10.html.

9. Perkins, *Oration upon Genius*, 8

10. Giorgio Agamben, "Genius," in *Profanations*, trans. Jeff Fort (New York: Zone Books, 2007), 9–18.

11. See "Genius, n. and adj.," *Oxford English Dictionary Online*, 3rd ed., Oxford University Press, December 2014. http://www.oed.com.proxy.lib.umich.edu/view/Entry/77607?redirectedFrom=genius (accessed March 14, 2015).

12. Thomas Paine, *Rights of Man* (1792; rep., New York: Penguin, 1985), 175.

13. I have real reservations about just what this technology in its present state can tell us, as it is notoriously rife with inaccuracies (indeed, from some spot checking I did, the graph of American English appears to be of questionable value, as many of the texts in its data set were actually British in origin).

14. On "talents," see John Carson, *The Measure of Merit: Talents, Intelligence, and Inequality in the French and American Republics, 1750–1940* (Princeton, NJ: Princeton University Press, 2007), 26–32.

15. On the notion of "fame" in the early republic, see Douglas Adair, "Fame and the Founding Fathers," [1967], in *Fame and the Founding Fathers*, ed. Trevor Colbourn (New York: W. W. Norton, 1974), 3–36.

16. I found 221,918 instances of "genius" in American newspapers indexed in *America's Historical Newspapers* Readex database between 1750 and 1860, and 157 instances in the *African American Periodicals* Readex database between 1825 and 1860. However in the *Accessible Archives African American Newspapers* database I found 1,961 instances of "genius" between 1825 and 1860.

17. Samuel Johnson, *A dictionary of the English language: in which the words are deduced from their originals, and illustrated in their different significations by examples from the best writers. To which are prefixed, a history of the language, and an English grammar. By Samuel Johnson, A.M. In two volumes*, vol. 1, 2nd ed. (London, 1755–1756), n.p. Eighteenth Century Collections Online, Gale. University of Michigan March 14, 2015. http://find.galegroup.com.proxy.lib.umich.edu/ecco/infomark.do?&source=gale&prodId=ECCO&userGroupName=umuser&tabID=T001&docId=CW3311286175&type=multipage&contentSet=ECCOArticles&version=1.0&docLevel=FASCIMILE.

18. *Encyclopædia Britannica; or, a dictionary of arts and sciences, compiled upon a new plan...Illustrated with one hundred and sixty copperplates. By a Society of gentlemen in Scotland. In three volumes*, vol. 2 (Edinburgh, 1771), 672. Eighteenth Century Collections Online, Gale. University of Michigan. March 14, 2015 http://find.galegroup.com.proxy.lib.umich.edu/ecco/infomark.do?&source=gale&prodId=ECCO&userGroupName=umuser&tabID=T001&docId=CW3326042865&type=multipage&contentSet=ECCOArticles&version=1.0&docLevel=FASCIMILE.

19. Thomas Dobson, *Encyclopædia: or, A dictionary of arts, sciences, and miscellaneous literature; constructed on a plan, by which the different sciences and arts are digested into the form of distinct treatises or systems, comprehending the history, theory, and practice, of each, according to the latest discoveries and improvements; and full explanations given of the various detached parts of knowledge, whether relating to natural and artificial objects, or to matters ecclesiastical, civil, military, commercial, &c., including elucidations of the most important topics relative to religion, morals, manners, and the œconomy of life; together with a description of all the countries, cities, principal mountains, seas, rivers, &c. throughout the world; a general history, ancient and modern, of the different empires, kingdoms, and states; and an account of the lives of the most eminent persons in every nation, from the earliest ages down to the present times*, vol. 7 (Philadelphia, 1798), 623–24.

20. Dobson, *Encyclopædia*, 624.

21. Noah Webster, *An American Dictionary of the English Language: Intended to Exhibit, I. The origin, affinities and primary signification of English words, as far as they have been ascertained. II. The genuine orthography and pronunciation of words, according to general usage, or to just principles of analogy. III. Accurate and discriminating definitions, with numerous authorities and illustrations. To Which Are Prefixed, an Introductory Dissertation on the Origin, History and Connection of the Languages of Western Asia and of Europe, and a Concise Grammar of the English Language*, vol. 1 (New York, 1828), 818.

22. Noah Porter, ed., *Webster's International Dictionary of the English Language. Being the Authentic Edition of Webster's Unabridged Dictionary, Comprising the Issues of 1864, 1879, and 1884* (Springfield: G. & C. Merriam, 1898), 619–20.

23. See Agamben, "Genius," esp. pp. 13–14; Darrin M. McMahon, *Divine Fury: A History of Genius* (New York: Basic Books, 2013), esp. ch. 4.

24. See Carson, *Measure of Merit*, esp. 14–20, 44–52.

25. Alexander Pope, "Intended for Sir Isaac Newton, in Westminster-Abbey," in *The Works of Alexander Pope*, vol. II (London, 1822), 379.

26. See Carson, *Measure of Merit*, esp. 26–32.

27. Robert Musil, *The Man without Qualities*, vol. 1: *A Sort of Introduction the Like of It Now Happens (I)*, trans. Ethne Wilkins and Ernst Kaiser (London: Secker & Warburg, 1953), 47.

28. This is clear in Francis Galton's earliest presentations of his statistical understanding of genius. Francis Galton, *Hereditary Genius: An Inquiry into Its Laws and Consequences* (London, 1869). For discussions of the domestication of genius, see Carson, *Measure of Merit*, ch. 5; Raymond Fancher, *The Intelligence Men: Makers of the IQ Controversy* (New York: W. W. Norton, 1985), 18–40; Theodore M. Porter, *The Rise of Statistical Thinking, 1820–1900* (Princeton, NJ: Princeton University Press, 1986), 128–46, 270–314.

29. Carson, *Measure of Merit*, 255.

30. For some contemporary examples extolling Einstein's genius, see, for example, Emil Ludwig, "Are There Great Men Today?," *New York Times*, August 28, 1927; "Einstein Receives Keys to the City," *New York Times*, December 14, 1930; "Sees a New Science

Mapped by Einstein," *New York Times*, August 21, 1931. For scholarly analysis, see Marshall Missner, "Why Einstein Became Famous in America," *Social Studies of Science* 15 (May 1985): 267–91; Jozsef Illy, ed., *Albert Meets America: How Journalists Treated Genius during Einstein's 1921 Travels* (Baltimore, MD: Johns Hopkins University Press, 2006).

31. Missner, "Why Einstein Became Famous," 288.
32. See Gary Kornblith and John M. Murrin, "The Making and Unmaking of an American Ruling Class," in *Beyond the American Revolution: Explorations in the History of American Radicalism*, ed. Alfred F. Young (DeKalb: Northern Illinois University Press, 1993), 27–79; Wood, *Creation of the American Republic*, esp. 70–75, 471–518; Morton G. White, *The Philosophy of the American Revolution* (New York: Oxford University Press, 1978).
33. John Adams, "Defence of the Constitutions of Government of the United States (1787)," in *The Works of John Adams*, vol. 4, ed. Charles Francis Adams (Boston, MA, 1850–1856), 391.
34. Thomas Jefferson, "Notes on the State of Virginia (1781–1785)," in *The Portable Thomas Jefferson*, ed. Merrill D. Peterson (New York: Penguin, 1977), 196.
35. Jefferson to John Adams, October 28, 1813, *Adams-Jefferson Letters*, 388.
36. See Carson, *Measure of Merit*, ch. 1.
37. Madison argues this point explicitly in *Federalist* No. 10.
38. See, for example, Carl F. Kaestle, *Pillars of the Republic: Common Schools and American Society, 1780–1860* (New York: Hill & Wang, 1983).
39. See Linda K. Kerber, *Women of the Republic: Intellect and Ideology in Revolutionary America* (Chapel Hill: University of North Carolina Press, 1980).
40. Perkins, *Oration upon Genius*, 10.
41. James G. Carter, *Essays upon Popular Education, Containing a Particular Examination of the Schools of Massachusetts and an Outline of an Institution for the Education of Teachers* (1826; rep., New York: Arno Press, 1969), 20.
42. See Wood, *Creation of the American Republic*, esp. 70–75; Wood, *Radicalism of the American Revolution*, 180–86.
43. See Carson, *Measure of Merit*, chs. 1–2.
44. Andrew Jackson, "Veto Message," quoted in Richard Hofstadter, *The American Political Tradition* (New York: Vintage, 1948), 62.
45. Jefferson, *Notes on the State of Virginia*, 198.
46. James Madison, *Federalist* No. 58, "Objection That the Number of Members Will Not Be Augmented as the Progress of Population Demands Considered," [1788]; at http://thomas.loc.gov/home/histdox/fed_58.htm.
47. See Frederick Rudolph, *The American College and University: A History* (New York: Vintage, 1962); David B. Potts, "Curriculum and Enrollment: Assessing the Popularity of Antebellum Colleges," in *The American College in the Nineteenth Century*, ed. Roger Geiger (Nashville: Vanderbilt University Press, 2000), 37–45.
48. Mary Kelley, *Empire of Reason: The Making of Learned Women in America's Republic* (Chapel Hill: University of North Carolina Press, 2006).
49. See Sean Wilentz, *Chants Democratic: New York City and the Rise of the American Working Class, 1788–1850* (New York: Oxford University Press, 1986).
50. Hannah Mather Crocker, *Observations on the Real Rights of Women, with Their Appropriate Duties, Agreeable to Scripture, Reason and Common Sense* (1818), reprinted in *Sex and Equality* (New York: Arno Press, 1974), 5.
51. See *Freedom's Journal*, vols. 1–2 (1827–1829); *The Colored American* vols. 1–3 (1837–1839), n.s. vols. 1–2 (1840–1841); Carson, *Measure of Merit*, 93–95; Mia Bay, *The White Image in the Black Mind: African-American Ideas about White People, 1830–1925* (New York: Oxford University Press, 2000), chs. 1–2; Bruce Dain, *A Hideous Monster of the Mind: American Race Theory in the Early Republic* (Cambridge, MA: Harvard University Press, 2002).
52. See W. E. B. Du Bois, "The Talented Tenth," in *The Negro Problem: A Series of Articles by Representative Negroes of To-day* (New York: James Pott, 1903).
53. See J. G. A. Pocock, *Virtue, Commerce, and History: Essays on Political Thought and History, Chiefly in the Eighteenth Century* (Cambridge: Cambridge University Press, 1985).

54. See Gordon S. Wood, "Interests and Disinterestedness in the Making of the Constitution," in *Beyond Confederation: Origins of the Constitution and American National Identity*, ed. Richard Beeman, Stephen Botein, and Edward C. Carter II (Chapel Hill: University of North Carolina Press, 1987), 69–109; Pocock, *Machiavellian Moment*.

55. See, for example, Henry Lee, "Funeral Oration in Honour of the Memory of George Washington," *The Maryland Gazette*, January 16, 1800; "Extract from a Sermon, on the Death of General Washington, Preached at Burlington, N. J. by the Rev. Dr. Wharton," *Gazette of the United States*, January 8, 1800, vol. XVII; "Judge Minot's Eulogy on Gen. George Washington," *Thomas's Massachusetts Spy*, January 29, 1800, vol. XXVIII; "Eulogy on the Late Illustrious Citizen, George Washington. Delivered in Lexington, on Saturday the 25th," *Stewart's Kentucky Herald*, February 11, 1800, vol. V; Gouverneur Morris, "An Oration, upon the Death of General Washington, Delivered at the Request of the Corporation of the City of New-York," *The Providence Journal, and Town and Country Advertiser*, February 12, 1800, vol. II; "New-York; Friday, February 14, 1800," *Commercial Advertiser*, February 14, 1800, vol. III; Samuel Stanhope Smith, "An Oration upon the Death of Gen. George Washington," *The Centinel of Liberty, and George-Town and Washington Advertiser*, March 18, 1800, vol. V.

56. "The Sun of our glory has set forever: WASHINGTON is no more!" announced *Thomas's Massachusetts Spy*. "Capt. Dunham's Funeral Oration," *Thomas's Massachusetts Spy*, February 19, 1800, vol. XXVIII.

57. See Carson, *Measure of Merit*, chs. 1–3.

58. See Ibid., 52–60.

59. See John Stauffer, *The Black Hearts of Men: Radical Abolitionists and the Transformation of Race* (Cambridge, MA: Harvard University Press, 2002).

60. Francis Wayland, *Thoughts on the Present Collegiate System in the United States* (Boston, MA: Gould, Kendall and Lincoln, 1842), 7.

61. Tocqueville, *Democracy in America*, vol. 1, pt. 2, chs. 7–8.

5

Genius and Obsession: Do You Have to Be Mad to Be Smart?

Lennard J. Davis

I intend in this chapter to focus on one specific side of genius—its relation to psychological states and diagnoses, most particularly obsessive thinking and compulsive behaviors. My interest is less to locate madness in any one person and more in observing the change of certain kinds of epistemological categories that reshape the nature of knowledge about madness and genius and the instantiation of that knowledge within culture.

My claim is that one of the key factors in the rise of the idea of the genius is a type of ruminative, obsessive thinking combined with a compulsive type of repetition and practice. In other words, although genius may have been around for a very long time, it seems our modern sense of genius, beginning in 1750 or so, is tied up with a new notion of obsession, and both of these terms—genius (as in "he is a genius") and obsession—arose in tandem in the latter part of the eighteenth century through the nineteenth century. In linking with this volume's theme, I will also be claiming that the development of obsession is in fact part of a democratizing of madness.

Linking genius and madness is not a unique or original claim. Is it not the case that madness and genius have had a long and documented history? We know that Plato links poetry to divine madness in the *Phaedrus*, although let us be clear that he is not talking about genius in our modern sense but more likely divinely inspired frenzy (using the word *manike*, which better translates as "mania"). Aristotle, or rather his student Theophrastus, asks "why is it that all men who are outstanding in philosophy, poetry, and the arts are melancholics?" Indeed, melancholia had a long and detailed history in its association with creativity. Melancholia and mania were categories that held sway until the eighteenth century and tended to dominate the *Diagnostic and Statistical Manual of Mental Disorders (DSM)* equivalent of the time. All mental distress ultimately funneled into these two categories depending on whether the madness was passive or active. Indeed, the famous sculpture over the entrance to the London hospital Bedlam depicted these two states of being.

I am describing a radical change in the way mental distress was conceptualized, which I study in more detail in my book *Obsession: A History* (2008), from the Aristotelian and Galenic notion of human psychology to a new one. This new view abandons the regnant distinction between passive and active (melancholic and manic—il penseroso and l'allegro, as Milton would have put it). This new view also shifts from a world in which madness was a rare thing that dominated one's entire sensorium to a diagnosis that was endemic to humans, could be partial, and was found in not just abject beings but actually the best and the brightest, the cream of society and culture. Another way of saying this is that the madness that got people thrown into Bedlam became the madness that got people to write dictionaries, novels, compile statistics, and the like. Along with this broadening of the concept of madness came a kind of democratization of madness. Allowing everyone to be mad then allowed, by extension, everyone to become a kind of genius. Indeed, Dr. Johnson makes it sound as if it is an imperative for each person to try to be a genius. "Since a genius, whatever it be, is like fire in the flint, only to be produced by collision with a proper subject, it is the business of every man to try whether his faculties may not happily cooperate with his desires; and since they whose proficiency he admires, knew their own force only by the event, he needs but engage in the same undertaking, with equal spirit, and may reasonably hope for equal success."[1] A larger question to ask is whether the democratization of madness led to the democratization of genius (itself a contradiction that could undo the very category of genius).[2]

Perhaps what I am saying is that madness is not one thing but a generic term for various behaviors and symptoms that vary from period to period. The kind of madness we see in Shakespeare's plays is one that comes on in a moment and is a total alienation from meaning and the world (although there might be truth in that madness, or as Polonius says, "method"). But in the new view of madness (the one I am relating to genius), madness is actually a method, a way of being in the world very much tied up to the development of the early modern zeitgeist.

Alexander Anderson in 1796 allows for a continuum between madness and genius, writing "that we can scarcely say where rationality ends and folly begins. No less difficult would the task be to determine the point at which madness commences, since very inordinate indulgence of the passions partakes of it, and even low spirits and absence of mind may be reckoned as slighter degrees of the same affection." He goes on to acknowledge that great genius is itself like madness, and both Christ and St. Paul were accused of being "demoniac, or in other words, a madman." Echoing Plato, he continues: "The transition from poetic ardor to madness is easy; hence some of the most sublime of imagination have been the productions of a disordered mind." Anderson here reflects not the new view of madness but the old one—the Platonic notion of frenzy or the lethargy of melancholy. And more tellingly he sees madness as a "disordered mind." But, in fact, the new madness, what came to be called obsession, is not disordered at all but hyper-ordered, with that super-organized or attentive part taking over the rest of the mind.[3]

In that regard, many people saw this new madness as tied up with scholarly study, reading, and repetitive activities. For example, Samuel-Auguste Tissot writes that "the brain of Blaise Pascal was so vitiated by passing his life in the laborious exercises of study, thought, and imagination, that certain fibers, agitated by incessant motion, made him perpetually feel a sensation which seem'd to be excited by a globe of fire being plac'd on one side of him; and his reason being overpower'd by the disorder of his nerves, he could scarce banish the idea of the fiery globe being actually present."[4] It is worth pointing out that Pascal's "disorder" is no longer of the mind but of the nerves—a very different concept. Rather than the mind's categories being thrown out of whack, the nerves are the culprits that energize or enervate the mind. In this new madness, the mind is not at all disordered, but one faculty of the mind predominates. This new activation or enervation model was called, appropriately, monomania. The mania is now no longer totalizing but is located in a particular ability or faculty of the mind. So, thoughts are not disordered but their equality is—with one taking a superior or dictatorial role. Just at the moment when equality and democracy is being touted as primary human rights, the problem with monomania is that one faculty now becomes, as it were, the tyrannical ruler over the others.

Thomas Arnold writes in 1782 that "it has been commonly asserted, that persons of greater abilities, and genius, are more liable to madness than men of inferior understandings... it is true, that persons of great inventive genius, of fine imagination, and of lively feeling, if not blessed with great judgment, as well as with the best moral dispositions, are so situated up on the verge of madness, that they easily fall into it."[5] In this statement we see that those most likely to become mad are geniuses, and this is because their faculties are that much more powerful than those of ordinary people, so when the democracy of the mind becomes overthrown, the power of an individual faculty can tyrannize.

French aesthetic theory, according to Kinneret Jaffe, bears out this trajectory from a notion that the genius is a person who is rational to the person who is a genius because of emotions and enthusiasm. In this latter case, the genius must be careful because the very thing that powers his or her way of creating is the very thing that can drive that person mad. In fact, Diderot says that the genius is mad. In that he points to enthusiasm as a productive force, even if it carried some of the elements of madness that Swift satirized in his "Mechanical Operation of the Spirit."[6]

This worry about enthusiasm translates itself into worries about extreme devotion to anything. Thomas Trotter in 1807 observes of studious men that "the mind itself by pursuing one train of thought, and poring too long over the same subject becomes torpid to external agents... Hence the numerous instances of dyspepsia, hypochondriasis and melancholia, in the literary character."[7] Pursuing a single train of thought becomes the cause of monomania, which is itself the disease of pursuing a single train of thought. So the cause of the disease and the symptoms are the same. And the activity most often cited for the development of monomania or obsession is too much reading and thinking. Thus the scholar, writer, critic, and artist were all the ones most likely to suffer this new, particular kind of madness. Indeed, people began to describe themselves willingly as suffering from such a condition, as did Sir Walter Scott who wrote of himself that he suffered from *"morbus eruditorum* [scholar's disease]."[8]

What I am pointing to is a new emphasis on thinking—obsessive, habitual thinking—combined with obsessive, habitual reading and writing. Diderot, writing about genius, links it to the power of observation. "When I speak of the power of observation I don't mean the petty daily espionage of words, acts, and expressions, this tact so familiar to women, who possess it to a greater degree than the most intelligent men, the greatest souls, the most vigorous geniuses. This subtlety, which I would compare to the art of passing grains of millet through the eye of a needle, is a miserable daily study whose usefulness is domestic and trifling." As with the other examples, genius is seen as having an obsessive and compulsive quality. It is a ruminative quality that becomes second nature so that "he knows this without having calculated the probabilities for or against. This calculation is entirely done in his head."[9]

And William Sharpe notes that "the power of thinking constitutes the essence of genius."[10] But it is not simply thinking but a very focused and disciplined thinking. As Sharpe notes, genius "depend[s] upon the habit and constancy of its action, and its intensity is confessedly the result of its application. And the greater its application and acquisitions, the more capacious is Genius."[11] Today many theories of genius talk about how such people must spend a magical ten years of their lives in deep, continuous, self-contained rumination to achieve their eureka moments. Edison's oft quoted "inspiration is 99 per cent perspiration" is but another version of this idea.

It was not always the case that continuous study and continuous writing were part of human life. But in the eighteenth century the dedicated man and woman of letters arose as a distinct entity. Dr. George Cheyne, who invented "the English Malady"—the nervous disorder that publicized this new democratized madness—wrote to Boswell to say that his "sedentary life and thinking attentively" had caused his "wasted and relaxed nerves." Cheyne recommended that Boswell "never apply [himself]...long at a time."[12] And Andrew Harper in 1789 could write that the cause of madness was too fixed attention to specific things: "If the mental faculty happens to be particularly occupied and engaged by the presence and operation of some separate exclusive object, affection or idea, or even peculiar train of uniform ideas, the mind, by being thus pitched upon a specific note and its nervous motions circumscribed within the limits of a certain modulation, receives too deep an impression, from this unchanging effect, in the tone of its movements."[13]

I could continue to recite many more quotations of this period that emphasize over and over again that too focused attention to a specific thing will make you crazy. Thomas Arnold, at the end of the eighteenth century, writes "that the ablest heads, and soundest judgments, may be deranged by too intense an application of the mind." He also notes that thinking too much requires inactivity, late hours, and solitude. All features of what "genius theorists" have characterized as the requirements that turn talent into genius.[14]

This possibility that specialization (let's call it that) can lead to an obsessive attention to a subject, which in turn can create what will come to be called "monomania," leads us to the notion that anyone can become mad if one puts one's mind to it. Indeed, in *Rasselas*, Johnson has Imlac say that "disorders of intellect...happen much more often than superficial observers will easily believe. Perhaps, if we speak with rigorous exactness, no human mind is in its right state." Johnson's point is that all humans are to a degree mad in this new and partial way. What causes this "degree of insanity" according to Imlac is "too much silent speculation."[15]

While the Renaissance discussed the conflict between reason and passion, emphasizing the need for reason to control passion, this new form of madness is one in which reason and passion exist on the same level—the disease is a kind of passion of reason—obsession is, after all, a disease of rationality. On one hand, it is caused by too much thinking, and on the other, it exists as a problem because one is rationally aware of the behavior and fruitlessly wants to stop it. Sir Henry Holland wrote that this type of disease is caused by "too frequent and earnest direction of the mind inwards upon itself."[16]

Of course, this kind of introspection is a likely product (or even a cause) of a new culture of reading, philosophical speculation, and greater interest in the workings of the mind and the emotions. I have made the point elsewhere that the distinction between disease and cultural activity is one that is difficult to make clearly, and that the making of that distinction is itself an act that is part of the process I am discussing, not outside or tangential to that process. Thus we might want to consider Locke's devotion to introspection, and the elevation of the writer, the poet, the critic, the historian, and the mathematician in the eighteenth century—the rise of the concept of genius not as one's personal muse or daemon but as the exceptional, the unique, the sine qua non, the ne plus ultra. This is an era of distinct change toward being one's profession, as opposed to what has been called being a renaissance man.[17]

Esquirol, who, along with Pinel, came to solidify the diagnosis of monomania and partial insanity believed that geniuses were exempt from monomania, that they had some special endowment that immunized them from the dangers of introspection and doing one thing too much. Esquirol's fear was that artists and scholars of lesser fortitude were the ones who were most in danger. He wrote that "the great part of painters, also of poets and musicians, impelled by the need of emotions, abandon themselves to numerous errors of regimen."[18] In the case of scholars of lesser capacity, he notes "the understanding takes an exclusive direction; and the man meditates without cessation, upon subjects connected with metaphysical speculations, and confines himself to them, with a determination proportionate to the efforts that are made to divert his mind...He neglects the most important personal attentions, condemning himself to practices which seriously affect his constitution."[19] Stories of learned men who go mad abound. Tissot mentions one:

I must still grieve for a friend of penetrating genius...with too great a love of learning, and in particular of the medical science, by reading night and day, observing, making experiments, and mediating who became mad and "never recovered his reason."[20]

This friend clearly becomes ill because of his specialization—his flaw perhaps being his "too great a love of learning." The idea of the nervous breakdown as a result of too much work is a recurrent theme in nineteenth century novels and memoirs. It was, indeed, invented in that era since we don't see such accounts before. And interestingly no memoir is complete without a nervous breakdown—because it is a mark of accomplishment that indicates sensitivity and perhaps genius. When Tissot elaborates that "most studious men lose their time, and break their constitutions to no purpose,"[21] we see a different kind of critique than we might have observed in the past. Now it is the disease of attention and the professions that exist as a result of that attention that take prominence. Now with the explanation of "nerves" a seemingly material link is created between mental disease and genius. Jacques-Joseph Moreau created a "tree of nervosity" in which the branch for exceptional intelligence is connected to the branch of "lesions of the central nervous system" and just above the branch for "neuroses."[22] Linked to the exceptional intelligence branch springs sciences and letters. So a rather complete genealogy of arts and sciences contains, without apology or embarrassment, nervosity.

A related phenomenon in the nineteenth century was what was labeled as graphomania—one of the many monomanias detailed by Esquirol. We can best see this phenomenon by defamiliarizing something we know all too well—nineteenth-century novels and their prolific authors. Names such as Dickens, Balzac, Trollope, and Zola, to name a few, were engaged in a single-minded work project that had no precedent—the continuous, cumulative production of words. These writers engaged full time not only in novel writing but also in journalism, criticism, and letters—they were, in effect, writing all the time. They had become obsessive in the cause of letters.

This is not to say that earlier writers did not devote themselves to writing, but few, if any, of them occupy as much sheer shelf space as these writers. In order to produce such a volume of writing, these authors had to develop consistent and compulsive habits. Indeed, Zola had inscribed on his mantelpiece the phrase *nulla dies sine linea*, "no day without a sentence." Like the members of the proletariat who exchanged older desultory models of work for the efficient and repetitive industry of the factory, so did writers; those who had previously written when the muse struck them, or when they needed money, now engaged in a kind of marathon writing that often outpaced any monetary or inspirational need. The case of Anthony Trollope's mother, Frances, was not unusual. From the age of 50 until 76 she wrote 114 novels.[23] Trollope himself, by comparison, wrote a mere 47, as well as 16 other books on various subjects. Sir Walter Scott authored over 60 works. Balzac sat at his desk each day from 15 to 18 hours, ultimately inventing over 3,000 characters in his massive *Comédie humaine*.[24] Freud worked 8 a.m. to 8 p.m. in psychoanalytic sessions while managing to write over 150 books and articles as well as 20,000 letters, mainly at night.

Bulwer-Lytton, who wrote 29 novels, three books of verse, and three plays, had a nervous breakdown as a result of writing too much. He blames his breakdown on the fact that children are told "to read and read and read." Of himself he wrote "I began to write and to toil" when just a child so that "the wear and tear went on without intermission." He was caught in a paradox—the obsessive process was making him ill, but "as long as I was always at work, it seemed that I had not leisure to be ill."[25]

Or take Zola who wrote 37 novels, ten critical works, and countless pieces of journalism, art, criticism, and letters. In addition, Zola was probably the first author to allow himself to be analyzed by science; and the result of a very detailed psychometric and physiological exam, which was published, produced the diagnosis that Zola suffered from "a lack of nervous equilibrium" caused by his "intellectual superiority," which was, in turn, caused by "exercise of brain and mind."[26] Edouard Toulouse, Zola's personal physician, noted "he [Toulouse] has never seen an obsessed or impulsive person who was so well balanced."[27] While this sounds like a punch line, it is telling in that the relation between genius and neurosis was so close that the question became not whether someone *was* neurasthenic but really *how* someone was neurotic. In this case, Zola's genius is reconciled with the physical and mental facts of what would, at the time, have been called a degenerative personality, and indeed the author of the medical study writes, "Although he [Zola] has many nervous troubles, the term 'degeneracy' does not apply to him wholly."[28] The hedge in the use of the word "wholly" plucks Zola from the jaws of insanity. Yet, the study goes on to say that Zola is classed "among those degenerates who, though possessing brilliant faculties, have more or less mental defects," and concludes, "Zola is a neuropath" and "heredity seems to have caused this tendency" along with "constant intellectual work [which] affected the health of his nervous tissues."[29]

More interesting than the diagnosis is the question asked by this study: "Now, it is a question whether this neuropathical condition is not an excitation that has given rise to the intellectual ability of Zola. Whether a diseased nervous system is a necessary cause of great talent or genius?"[30] Is Zola a genius because of his nervous condition, or is his nervous condition a result of his genius? This chicken versus egg question is one that haunts the discussion of genius and madness in this era.

Zola himself was clearly fascinated by this question of the relation of genius to madness and obsession. His novel *L'Oeuvre* (*The Masterpiece*) ponders, even in its title, the relationship between work, in this obsessive sense, and the masterpiece, the artistic work of genius. The main character Claude Lantier devotes himself to his masterpiece in a dangerous, in the sense we have been observing, way—his day involved "spurning meat and drink, working like a madman in an endless struggle with nature."[31] Claude degenerates under the weight of his obsession and ultimately hangs himself in front of his painting, which itself has become an unintelligible mess after he has stabbed it, punched it through, scraped off all the paint, and torn it to pieces. The epitaph of the novel, spoken by Sandoz, Claude's friend and the literary stand-in for Zola himself, summarizes the nature of this obsessive life in the modern world.

> The thing is, work has simply swamped my whole existence...It's like a germ planted in the skull that devours the brain...It's so completely merciless that once the process of creation is started, it's impossible for me to stop it...Outside that, nobody exists...So there we are, cribbed and confined together, my work and me. And in the end it'll devour me, and that will be the end of that.[32]

Indeed, Sandoz has the last words of the novel, said at the end of Claude's funeral; I would say one of the most telling lines in modern literature. As the casket is laid in the grave, Sandoz pronounces: "And now back to work."[33]

In addition to Zola as an example of the genius whose very existence as such is bound up with obsession, it might make sense to look at Sir Francis Galton. Galton, best known as the founder of eugenics, combined many of these compulsive aspects with a dazzling breadth of knowledge and invention. Indeed, he was so interested in our subject that he wrote a book on hereditary genius. (See also chapter 6: Janet Browne, "Inspiration or Perspiration: Francis Galton's *Hereditary Genius* in Victorian Context," in this volume.) In his memoir, Galton traces his genetic genius-endowment back to his illustrative relatives including Erasmus Darwin (and we may note that Galton's cousin was Charles Darwin). As a biographical correlate to what we have been discussing, both Francis and Charles had breakdowns. Galton described having in his third year at Oxford a breakdown that included "a variety of brain symptoms of an alarming kind. A mill seemed to be working inside my head; I could not banish obsessing ideas." The reason given for this breakdown is the by now expected one: "I had been much too zealous, had worked too irregularly in too many directions, and had done myself harm." He adds, using the nineteenth-century mechanistic explanation that would signal neurasthenia to his readers, "It was as though I had tried to make a steam-engine perform more work than it was constructed for, by tampering with its safety valve and thereby straining its mechanism."[34] Mill and machine pick up on the obvious connection equating this kind of work to factory labor. Galton recovered from this bout, but found himself in 1866, at age 44, with a more serious episode. His symptoms now were "small problems, which successively obsessed me day and night, as I tried in vain to think them out." He adds that "these affected mere twigs, so to speak, rather than large boughs of the mental process, but for all that most painfully."[35] Using the language of obsession, Galton is saying that he was not crazy writ large, but crazy in lowercase—the major functions of his brain were not affected, only the smaller ones. But the effects of these functions, the obsessive, repetitive ones that affect process rather than content, were nonetheless painful and problematic. In other words, Galton acknowledges the kind of obsessive disorder that we have seen as characterized by being partial—the consumerist, democratic kind of breakdown that links the genius with all the other hardworking, intelligent, neurasthenics who make up the elites and increasingly the working classes as well.

Rather than seeing the breakdowns as deviations from Galton's path as a genius scientist, we might say they are part of the process. If we look at Galton's scientific work, might we not see the traces of obsession? Galton decides to perform an experiment calibrating the change in facial color. In an article on the subject published in *Nature* he wrote:

> A curious sight caught my attention...[at the racetrack]. I was on the side of the course that faced the distant [viewing] stand, and amused myself while waiting in studying the prevalent tint of the faces upon it. At length the horses were off, but it was hot, and I was contented to remain in quiet where I was. When the horses approached the winning post, the prevalent tint of the faces in the great stand changed notably, and became distinctly more pink under the flush of entertainment.[36]

His scientific experiment involved having observers track the changes in facial color somewhat objectively. What might have been seen as an eccentric attention to detail a 100 years earlier, easily dealt with in parlor chatter, now becomes science—now that observation and statistics begin to dominate knowledge. Another example: Galton, having decided that "many mental processes admit of being roughly measured," decided to measure human boredom by counting the number of times a group of people fidgeted. As a member of the Royal Geographical Society, he had the occasion to observe attendees at the meetings, where, as Galton wryly noted, "even there dull memoirs are occasionally read." His experiment consisted of selecting a section of two or three rows in the observer gallery bounded by two wrought iron pillars as a "convenient sample." Galton would count the number of fidgets in each group bounded by the pillars per minute and then calculate the average number of fidgets per person. Since he did not want to create an observer effect, he had to come up with a way to measure each minute without obviously looking at his watch. He writes, "so I reckon time by the number of my breathings of which there are fifteen in a minute. They are not counted mentally, but are punctuated by pressing with fifteen fingers successively. The counting is reserved for the fidgets."[37] I think Galton must have been a genius for this alone—try it yourself, it is not easy. But for Galton this compulsive behavior was one with which he "often amused myself."[38] This obsessive-compulsive breathing/counting behavior now serves the interest of scientific progress and comes to be printed in an academic journal without comment on its obsessive nature. Science is after all what one deliberately does; obsession is what one cannot help doing—a nice distinction that collapses rather frequently.

It is no coincidence that Galton's attention to his own breathing became, in turn, a bodily activity that could be grist for his obsessive mill. In many moments in his life the scientific and the personal crossed over the bridge of his obsession. Galton recalled that "in the days of my youth I felt at one time a passionate desire to subjugate the body by the spirit, and among other disciplines determined that my will should replace automatism by hastening or retarding automatic acts." To do so, young Galton became hyperaware of his own breathing as he attempted to make every breath a conscious act. As a result, "every breath was submitted to this process, with the result that the normal power of breathing was dangerously interfered with."[39]

Not simply a whimsy of a compulsive childhood, interfering with breathing played a prominent role in his adult life. He experimented with the sensation of suffocation and was "surprised at the absence of that gaping desire for air" that most people feel. Galton said he felt ill at the point of fainting, but nothing more. He then had himself fitted out with prescription goggle-glasses made for him so he could "read the print of newspaper perfectly under water." And "amused myself very frequently with this new hobby, and being most interested in the act of reading, constantly forgot that I was nearly suffocating myself."[40]

Am I describing an eccentricity or part of a pattern of being a genius, being in touch with the new motor of creativity that obsessive activity had become as part of the rise of science and a world based on measurement and exact time? (Galton ended up at the Observatory at Kew where he was in charge of coordinating all clocks in England.) Galton's eugenic method consisted in large part of measuring the bodies and minds of humans. He describes "the pressing necessity of obtaining a multitude of exact measurements relating to every measurable faculty of the body or mind" as central to his project.[41] He even went so far as creating a "beauty map" of the British Isles. His method is again a somatic tic combined with detailed observation. He groups women into three simple categories of attractiveness—"good, medium, and bad." He would hold in his hand a paper with the date and place written on it, and which he had torn into the shape of a cross. In his other hand he would carry a pin, and then he would walk along the streets "classifying the girls...as attractive, indifferent, or repellent" by sticking his pin into different parts of the cross. (Where to begin analyzing this?) The results were that London had the prettiest women and Aberdeen the most unattractive. He judged his result "consistent" since he could repeat the statistics at various times and places, coming up with the same results.[42]

One more example should suffice. In South Africa he was rather taken with the figure of an African woman and wanted to measure her (he says that as a "scientific man" this was his natural inclination). Knowing he did not speak her language, he realized he could "never therefore have explained to the lady what the object of my foot rule could be; and I really dared not to ask my worthy missionary host to interpret for me." So he turned to other methods. "The object of my admiration stood under a tree, and was turning herself about to all points of the compass, as ladies who wish to be admired usually do." He then employs his sextant and takes "a series of observations upon her figure in every direction, up and down, crossways, diagonally, and so forth, and I registered them carefully upon an outline drawing for fear of any mistake: this being done, I boldly pulled out my measuring tape, and measure the distance from where I was to the place where she stood, and having thus obtained both base and angles, I worked out the results by trigonometry and logarithms."[43]

Galton's social ineptitude, combined with his colonialist-imperialist-masculine assumptions, make for a funny moment tinged with darkness. One way of understanding geniuses such as Galton is to fast-forward to a television show like *The Big Bang Theory* with its convenient diagnosis of Asperger's syndrome. In a sense, today we still believe that genius is attended by diagnosable mental conditions. And the fact that we can laugh about such situations among geeky roommates, does not really change the picture. There is a gradual process involved in which we shift, from seeing madness as something that removes you from the human community and is quite separate from the ordered and reasoned mind that the genius must have, to a more democratic notion that madness and genius are very closely allied and that most humans are mad (it feels better to us now to say "neurotic"). The only difference is that geniuses are smarter and more neurotic than most.

Which brings us to the paradox of genius being both a sign of the democratic impulse—displacing hereditary nobility by a meritocracy—and a sign of exclusivity, since the genius is a member of the intellectual and cultural nobility. If everyone were a genius, then no one would be (just as all small children are artists so, by definition, none of them are). So genius is unique, even to itself, as Jacques Derrida suggests: "What of this common noun that claims to name that which is least common in the world? The noun 'genius', one supposes, names that which never yields anything to the generality of the nameable. Indeed the genius of the genius, if there is any, enjoins us to think how an absolute singularity subtracts itself from the community of the commons...and thus from the shareable."[44] So genius stands in a strange relationship to democracy. It implies that anyone can be a genius, regardless of class. Shakespeare could be a genius, as could Dr. Johnson, while King George III might not be a genius at all. On the other hand, the meritocratic nature of genius is displaced by its exclusivity. Only some people, very, very few, can get into the pantheon, and all the hard work you might put in will never get you into the empyrean of accomplishment.

My concluding point is that genius is part of a larger view of the human mind that developed over time. If obsessive behavior becomes a hallmark of our culture—both a goal and a disease—the genius is the one who best combines the contradictory impulse behind that dual contradictory imperative. If society is driven by the motor of obsession and compulsion, then the genius is the one who is the symptom bearer and the hero. Like Michael Phelps whose swimming seems effortless but is backed by millions of hours of repetitive, driven underwater activity, the genius conceals the hard work, obsession, and repetition with the seemingly natural and unscripted brio and sprezzatura that makes it possible for each citizen to believe that genius is both unreachable and already within one's grasp. That the germs of greatness lie in the neurotic miasma within each and every one of us.

Notes

1. Samuel Johnson, *The Rambler* 25, June 12, 1750.
2. Lennard Davis, *Obsession: A History* (Chicago: University of Chicago Press, 2008), 48.
3. Alexander Anderson, *An Inaugural Dissertation on Chronic Mania* (New York: T. and J. Swords, 1796), 6.
4. S. A. Tissot, *An Essay on Diseases Incidental to Literary and Sedentary Persons with Proper Rules for Preventing Their Fatal Consequences* (London: Edward and Charles Dilly, 1768), 39.
5. Thomas Arnold, *Observations on the Nature, Kinds, Causes and Prevention of Insanity, Lunacy, or Madness* (London: G. Robinson, 1882), I, 106, 108.
6. Kinneret S. Jaffe, "The Concept of Genius in Eighteenth Century French Aesthetics," *Journal of the History of Ideas* 4 (1980): 596.
7. Cited in Anderson, *Dissertation on Chronic Mania*, 6.
8. Walter Scott, *The Journal of Sir Walter Scott: Volume 1: From the Original Manuscript at Abbotsford*, ed. David Douglas (Cambridge: Cambridge University Press, 1890), 45.
9. http://www.marxists.org/reference/archive/diderot/17xx/on-genius.htm.
10. William Sharpe, *A Dissertation upon Genius* (London: C. Bathurst 1755), 47.
11. Ibid., 55.
12. Cheyne to Richardson, July 1742, in *The Letters of Doctor George Cheyne to Samuel Richardson (1733– 1743)*, ed. Charles F. Mullett (New York: Columbia University Press, 1943), 104.
13. Andrew Harper, *Treatise on the Real Cause and Cure of Insanity* (London: C. Stalker and J. Walter, 1789), 33.
14. Arnold, *Observations on the Nature*, I, 110.
15. Samuel Johnson, *Rasselas: Prince of Abyssinia* (Chicago: McClurg, 1889), 172.
16. Henry Holland, "On Dreaming, Insanity, Intoxication, etc.," in *Medical Notes and Reflections* (London: Longman, 1839), 240.
17. Davis, *Obsession*, 77. See also John Locke, *An Essay Concerning Human Understanding* (London: William Tegg, 1849), 94.
18. Étienne Esquirol, *Mental Maladies: A Treatise on Insanity*, trans. E. K. Hunt (Philadelphia: Lea and Blanchard, 1845), 39.
19. Ibid.
20. Tissot, *Essay on Diseases*, 41.
21. Ibid., 108.
22. J. J. Moreau (de Tours), *La psychologie morbide* (Paris: Victor Masson, 1859), 53.
23. Anthony Trollope, *An Autobiography* (London: Oxford University Press, 1923; repr., 1936), 30.
24. Werner Muensterberger, *Collecting: An Unruly Passion* (Princeton, NJ: Princeton University Press, 1994), 119, 121.
25. Edward Bulwer-Lytton, *Confessions of a Water Patient* (London: H. Bailliere, 1848), 15–18.
26. Arthur MacDonald, *Émile Zola: A Study of His Personality* (Washington, DC, 1898), 478.
27. Ibid., 484.
28. Ibid.
29. Ibid.
30. Ibid.
31. Émile Zola, *The Masterpiece*, trans. Thomas Walton (Oxford: Oxford University Press, 2008), 41.
32. Ibid., 285.
33. Ibid.
34. Francis Galton, *The Art of Travel* (London: John Murray, 1872; rpt., London: Phoenix Press, 2000), 79.
35. Francis Galton, *Memories of My Life* (London: Methuen, 1908), 154.
36. Ibid., 179.

37. Ibid., 278.
38. Ibid.
39. Ibid., 276.
40. Ibid., 185–86.
41. Ibid., 244.
42. Ibid., 315.
43. D. W. Forrest, *Francis Galton: The Life and Work of a Victorian Genius* (New York: Taplinger, 1974), 45; citing F. Galton, *Narrative of an Explorer in Tropical South Africa* (London: John Murray, 1853), 115.
44. Jacques Derrida, *Geneses, Genealogies, Genres, and Genius: The Secrets of the Archive* (New York: Columbia University Press, 2003), 1.

6

Inspiration to Perspiration: Francis Galton's *Hereditary Genius* in Victorian Context

Janet Browne

In his classic text *The Mirror and the Lamp*, published in 1953, the literary critic Meyer Abrams described the concept of genius in the Romantic imagination. Genius, he said, was believed to have specific features: it was sudden and effortless; it was involuntary; it generated intense mental excitement; and the completed musical, visual, or conceptual achievement sometimes seemed unfamiliar to the author, almost as though it were produced by someone else.[1] Inspiration was a visitation from somewhere outside the body entirely. Shelley was Abrams's typical example, although he could as easily have cited individuals from other spheres, such as Mozart, Goethe, or Johann Friedrich Gauss, one of the greatest theoretical mathematicians of the period. Much of this rhetoric of genius, Abrams argues, was prevalent in Europe and North America through the first two decades of the nineteenth century. It was strikingly echoed in pictorial form by Casper David Friedrich's painting "The Wanderer above the Sea of Fog" (1818). The solitary figure, viewed from behind, is caught in an instant of sublimity, an enlargement of the spiritual self through the contemplation of nature.

But as in so many things, the Victorians were to think differently. Only a few years further into the nineteenth century, the idea of genius had mostly moved away from the intense emotional and aesthetic experiences of the Romantic era and was becoming very much more prosaic.[2] Francis Galton, the founder of the eugenics movement, was one of the individuals who lowered the tone, an oddball individual in Victorian science who pushed "genius" off the romantic mountaintop, made it predictable through statistics, and brought it inside, into the middle-class Victorian home. One large painting in the collection of the Wellcome Library, London, speaks to this shift. It depicts a number of elite scientific and medical men at a garden party held during the International Medical Congress of 1881. The painting included Louis Pasteur (1822–1895), the acknowledged scientific genius of the era, and other preeminent individuals such as Jean-Martin Charcot (1825–1893) and Joseph Lister (1827–1912). It shows how the representation of men with superior intellects and insights had changed in Europe from one of great mental intensity to one of sobriety—or putting it another way, from a highly idiosyncratic and unaccountably inspired insight in one individual to a more sober and rational possession of knowledge that might be found in a number of people. John Carson describes this process as the democratization of the idea of excellence.[3] While Galton was hardly responsible on his own for the rise of the Victorian bourgeoisie, his scientific work took much of its reach and content from the emerging consolidation of the respectable classes. This chapter assesses Galton's role in the "biologization" of the human mind and explores the democratization and even domestication of the idea of genius during the later Victorian period.[4]

Francis Galton (1822–1911) was an exceptionally wide-ranging intellectual who contributed to many fields characteristic of the emerging high Victorian academic world, including statistics, heredity, criminology, anthropometrics, intelligence studies, photography, and eugenics. Scholars have struggled to render a complete picture of his interests.[5] It is perhaps most helpful to link these different fields of inquiry together through Galton's urge to render natural phenomena into numbers that could be tabulated and compared, as was becoming a key feature of Victorian science.[6] He began publishing in the middle years of the century and his work was soon recognized by a prestigious Founder's Medal from the Royal Geographical Society (of London) and election as a Fellow of the Royal Society in 1856. One of his earliest works was *Hereditary Genius*,[7] published in 1869, the same year as the opening of the Suez Canal and publication of Mill's *Subjection of Women* and Tolstoy's *War and Peace*.[8] The book was intended to be modern and forward-looking. In it, Galton proposed that ability ran in families, through the male line, and that talent, or genius as he called it, was inherited as a biological factor, just like any other biological phenomenon such as eye color. In the opening pages, he stated that "a man's intellectual abilities are derived by inheritance, under exactly the same limitations as are the form and physical features of the whole organic world."[9]

In the pages that followed, he rejected the notion that genius was a mysterious force originating outside the individual. Instead, for him, it was an innate mental trait that ran in families, could be rendered statistically, and was sometimes squandered by those who did not make full and energetic use of it.[10] Only those people who combined innate ability with zeal and application truly deserved the name of genius, he said. In other words, the biology of inheritance was fundamental in determining the level of intellect that any person would possess and that a high level of ability, when combined with hard work and energy, could occasionally lead an individual man to genius.[11] Like many Victorian men, he was ambivalent about the notion of female intellectual ability. These notions were eventually expressed in full in Galton's *Inquiries into Human Faculty and Its Development* (1883).

Hereditary Genius

Galton's *Hereditary Genius* was based on statistical techniques, supported by data that we now regard as problematic but from which his inferences were confidently drawn.[12] Each chapter addressed a particular professional group of the day, such as military commanders, judges, statesmen, musicians, scientists, and so forth; and under these headings Galton supplied information drawn from published sources such as biographical dictionaries and alumni records at Oxford and Cambridge Universities. Later on he adopted the practice of circulating printed questionnaires. His sample size for *Hereditary Genius* was not very large, about 1,000 people in all. He focused on those families that presented several generations of men who followed a particular profession and were sufficiently notable to be included in published dictionaries. Indeed his book can be read as a collective biography of the masculine Victorian elite in the middle decades of the nineteenth century. Nearly every male member of the British intelligentsia could read about himself and confirm the pleasing thought that ability ran in his family line. A later book of Galton's developed this research and addressed the family backgrounds of *English Men of Science: Their Nature and Nurture* (1874). Both this and *Hereditary Genius* bear a significant relationship to his future work in eugenics.

While Galton's opinions were generally more sophisticated than usually assumed, there can be no denying the naiveté with which he defended the idea that ability was an innate, inheritable quality. To our eyes, he seems unwilling to recognize that social structure, education, and inherited wealth must play substantive roles in the attainment of high position in Victorian society, although he did devote space to explaining why class and social rank were not the only qualifying features in his choice of individuals.[13] He similarly looks myopic on the question of gender. He discussed the problem of accounting for inheritance through the female line with tables that showed how the female kin of eminent men tended not to marry, or bear children, and thus intellectual qualities in the family were not passed on—were "lost" for the next generation.[14] He also included remarks couched in the gendered terms of his day about the value of women:

> It therefore appears to be very important to success in science, that a man should have an able mother. I believe the reason to be, that a child so circumstanced has the good fortune to be delivered from the ordinary narrowing, partisan influences of home education...Happy are they whose mothers did not intensify their naturally slavish dispositions in childhood, by the frequent use of phrases such as, "Do not ask questions about this or that, for it is wrong to doubt;" but who showed them, by practice and teaching, that inquiry may be absolutely free without being irreverent, that reverence for truth is the parent of free inquiry, and that indifference or insincerity in the search after truth is one of the most degrading of sins...Of two men with equal abilities, the one who had a truth-loving mother would be the more likely to follow the career of science.[15]

Intelligence and ability were biological traits, he went on to claim, the product of nature not nurture. Galton's subsequently famous phrase "nature not nurture" first appeared in *English Men of Science* (1874), but here in *Hereditary Genius* he set out the dialectic that would later become codified in this form of words.[16] It came from Shakespeare's *Tempest*, where Prospero describes Caliban as "a born devil, on whose nature nurture cannot stick."[17]

Perhaps the book on genius was misleadingly titled. Galton was mostly interested in the general distribution of natural ability in a population (or what he called a natural power of intellect), and genius *qua* genius formed part of his discussion only in the sense that this state of mind occurred at the extreme upper end of his bell curve of distribution. In his introduction, Galton claimed to be the first person to treat the topic of intellectual inheritance in a statistical way. In retrospect, the Belgian statistician Adolphe Quetelet probably has as strong a claim.[18] Nevertheless, Galton wanted to render genius predictable. Unusual abilities were not aberrations or freaks of nature to him, but fell firmly within the statistical run of things. In Galton's vision, there would still be Mozarts and Napoleons appearing more or less regularly in a population. But there would also be plenty of space for people who could capitalize on any natural inborn ability through zeal and a capacity for intense intellectual engagement. He cited the case of the French mathematician Jean Le Rond d'Alembert (1717–1783), who was a foundling child and yet rose to great eminence.[19] Galton seemingly was the first to reformulate the notion of genius and make it available to the Victorians under the new label of hereditary talent.[20]

Much of Galton's underlying intent in *Hereditary Genius* was to eulogize the British national character at a time of expanding empire. Patriotically, he thought that British nationals possessed superior inborn traits. To that end, he included a chapter on the comparative worth of different nations as assessed by the purported ability of each nation's most prominent public figures.[21] Here he also signalled his larger imperial and racial concerns by comparing the abilities of different "races." He compared whites with blacks, and ancient Greeks with modern Englishmen, arguing in each case that superior achievements were due to superior natural ability.[22] These pages show that from a very early stage Galton adopted the idea of a hierarchy of human races based on supposedly innate biological differences, in which the northern Europeans were positioned at the top.[23] Galton already had some empirical experience with questions of racial identity, having travelled in Africa during the 1850s and authored *The Narrative of an Explorer in Tropical South Africa* (1853) and *The Art of Travel: Or, Shifts and Contrivances Available in Wild Countries* (1855).[24] Only a few years later, he began to develop the system of comparative bodily measurement—anthropometry—that became the method of choice for early anthropologists for standardizing so-called racial types and their defining characteristics.[25] These anthropometric methods and the complementary practice of craniometry—the measurement of skulls—were intended by Galton to obtain a typology of physical difference between ethnic groups that could be measured, photographed, and arranged on a scale of absolute value.[26] In the 1880s Galton extended these ideas to criminology in the form of photographic record cards, intermeshing with Alphonse Bertillon's system of police identification cards.[27] In similar vein, he proposed that fingerprints were not only uniquely special to individuals but also revealing of mental traits such as criminality.[28] Like Quetelet, he was gripped by a search for the characteristics of *"l'homme moyen."*[29] In this research, he created a series of composite photographs that have subsequently fascinated photographic historians. He called these "generic images." They consisted of overlaid portraits of members of the same family group that revealed the "average" physical features of the group, whether human families, groups of racehorses, or Roman portrait coins.[30] Activities such as these, seemingly so miscellaneous, were united by his emphasis on the identification of the physical and mental characteristics that made an individual simultaneously unique and a member of an interconnected group.

Heredity and eugenics

Galton's interest in heredity was already evident in scientific circles before he published *Hereditary Genius*. Early in the 1860s he wrote in *Macmillan's Magazine* a pair of papers on "Hereditary Talent," arguing that intellect ran in families and employing techniques derived from Quetelet to establish the point.[31]

He simultaneously developed a theory of heredity that described every individual as carrying a proportional fraction of characteristics inherited from each of his or her ancestral lines. It should be noted that this was before the development of classical Mendelian genetics. As proposed by Galton, his "Law of Ancestral Heredity" suggested that the traits and characteristics of every individual were a composite of those possessed by his or her ancestors, where one half of the offspring's inherited material came from each of the parents, which included, in turn, one eighth from each of the grandparents, one sixteenth from great-grandparents, and so forth back through the family line. Any talents or abilities would therefore stay in the family either until they were lost by breeding out or diminution, or were reinforced or improved by marriage into another talented line.[32]

In a single statistical stroke, Galton thus managed to explain the irregular transmission of traits, some skipping several generations, others seemingly dying out. He also established a practical rationale for the observable fact that some characteristics ran in families. These notions became the foundation of Galton's subsequent work in what is now recognized as early inheritance studies. They also provided the grounding on which he based a series of experiments intended to prove Charles Darwin's theory of pangenesis, first set out in Darwin's book *The Variation of Animals and Plants under Domestication* (1868). Darwin postulated the existence of "gemmules" that circulated in the living body and were transmitted to offspring via the reproductive cells.[33] Galton explored some of these ideas in *Hereditary Genius*.[34] Between 1869 and 1871 he attempted to demonstrate Darwin's proposal by transfusing blood between differently colored rabbits. If the gemmules circulated in the blood, then the offspring of a mated pair should display some of the color of the transfused parent. When this experiment failed, Galton realized that he had unintentionally disproved Darwin's theory.[35] By the late 1870s he had moved on to other preoccupations such as regression to the mean and statistical correlations.[36]

Pangenesis aside, Galton's work in this area inspired a significant group of biological researchers in England at the very end of the nineteenth century who used his techniques to assess the rate of evolutionary change. The "Biometricians" based at University College London specialized in measuring very small changes in successive generations of organisms that would—they hoped—prove that evolutionary change proceeded in a gradual and statistically measurable manner. These biometricians, headed by Karl Pearson, were leading critics of Gregor Mendel's principles.[37] As is now well established, Mendel's achievements were not recognized by biologists until 1900, and even then his ideas were not immediately incorporated into existing hereditary research. A clash between Biometricians and Mendelians emerged in Britain that embraced many social and political differences as well.[38] It dominated most thinking about heredity in the United Kingdom for more than a decade: the London-based Biometricians grouped around Galton's protégé, Karl Pearson, and grounded their work on the investigation of continuous small changes in organisms, such as the carapaces of Crustacea; whereas the new Mendelians, mostly operative at Cambridge University, with William Bateson at the center of the group, favored a saltatory view of evolutionary change. The latter adopted Mendel's theories of the transmission of particulate "traits" that could segregate during the reproductive process and recombine. The two fields were consequently at odds with each other as regards the way they regarded evolutionary change taking place in nature—one group opting for discrete changes and the other for continuous. The debate was only resolved in 1918 by Ronald Fisher. Over in the United States, it similarly was unclear to practicing biologists how Mendel's ideas might fit with current work arising from the chromosomal theories and mutation studies undertaken by Thomas Hunt Morgan and the experimenters in Morgan's laboratory at Columbia University, New York.[39] In retrospect it can be seen that Galton's law of ancestry was somehow a precursor to each of these movements: the statistical, the saltationist, and the particulate.[40] Galton's collaboration with Karl Pearson also formalized the apparatus of modern statistics—including chi-square, regression, and correlation.[41]

As discussed by Kevles and others, Galton's interests in heredity drew him to the study of human society and then onward to define the field of eugenics.[42] Galton coined the term "eugenics" in 1904: "Eugenics is the science which deals with all influences that improve and develop inborn qualities of a race."[43] These ideas had first been elaborated by him in *Inquiries into Human Faculty* (1883) and lasted through the rest of his life: in 1911, just before his death, he even unsuccessfully attempted to publish a eugenic novel called *Kantsaywhere*. He worked hard to establish eugenics as an area of significant scientific and social investigation in Britain—what he called "the cultivation of race."[44]

In its early phases, Galton's eugenics rested on a number of principles. He felt it was essential to disseminate knowledge of the laws of heredity. He recommended careful study of demography as an indication of "national rise and decline" and the systematic collection of facts relating to the "circumstances in which large and thriving families have most frequently originated." The aim of the enterprise was to "represent each class or sect by its best specimens, causing them to contribute *more* than their proportion to the next generation."[45] Here lay the basic structure of his ideas about "positive" and "negative" eugenics. Galton was already a strong believer in Darwin's principle of natural selection, as well as its counterpart of artificial selection, and applied the latter in several instances as an explanation for shifts in the characteristics of domesticated animals and plants. As far as humans were concerned, he thought that people should take breeding into their own hands in order to maintain and improve the human race. He stated that "what nature does blindly, slowly and ruthlessly, man may do providently, quickly and kindly."[46] The eugenics movement was rapidly taken up in Britain, continental Europe, and the Americas. This history and its consequences have been well documented.[47]

To further his eugenic aims, Galton founded an Anthropometric Laboratory in 1885 in South Kensington, London, whose function was to measure the physical details of individual volunteers. The laboratory moved a few years later to University College London (UCL) as the primary site in the United Kingdom for the collection of eugenic data.[48] On Galton's death in 1911, his will provided £45,000 to UCL for the continuation of anthropometric study and the creation of a Chair of Eugenics.[49] As a result, his directives on anthropometrics are noted now as a leading feature of late nineteenth-century thinking about racial typologies and eugenics in general. These directives were highly influential in the general trend toward biological reductionism, especially in treating brains and bodies as objects to be measured and compared. Galton needs to be included in any study of the historical concept of genius, not only as a founding father of intelligence studies and the measuring movement that led to the concept of IQ, but also as a significant promoter of eugenics. He spent the last decades of his life expounding on eugenics as a social, political, and secular creed.[50]

The biology of genius

Galton read Charles Darwin's *On the Origin of Species* on publication in 1859.[51] He and Darwin were cousins, and this gave Galton a sense of intellectual pride in his family's contribution to science. And in truth, Galton assembled some striking materials in *Hereditary Genius* in order to establish the point about ability running in family lines. He went through scores of biographical dictionaries and encyclopedias containing the history of western civilization to compile a database of some 1,000 prominent male individuals along with their ancestral kinship details. He invented arithmetic formulae to indicate the degrees of relationship of the people in each category. The most notable aspect of this research from today's perspective is his emphasis nearly exclusively on male inheritance. He was particularly impressed by uncles, male cousins, and nephews, finding that collateral lines were the most statistically significant for his purposes. For example, of the 32 military individuals that he included in *Hereditary Genius*, 27 were related by collateral descent to another male in the same professional category. In the section dedicated to "Men of Science," he included the astronomical Herschels, father and son, the anatomical Geoffroy Saint-Hilaires, several generations of the botanical Jussieus, and the geological de Saussures, among others. Charles Darwin was in the book, along with his grandfathers Erasmus Darwin and Josiah Wedgwood, his father Robert Waring Darwin, and several scientific uncles and cousins from the Wedgwood-Darwin family dynasty. Galton, who regarded himself as a scientific man and was directly related to Darwin through Erasmus Darwin (their mutual grandfather), did not include his own name. It can be suggested, though, that he felt he should be included. In a pamphlet published in 1904, entitled *Index to Achievements of Near Kinsfolk of Some of the Fellows of the Royal Society*, he did include himself in the list of Darwin and Wedgwood relatives who displayed scientific ability.[52]

Galton had every reason to muse on family ability. His personal circle comprised a close-knit stratum of the scientific intelligentsia of the high Victorian era.[53] In general intellectual terms, he was sympathetic to John Stuart Mill's idea of a "learned elite" and Thomas Carlyle's "aristocracy of talent."[54] It was in Carlyle that Galton found the phrase about genius being an infinite capacity for taking pains. Most members of this intellectual elite associated themselves with the rising ideologies of meritocracy and utilitarianism, as well as accepting the ideas about "character," personal effort, self-help, and individual drive that were promoted in Britain by the popular author Samuel Smiles.[55] Like Smiles, Galton applauded merit and industry wherever in the social landscape it appeared. He endorsed civic duty and social progress in the laboring classes as well as in the middling sectors of the British social order, while considering himself a member of refined society. He felt he was a liberal thinker in the political terminology of the time, and had no guilt about being an elitist.

Looking more widely at the cultured classes of high Victorian Britain, the family can also be seen as the primary institution in which the meanings of individual lives were constructed and transmitted over the generations—the lines of descent in a family were felt to be a significant repository of personal history and character.[56] Both of Galton's grandfathers, Erasmus Darwin and Samuel Tertius Galton, for example, were prominent in the British industrial revolution and members of the Lunar Society, an informal yet prestigious group of practical men located in the technological heartland of the United Kingdom who promoted progress in science and engineering.[57] Galton thought that his scientific ability was inherited from these two grandfathers. Everywhere he looked, indeed, he saw the reinforcements of family lines that were repeated in his own circle through marriage and extended familial relationships. There was every apparent reason for him to believe that the transmission of biological and mental characteristics in family lines was a real phenomenon.[58]

One of the most telling biographical details about Galton's life story was his long-term interest in ascertaining the defining characteristics of the men who occupied the inner circles of Victorian science—perhaps also in some way a personal investigation of himself and his mental achievements. In later work he extended the program mapped out in *Hereditary Genius* by addressing the preponderance of fellowships of the Royal Society in certain families, his own Darwin-Wedgwood-Galton family being of central concern here.[59] Yet despite his own FRS awarded early in his lifetime, he did not appear to be an acknowledged member of those inner circles. He danced attendance on leading scientists such as Thomas Henry Huxley, William Spottiswood, John Tyndall, Herbert Spencer, and the rest. He would have liked to be a member of the group of scientists self-styled as the X Club: his views were just as secular and progressive as theirs; and he identified with their professionalizing mission in life.[60] For example, in 1864, he joined company with Spencer, Huxley, John Lubbock, Norman Lockyer, and a number of others to purchase and edit *The Reader*, a journal of literature, science, and art that, unfortunately, soon failed.[61]

He also made plain his religious skepticism through a number of showcase activities. He made the first statistical study of the efficacy of prayer (completely seriously), showing that British royalty did not live any longer than the norm, even though many thousands of British citizens prayed for their health every Sunday in church.[62] The same form of rational skepticism was reflected in his agreement with Huxley that contemporary spiritualism was a sham. Galton was one of the organizers of a séance in 1874 attended by Huxley and others in order to test whether the manifestations were genuine.[63] In these activities, Galton displayed a strong belief in social hierarchy, evolution, secularism, and biological reductionism, as we would now term it. Yet he was only ever allied with the scientific avant-garde, but not one of them.

Genius as hard work

Galton sent a copy of *Hereditary Genius* to Charles Darwin in 1869, just after publication. The argument certainly caught Darwin's eye. "I do not think I ever in my whole life read anything more interesting & original," he admitted.[64] The point brought Darwin up sharp. He was, of course, famous for his statements on the power of natural selection to generate the adaptedness of all living beings. Yet at this point in his intellectual trajectory, ten years after the first edition of the *Origin of Species* had been published, Darwin was increasingly accommodating toward allowing the environment to have some effect in evolutionary change, as evidenced in his work on the domestication of plants and animals.[65] Actually Darwin had always allowed for certain influences of the environment while maintaining his strong conviction in the power of heredity and ancestral family trees.[66] He had not expected Galton to show so definitively that an ephemeral quality like talent ran in human families. He wrote to Galton that "I have always maintained that, excepting fools, men did not differ much in intellect, only in zeal & hard work."[67] He was surprised to see that ability did seem to run in families just as Galton proposed.

Generally speaking, Darwin was not overly concerned with the concept of genius as a category for research, at least as conventionally understood. Here and there in his *Descent of Man* (1871), he referred to commonplace ideas about exceptional intellect. Personally, he believed that genius was an infinite capacity for taking pains, and occasionally mentioned this doctrine as one of his own distinctive characteristics. His son Francis Darwin, when composing recollections of his father, said that Darwin "used almost to apologise for his patience, saying that he could not bear to be beaten, as if this were rather a sign of weakness on his part. He often quoted the saying, 'It's dogged as does it;' and I think doggedness expresses his frame of mind almost better than perseverance. Perseverance seems hardly to express his almost fierce desire to force the truth to reveal itself."[68] In *Descent of Man*, Darwin discussed genius in much the same terms: "for genius has been declared by a great authority to be patience, and patience, in this sense meaning unflinching, undaunted perseverance."[69]

More particularly, he cited Galton's *Hereditary Genius* as evidence for the superiority of the male mind over that of the female. "We may also infer, from the law of the deviation of averages, so well illustrated by Mr. Galton, in his work on 'Hereditary Genius,' that if men are capable of decided eminence over women in many subjects, the average standard of mental power in man must be above that of woman."[70] Like Galton, Darwin thought that mental excellence was principally to be found in the human male, and in the *Descent of Man* he tried to show how his concept of sexual selection could provide an explanation for this.

> The chief distinction in the intellectual powers of the two sexes is shewn by man attaining to a higher eminence, in whatever he takes up, than woman can attain—whether requiring deep thought, reason, or imagination, or merely the use of the senses and hands. If two lists were made of the most eminent men and women in poetry, painting, sculpture, music,— comprising composition and performance, history, science, and philosophy, with half-a-dozen names under each subject, the two lists would not bear comparison.[71]

In this, the two cousins were entirely men of their time. When periodical writers of the day discussed intellectual eminence, they, too, usually meant the male version. Literary critics sometimes—but infrequently—applied the term "genius" to successful women writers such as Madame de Staël or Maria Edgeworth, but generally British authors seem to have assumed that if female genius existed, it was less powerful and less extensive than male genius, and that women could only reach beyond the normal when addressing subjects that engaged the emotions and feelings, popularly supposed to be typical of the female mind.[72] In other words, if women possessed genius, it was of a special type, and not as elevated as that possessed by men. Mary Somerville was sometimes cited as a rare counterexample.[73] These notions show how far the idea of genius had moved away from personal inspiration, a characteristic that might perhaps be supposed to be shared by both men and women, toward that of rational intellect, a trait presumed to be chiefly found in the masculine mind. One small moment in the Darwin story reflects this gendered view of genius. The first French translation of Darwin's *Origin of Species* was published in 1862 by Clémence Royer, a clever, politically active author, and scientific thinker.[74] Royer seemingly overstepped her prescribed role as a woman so completely that she was referred to as "almost a man of genius."[75]

Darwin therefore appears to have endorsed Galton's vision of hard work and perseverance as a necessary aspect of high ability. Writing in the *Descent of Man*, in 1871, he expressed this in the words of John Stuart Mill as "plodding and long hammering at single thoughts," emphasizing that the higher orders of intelligence rested on persistence and mental labor.[76] Interestingly for historians of Darwinism, this is how Darwin went on to describe himself in his autobiographical reminiscences begun in the middle years of the 1870s. In these reminiscences, Darwin remarked that he thought his greatest gift was perseverance; and the same set of tropes came into play after his death when he was celebrated as a great national figure and as a genius of a particular sort. After his death, Darwin was revered as an independent and tireless thinker dedicated to his work. Obituaries and other forms of commemorative literature, including increasing numbers of biographies of Darwin, made the point that his was a life in which individual effort and personal virtue featured heavily.[77] Even the portraits and sculptures produced to commemorate his role in British science reflected something of this understanding: that Darwin's chief characteristics were sober respectability, hard work, and patience.[78] The Christian imagery of saintly self-dedication and austerity were here transferred to the idealized man of science.[79]

Nowadays we see much of this Victorian emphasis on dedication and hard work as the nineteenth-century equivalent of the credit-building processes described by Steven Shapin in seventeenth-century science.[80] It was important for Victorians to believe that science was carried out by trustworthy, hardworking, sincere individuals who carefully explored natural phenomena—men who did not seek to overthrow the status quo of the church or the political establishment. Scholars such as Adrian Desmond and James Secord demonstrate the social and political dangers that were thought to emerge should science be adopted by politically radical thinkers.[81]

Pedigree

The visual representation of the Wedgwood-Darwin-Galton family tree came to have an extended lifespan as an exemplar of the inheritance of genius.

By the turn of the century, this pedigree chart was one of the best known of the early eugenics movement. Indeed it served as a model for the outburst of diagrammatic pedigree charts in the early decades of the twentieth century that not only documented the supposed Mendelian inheritance of family abilities of different kinds but also the transmission of inherited diseases and many presumed medical conditions, such as mental disorders, alcoholism, and epilepsy. Here the concept of the inheritance of "genius" was easily incorporated into the emerging field of classical genetics. And the word "genius" was expanded to include skill of all kinds. One pedigree chart produced by the American Eugenics Record Office in Cold Spring Harbor, under the direction of Charles Davenport, for example, recorded the transmission of craftsmanship in the Herreshoff family of boat builders located in Rhode Island, United States. The label on the Herreshoff chart shows the interchange of the word "genius" with that of "ability" in the early years of the twentieth century. Here Galton's notion of inherited genius or talent comprised not only genetic transmission but also what we now consider to be primarily learned or acquired skills.

These same notions of heredity and family background became important factors in later work on intelligence. The American psychologist Lewis Terman was Galton's most formidable successor, bringing Galton's ideas about innate intelligence to Stanford in the first decade of the twentieth century and merging them with Alfred Binet's procedures for educational testing. In 1910, while Galton was still alive, Terman initiated a large-scale study of California schoolchildren to inquire into genius: its nature, its origin, and its cultivation.[82] "It is hardly too much to say that this field at present is the 'Darkest Africa' of education," claimed Terman.[83] Terman's team collected data on more than 1,400 children, each of whom ranked within the top 1 percent of the school population, and carried out prolonged educational tests on about 650 of these. The crucial, Galtonian, part of the study was to take extensive notes on the ancestry of the most gifted children, resulting in comparative tables of intellect according to kinship and ethnic origin. From studies like these the Stanford-Binet test was derived, the primary tool of the developing IQ movement and an important (if unfortunate) element in establishing eugenic rationales and procedures.[84]

In Britain, Galton's ideas were primarily pursued by Havelock Ellis in his *Study of British Genius*, published in 1904, again while Galton was still alive.[85] Ellis's aim was similar to Galton's in that he wished to describe in statistical form the national character and supposed British racial superiority. His methodology was similar to Galton's, too, in that he used for his database the 30,000 entries in the British *Dictionary of National Biography (DNB)*, edited by Leslie Stephen, of which the first series was completed in 1900, and subsequently extended to include supplements and a volume of errata in 1904.[86] Ellis's intention was to identify the most intellectually notable people as represented by public prominence sufficient to be described in a national dictionary. Yet he realized that 30,000 entries were several thousands too many for statistical manipulation and devised what he considered an appropriate selection system. To this end, he rejected those whose inclusion in the *DNB* came only by birth, such as aristocrats. He rejected those whose entries were less than three pages long and anyone categorized as a villain. He rejected women. With this list, which he considered highly objective, he tabulated ancestry, family size, and ethnic identity within the British Isles. He found that individuals of Anglo-Danish origin were numerically most prominent in the "genius" category. The people on his lists were also analyzed for their incidence in time, and Ellis was disconcerted to discover that the number of talented people appeared to be in decline at the end of the nineteenth century, a sure indication for him of the presumed decadence and national degeneration that he discussed in other books and psychiatric studies.[87]

Conclusion

The chapters in this volume reaffirm that the concept of genius was an important organizing device for thinkers and social commentators from the 1750s onward. The emergence and consolidation of ideas about talent and ability that appeared in the industrializing world around the end of the nineteenth century edged cultural opinion away from the idea that genius consisted in an inspired state of mind and toward the notion that it was innate, that it was inherited, was characterized by persistence, energy, and industry, and that its distribution in a population could be considered collectively and statistically. For a few decades in Victorian Britain, the notion took on an industrious air that can be directly related to Francis Galton's writings. With hindsight we can see that he "naturalized" and "biologized" mental ability in a way that made it a characteristic feature of the technologically advanced, geographically expansive, colonial culture of his day—a feature that confirmed the moral codes and gender norms of the emerging middle classes and gave biological justification to the shifting social hierarchies of the day. He gave scientific credence to the concept of family talent. This "domestication" of the idea of genius can be added to the fertile mix of ideas about inborn abilities and national improvement that were taking shape in Britain during the later nineteenth and early twentieth centuries: ideas that went on to provide much of the substrate of intelligence studies and the discipline of genetics in the modern era.

Notes

1. M. H. Abrams, *The Mirror and the Lamp: Romantic Theory and the Critical Tradition* (New York: Oxford University Press, 1953), 189. I thank Scott Phelps for his research assistance with this chapter.
2. Darrin M. McMahon, *Divine Fury: A History of Genius* (New York: Basic Books, 2013). See also Laura C. Ball, "Genius without the 'Great Man': New Possibilities for the Historian of Psychology," *History of Psychology* 15 (2012): 72–83.
3. John Carson, *The Measure of Merit: Talents, Intelligence, and Inequality in the French and American Republics, 1750–1940* (Princeton, NJ: Princeton University Press, 2006).

4. For more on the biologization of the concept of genius, see Michael Hagner's study of the anatomy of brains, especially as conducted by Oskar Vogt: Michael Hagner, *Geniale Gehirne: Zur Geschichte der Elitegehirnforschung* (München: Deutsch Taschenbuch-Verlag, 2007), 177–81; Michael Hagner, *Homo cerebralis: Der Wandel vom Seelenorgan zum Gehirn* (Berlin: Berlin Verlag, 1997). See also Anne Harrington, "Beyond Phrenology: Localization Theory in the Modern Era," in *The Enchanted Loom: Chapters in the History of Neuroscience*, ed. Pietro Corsi (New York: Oxford University Press, 1991), 207–39; Robert J. Richards, *Darwin and the Emergence of Evolutionary Theories of Mind and Behavior* (Chicago: University of Chicago Press, 1989); Janet Browne, "Darwin and the Face of Madness," in *The Anatomy of Madness: Essays in the History of Psychiatry*, ed. W. F. Bynum, Roy Porter, and Michael Shepherd (London: Tavistock Press, 1985) 1, 151–65.

5. Michael George Bulmer, *Francis Galton: Pioneer of Heredity and Biometry* (Baltimore, MD: Johns Hopkins University Press, 2003); W. Milo Keynes, ed., *Sir Francis Galton, FRS: The Legacy of His Ideas* (Houndmills, Basingstoke, Hampshire: Macmillan; in association with the Galton Institute, 1993); D. W. Forrest, *Francis Galton: The Life and Work of a Victorian Genius* (Oxford: Taplinger, 1974); Nicholas Wright Gillham, *A Life of Sir Francis Galton: From African Exploration to the Birth of Eugenics* (Oxford: Oxford University Press, 2001).

6. Theodore M. Porter, *The Rise of Statistical Thinking, 1820–1900* (Princeton, NJ: Princeton University Press, 1986); Lorenz Kruger, Lorraine J. Daston, and Michael Heidelberger, eds., *The Probabilistic Revolution, Vol. 1: Ideas in History; Vol. 2: Ideas in the Sciences* (MIT Press, 1987); Ian Hacking, *The Taming of Chance* (Cambridge: Cambridge University Press, 1990).

7. Francis Galton, *Hereditary Genius: An Inquiry into Its Laws and Consequences* (London: 1869), reprinted in New York in 1870, 1871, and 1884. There was a second edition during Galton's lifetime in London 1892. The book is still being published: a reprint edition was issued in 2006 by Prometheus Press, Amherst, Massachusetts, in the series "Great Minds."

8. John Stuart Mill, *The Subjection of Women* (London: 1869); Leo Tolstoy, *Voyna i Mir* (Moscow: 1869), translated into English by Clara Bell, London, 1886 (London: Longmans, Green, Reader and Dyer, 1869).

9. Galton, *Hereditary Genius*, 1.

10. Ibid., 37–38.

11. Francis Galton, *Inquiries into Human Faculty and Its Development* (London: Macmillan, 1883), 25–27. On the combination of work and energy, see particularly, M. Norton Wise and Crosbie Smith, "Measurement, Work and Industry in Lord Kelvin's Britain," *Historical Studies in the Physical and Biological Sciences* 17, no. 1 (1986): 147–73; M. Norton Wise and Crosbie Smith, "Work and Waste: Political Economy and Natural Philosophy in Nineteenth Century Britain" *History of Science*, 27 (1989), Pt. I, 263–301; Pt. II, 391–449; Pt. III, 28 (1990), 221–61; Anson Rabinbach, *The Human Motor: Energy, Fatigue, and the Origins of Modernity* (Oakland CA: University of California Press, 1992).

12. Carlos López-Beltrán, "Storytelling, Statistics and Hereditary Thought: The Narrative Support of Early Statistics," *Studies in History and Philosophy of Science Part C: Studies in History and Philosophy of Biological and Biomedical Sciences* 37, no. 1 (2006): 41–58.

13. Galton, *Hereditary Genius*, 1870, 41–43.

14. Ibid., 3–4, 62–63.

15. Ibid., 196.

16. Galton also used it in "On Men of Science, Their Nature and Their Nurture," *Proceedings of the Royal Institution of Great Britain* 7 (1874): 227–36. See Ruth Schwartz Cowan, "Nature and Nurture: The Interplay of Biology and Politics in the Work of Francis Galton," *Studies in History of Biology* 1 (1977): 133; Dean Keith Simonton, *Origins of Genius: Darwinian Perspectives on Creativity* (Oxford: Oxford University Press, 1999), 111–12.

17. *The Tempest* IV, i, 188–89.

18. Adolphe Quetelet, *Sur l'homme et le dévelopment des facultés ou, Essai de physique sociale* (1835) and *Anthropométrie ou Mesure des différentes facultés de l'homme* (1871).
19. Galton, *Hereditary Genius*, 1870, 208–209.
20. Discussed in Kathleen R. Slaugh-Sanford, "Declaring Genius: Literary and Scientific Claims of Artistic Genius in Late-Victorian Britain," PhD, University of Delaware, 2012.
21. Galton, *Hereditary Genius*, 1870, ch. 20, "The Comparative Worth of Different Races."
22. "It follows from all this, that the average ability of the Athenian race is, on the lowest possible estimate, very nearly two grades higher than our own—that is, about as much as our race is above that of the African negro." Ibid., 342.
23. Authoritative general accounts of racial theory and hierarchy are given by Nancy Stepan, *The Idea of Race in Science: Great Britain, 1800–1960* (London: Archon Books, 1982) and Henrika Kuklick, *The Savage Within: The Social History of British Anthropology, 1885–1945* (Cambridge: Cambridge University Press, 1991). See also John P. Jackson and Nadine M. Weidman, *Race, Racism, and Science: Social Impact and Interaction* (New Brunswick, NJ: Rutgers University Press ABC-CLIO, 2004); Katya Gibel Azoulay, "Reflections on 'Race' and the Biologization of Difference," *Patterns of Prejudice* 40, no. 4–5 (2006): 353–79; Debbie Challis, *The Archaeology of Race: The Eugenic Ideas of Francis Galton and Flinders Petrie* (London: Bloomsbury Academic, 2013).
24. Raymond E. Fancher, "Galton in Africa," *American Psychologist* 37, no. 6 (1982): 713; Francis Galton, *The Narrative of an Explorer in Tropical South Africa* (London, 1853); Francis Galton, *The Art of Travel: Or Shifts and Contrivances Available in Wild Countries* (London, 1855).
25. Edward E. Hunt, "Anthropometry, Genetics and Racial History," *American Anthropologist* 61, no. 1 (1959): 64–87; Dudley Allen Sargent, *Anthropometric Apparatus: With Directions for Measuring and Testing the Principal Physical Characteristics of the Human Body*, 2nd ed. (London: Macmillan, 1887). There was apparently a steady trade in the apparatus for making anthropometric measurements. The Cambridge Scientific Instrument Company, managed by Charles Darwin's son Horace Darwin, was one such. See, *A Descriptive List of Anthropometric Apparatus: Consisting of Instruments for Measuring and Testing the Chief Physical Characteristics of the Human Body Designed under the Direction of Mr. Francis Galton, and Manufactured and Sold by the Cambridge Scientific Instrument Company* (Cambridge, UK: C.J. Clay, 1887).
26. Discussed in the wider framework of anthropology by Elizabeth Edwards, "Photographic 'Types': The Pursuit of Method," *Visual Anthropology* 3, no. 2–3 (1990): 235–58; Elizabeth Edwards, *Anthropology and Photography, 1860–1920* (New Haven, CT: Yale University Press, 1992); Elizabeth Edwards, "Evolving Images: Photography, Race and Popular Darwinism," in Donald, D. and Munro, J. eds. *Endless Forms: Charles Darwin, Natural Science, and the Visual Arts* (New Haven, CT: Yale University Press, 2009); Anne Maxwell, *Picture Imperfect: Photography and Eugenics, 1870–1940* (Brighton, UK: Sussex Academic Press, 2010); David Green, "Veins of Resemblance: Photography and Eugenics," *Oxford Art Journal* 7 (1984): 3–16; Douglas A. Lorimer, "Science and the Secularization of Victorian Images of Race," in *Victorian Science in Context*, ed. Bernard Lightman (Chicago: University of Chicago Press, 1997), 212–35; Christopher Pinney, *Photography and Anthropology* (London: Reaktion Books, 2011).
27. Alphonse Bertillon, *La photographie judiciaire: avec un appendice sur la classification et l'identification anthropométriques* (Paris: Gauthier-Villars, 1890); Alphonse Bertillon, *Signaletic Instructions: Including the Theory and Practice of Anthropometrical Identification* (Chicago: Werner, 1896); Nanette L. Fornabai, "Criminal Factors: 'Fantômas', Anthropometrics, and the Numerical Fictions of Modern Criminal Identity," *Yale French Studies* 108 (2005): 60–73; Josh Ellenbogen, *Reasoned and Unreasoned Images: The Photography of Bertillon, Galton, and Marey* (University Park, PA: Penn State Press, 2012). See also Melanie Sarah Jane Francis, "The Criminal Subject: Alphonse Bertillon and Francis Galton, Their Aesthetics and Their Legacies," PhD diss., University of Nottingham, 2013.

28. Francis Galton, "The Patterns in Thumb and Finger Marks: On Their Arrangement into Naturally Distinct Classes, the Permanence of the Papillary Ridges That Make Them, and the Resemblance of Their Classes to Ordinary Genera," *Proceedings of the Royal Society of London* 48, no. 292–95 (1890): 455–57; Francis Galton, *Finger Prints* (New York: Macmillan, 1892).

29. See Theodore M. Porter, "The Mathematics of Society: Variation and Error in Quetelet's Statistics," *British Journal for the History of Science* 18 (1985): 51–69, and Alain Desrosières, *The Politics of Large Numbers: A History of Statistical Reasoning* (Cambridge, MA: Harvard University Press, 1998).

30. Francis Galton, *Generic Images. Reprinted from Proceedings of the Royal Institution 9: 161–70 with Minor Variations* (London: William Clowes, 1879); Francis Galton, "Composite Portraits, Made by Combining Those of Many Different Persons into a Single Resultant Figure," *Journal of the Anthropological Institute of Great Britain and Ireland* 8 (1879): 132–44; Josh Ellenbogen, "Reasoned and Unreasoned Images: The Photography of Bertillon, Galton, and Marey," *History of Photography* 38 (2014): 202–204; David Burbridge, "Galton's 100: An Exploration of Francis Galton's Imagery Studies," *British Journal for the History of Science* 27 (1994): 443–63.

31. Francis Galton, "Hereditary Talent and Character," *Macmillan's Magazine* 12 (1865): 318–27; Ruth Schwartz Cowan, "Francis Galton's Statistical Ideas: The Influence of Eugenics," *Isis* 63 (1972): 509–28.

32. Ruth Swartz Cohen, *Sir Francis Galton and the Study of Heredity in the Nineteenth Century* (New York: Garland Press, 1985); Michael Bulmer, "The Development of Francis Galton's Ideas on the Mechanism of Heredity," *Journal of the History of Biology* 32 (1999): 263–92; Michael Bulmer, "Galton's Law of Ancestral Heredity," *Heredity* 81 (1998): 579–85.

33. Darwin's theory of pangenesis was described in Charles Darwin, *The Variation of Animals and Plants under Domestication* (London: John Murray, 1868), 2: 357–404, and also in *The Descent of Man: And Selection in Relation to Sex* (London: John Murray, 1871), 1: 280, 284.

34. Galton, *Hereditary Genius*, 1870, 365.

35. A classic description of the theory of pangenesis is given by G. L. Geison, "Darwin and Heredity: The Evolution of His Hypothesis of Pangenesis," *Journal of the History of Medicine and Allied Sciences* 24 (1969): 375–411. Darwin commented on Galton's experiments in *Nature,* 27 April 1871, pp. 502–503. Galton responded in *Nature,* May 4, 1871, pp. 5–6. See also Janet Browne, *Charles Darwin: The Power of Place* (London: Random House, 2003), 290–92.

36. Bulmer, *Francis Galton*, ch. 6.

37. Donald A. Mackenzie, "Biometrician Versus Mendelian," in his *Statistics in Britain 1865–1930: The Social Construction of Knowledge* (Edinburgh: Edinburgh University Press, 1981), 120–52; Robert Olby, "The Dimensions of Scientific Controversy: The Biometric-Mendelian Debate," *British Journal for the History of Science* 22 (1989): 299–320; Nicholas W. Gillham, "The Battle Between the Biometricians and the Mendelians: How Sir Francis Galton's Work Caused His Disciples to Reach Conflicting Conclusions about the Hereditary Mechanism," *Science & Education* 22 (2013): 1–15.

38. Contested by M. Eileen Magnello, "The Non-correlation of Biometrics and Eugenics: Rival Forms of Laboratory Work in Karl Pearson's Career at University College London," Part 1, *History of Science* 37 (1999): 79–106; Part 2, *History of Science* 37 (1999): 123–50.

39. See Robert J Kohler, *Lords of the Fly: Drosophila Genetics and the Experimental Life* (Chicago: University of Chicago Press, 1994) and James Schwartz, *In Pursuit of the Gene: From Darwin to DNA* (Cambridge, MA: Harvard University Press, 2010).

40. Kathy J. Cooke, "The Limits of Heredity: Nature and Nurture in American Eugenics before 1915," *Journal of the History of Biology* 31, no. 2 (1998): 263–78; M. Eileen Magnello, "Karl Pearson's Mathematization of Inheritance: From Ancestral Heredity to Mendelian Genetics (1895–1909)," *Annals of Science* 55, no. 1 (1998): 35–94; P. Froggatt and N. C. Nevin, "The 'Law of Ancestral Heredity' and the Mendelian-Ancestrian Controversy in England, 1889–1906," *Journal of Medical Genetics* 8 (1971): 1–36.

41. Bulmer, *Francis Galton*, ch. 6.
42. Daniel J. Kevles, *In the Name of Eugenics: Genetics and the Uses of Human Heredity* (Cambridge, MA: Harvard University Press, 1985), 95; John Charles William Waller, "The Social and Intellectual Origins of Sir Francis Galton's (1822–1911) Views on Heredity and Eugenics," PhD diss., University of London, 2001.
43. Francis Galton, "Eugenics: Its Definition, Scope, and Aims," *Nature*, May 26, 1904, 82.
44. Galton, *Inquiries into Human Faculty and Its Development*, 17.
45. Galton, "Eugenics," 82.
46. Francis Galton, *Essays in Eugenics* (London: Eugenics Education Society, 1909), 42.
47. Kevles, *In the Name of Eugenics*; Cooke, "The Limits of Heredity"; Challis, *The Archaeology of Race*.
48. Frans Lundgren, "The Politics of Participation: Francis Galton's Anthropometric Laboratory and the Making of Civic Selves," *British Journal for the History of Science* 46 (2013): 445–66; Benoît Godin, "From Eugenics to Scientometrics: Galton, Cattell, and Men of Science," *Social Studies of Science* 37, no. 5 (2007): 691–728.
49. Bulmer, *Francis Galton*, 84.
50. Francis Galton, *Probability: The Foundation of Eugenics* (Oxford: Clarendon Press, 1907); Francis Galton, *Local Association for Promoting Eugenics* (London: Eugenics Education Society, 1912). See Kevles, *In the Name of Eugenics*, ch. 5; Donald MacKenzie, "Eugenics in Britain," *Social Studies of Science* 6 (1976): 499–532.
51. Darwin Correspondence online (www.darwinproject.ac.uk), Francis Galton to Charles Darwin, December 9, 1859. Charles Darwin, *On the Origin of Species by Means of Natural Selection; Or the Preservation of Favoured Races in the Struggle for Life*. London, 1859.
52. Francis Galton, *Index to Achievements of Near Kinsfolk of Some of the Fellows of the Royal Society* (London, 1904), 11–12.
53. Noel Annan, "The Intellectual Aristocracy," in *Studies in Social History: A Tribute to G. M. Trevelyan*, ed. J. H. Plumb (London: Longmans, 1955), 241–87; William Whyte, "The Intellectual Aristocracy Revisited," *Journal of Victorian Culture* 10 (2005): 15–45.
54. Thomas Carlyle, "Aristocracy of Talent," in *Past and Present* (London: Chapman and Hall, 1843). Also discussed in Thomas Carlyle, *On Heroes, Hero-Worship, and the Heroic in History* (London: James Fraser, 1841). See Catherine Hall, "The Economy of Intellectual Prestige: Thomas Carlyle, John Stuart Mill, and the Case of Governor Eyre," *Cultural Critique* 12 (1989): 167–96; Alan S. Kahan, *Aristocratic Liberalism: The Social and Political Thought of Jacob Burckhardt, John Stuart Mill, and Alexis de Tocqueville* (New Brunswick, NJ: Transaction Publishers, 1992).
55. Samuel Smiles, *Self-Help; with Illustrations of Character and Conduct* (self-published, 1859). The second edition of 1866 added "Perseverance" to the title. See also Asa Briggs, "Samuel Smiles and the Gospel of Work," in *Victorian People* (Chicago: Chicago University Press, 1955), ch. 5; Adrian Jarvis, *Samuel Smiles and the Construction of Victorian Values* (Stroud: Alan Sutton Publishing, 1997); Anne Secord, "'Be What You Would Seem to Be': Samuel Smiles, Thomas Edward, and the Making of a Working-Class Scientific Hero," *Science in Context* 16 (2003): 147–73.
56. Leonore Davidoff and Catherine Hall, *Family Fortunes: Men and Women of the English Middle Class 1780–1850* (London: Hutchinson, 1987); Steven Mintz, *A Prison of Expectations: The Family in Victorian Culture* (New York: New York University Press, 1983).
57. Galton, *Hereditary Genius*, 1870, 193. Discussed in Jennifer S. Uglow, *The Lunar Men: The Friends Who Made the Future, 1730–1810* (London: Faber, 2002). See also Robert E. Schofield, *The Lunar Society of Birmingham: A Social History of Provincial Science and Industry in Eighteenth-Century England* (Oxford: Clarendon Press, 1963); Maureen McNeil, *Under the Banner of Science: Erasmus Darwin and His Age* (Manchester: Manchester University Press, 1987), 83–84; Christine MacLeod, *Heroes of Invention: Technology, Liberalism and British Identity, 1750–1914* (Cambridge: Cambridge University Press, 2007), 66.
58. Galton, *Hereditary Genius*, 1870, 209–10.
59. Francis Galton, *English Men of Science: Their Nature and Nurture* (London: Macmillan, 1874). See also Victor L. Hilts, "A Guide to Francis Galton's English Men of Science," *Transactions of the American Philosophical Society* 65, no 5 (1975): 1–85.

60. Ruth Barton, "'An Influential Set of Chaps': The X-Club and Royal Society Politics 1864–85," *British Journal of the History of Science* 23 (1990): 53–81; Ruth Barton, "'Huxley, Lubbock, and Half a Dozen Others': Professionals and Gentlemen in the Formation of the X Club, 1851–1864," *Isis* 89 (1998): 410–44; Adrian Desmond, "Redefining the X Axis: 'Professionals,' 'Amateurs' and the Making of Mid-Victorian Biology: A Progress Report," *Journal of the History of Biology* 34 (2001): 3–50; J. C. W. Waller, "Gentlemanly Men of Science: Sir Francis Galton and the Professionalization of the Life-Sciences," *Journal of the History of Biology* 34 (2001): 83–114; Bernard Lightman, "'The Voices of Nature': Popularizing Victorian Science," in *Victorian Science in Context*, ed. Bernard Lightman (Chicago: University of Chicago Press, 1997), 187–211; Bernard Lightman, *Victorian Popularizers of Science: Designing Nature for New Audiences* (Chicago: University of Chicago Press, 2009).

61. Karl Pearson, *The Life, Letters, and Labours of Francis Galton. Vol. I. Birth, 1822, to Marriage, 1853.* (Oxford: Oxford University Press, 1914), 67–68.

62. Francis Galton, "Statistical Inquiry into the Efficacy of Prayer," *Fortnightly Review*, new series, xii (1872): 125–35. See also Browne, *Charles Darwin*, 2, 289. Galton's contribution played a significant part in the "Prayer-gauge debate" that dominated the literary magazines through 1872 and involved several other authors. For a general account, see Robert Bruce Mullin, "Science, Miracles, and the Prayer-Gauge Debate," in *When Science and Christianity Meet*, ed. David C. Lindberg and Ronald L. Numbers (Chicago: University of Chicago Press, 2003), 203–24.

63. Pearson, *Life and Letters of Galton*, vol. 1, 66. See also Browne, *Charles Darwin*, 2, 404–405; Shane McCorristine, ed., *Spiritualism, Mesmerism and the Occult, 1800–1920* (London: Pickering & Chatto, 2012); Janet Oppenheim, *The Other World: Spiritualism and Psychical Research in England, 1850–1914* (Cambridge: Cambridge University Press, 1985); Richard Milner, "Charles Darwin and Associates, Ghostbusters," *Scientific American* 275, no. 4 (1996): 96–101.

64. Darwin Correspondence (www.darwinproject.ac.uk) Charles Darwin to Francis Galton, December 23, 1869.

65. Browne, *Charles Darwin*, 2, 200–201.

66. Peter J. Bowler, *Evolution: The History of an Idea* (Berkeley: University of California Press, 1984), 161, 178.

67. Darwin Correspondence (www.darwinproject.ac.uk) Charles Darwin to Francis Galton, December 23, 1869.

68. Francis Darwin, ed., *The Life and Letters of Charles Darwin* (London: John Murray, 1887), 1, 148, 149.

69. Darwin, *Descent of Man*, 2, 328. In this passage Darwin probably refers to Thomas Carlyle: "Genius…means transcendent capacity of taking trouble, first of all," from Thomas Carlyle, *History of Friedrich the Second Called Frederick the Great*, 8 vols., vol 4, iii (London: Chapman and Hall, 1858–1865).

70. Darwin, *Descent of Man*, 2, 327.

71. Ibid.

72. Brenda R. Weber, *Women and Literary Celebrity in the Nineteenth Century: The Transatlantic Production of Fame and Gender* (Aldershot: Ashgate, 2012).

73. John Hedley Brooke, "Does the History of Science Have a Future? Presidential Address," *British Journal for the History of Science* 32 (1999): 1–20; Kathryn A. Neeley, *Mary Somerville: Science, Illumination and the Female Mind* (Cambridge: Cambridge University Press, 2001); Claire Brock, "The Public Worth of Mary Somerville," *British Journal for the History of Science* 39 (2006): 255–72.

74. Charles Darwin, *De l'origine des espèces, ou des lois du progrès chez les êtres organisés*, trans. Clémence Royer (Paris: Guillaumin, 1862). Royer is discussed in Joy Harvey, *"Almost a Man of Genius": Clémence Royer, Feminism, and Nineteenth-Century Science* (New Brunswick, NJ: Rutgers University Press, 1997).

75. A remark made by Ernest Renan quoted by Joy Harvey, "'Strangers to Each Other': Male and Female Relationships in the Life and Work of Clémence Royer," in *Uneasy Careers*

and Intimate Lives: Women in Science, 1789–1979, ed. Pnina G. Abir-Am and Dorinda Outram (New Brunswick, NJ: Rutgers University Press, 1987), 165.

76. In Darwin, *Descent of Man,* 2, 328 footnote. Darwin referred to John Stuart Mill, *The Subjection of Women* (London: Longmans, Green, Reader and Dyer, 1869), 122: "the things in which man most excels women are those which require most plodding, and long hammering at single thoughts."

77. Janet Browne, "Making Darwin: Biography and the Changing Representations of Charles Darwin," *Journal of Interdisciplinary History* 40, no. 3 (2010): 347–73; Janet Browne, "Darwin's Intellectual Development: Biographies and the Changing Presentation of Character," in *Darwin: The Darwin College Lectures 2009,* ed. William Arthur Brown and A. C. Fabian, Darwin College Lectures 23 (Cambridge: Cambridge University Press, 2010), 1–30; Bernard Lightman, "The Many Lives of Charles Darwin: Early Biographies and the Definitive Evolutionist," *Notes and Records of the Royal Society* 64 (2010): 339–58.

78. Janet Browne, "Looking at Darwin: Portraits and the Making of an Icon," *Isis* 100 (2009): 542–70; Browne, *Charles Darwin,* 2, 199–203; Ludmilla J. Jordanova, *Defining Features: Scientific and Medical Portraits, 1660–2000* (London: Reaktion Books, 2000).

79. Janet Browne, "I Could Have Retched All Night," in *Science Incarnate: Historical Embodiments of Natural Knowledge,* ed. Christopher Lawrence and Steven Shapin (Chicago: University of Chicago Press, 1998), 240–87; Alan J. Friedman and Carol C. Donley, *Einstein as Myth and Muse* (Cambridge: Cambridge University Press, 1989).

80. Steven Shapin, *A Social History of Truth: Civility and Science in Seventeenth-Century England* (Chicago: University of Chicago Press, 1994), chs. 5 and 6.

81. Adrian Desmond, *The Politics of Evolution: Morphology, Medicine, and Reform in Radical London* (Chicago: University of Chicago Press, 1992); James A. Secord, *Victorian Sensation: The Extraordinary Publication, Reception, and Secret Authorship of Vestiges of the Natural History of Creation* (Chicago: University of Chicago Press, 2003).

82. Paul Davis Chapman, "Schools as Sorters: Testing and Tracking in California, 1910–1925," *Journal of Social History* 14 (July 1, 1981): 701–17.

83. Lewis Madison Terman, *Mental and Physical Traits of a Thousand Gifted Children* (Stanford: Stanford University Press, 1926), vi.

84. See particularly Carson, *The Measure of Merit.* Also addressed by Leila Zenderland, *Measuring Minds: Henry Herbert Goddard and the Origins of American Intelligence Testing* (Cambridge: Cambridge University Press, 2001); Raymond Fancher, *The Intelligence Men: Makers of the IQ Controversy* (New York: W. W. Norton, 1985); Corwin Boake, "From the Binet–Simon to the Wechsler–Bellevue: Tracing the History of Intelligence Testing," *Journal of Clinical and Experimental Neuropsychology* 24 (2002): 383–405.

85. Havelock Ellis, *A Study of British Genius* (London: Hurst and Blackett, 1904).

86. Leslie Stephen and Sidney Lee, eds., *Dictionary of National Biography,* 63 vols. (London: Smith, Elder, 1885–1900; Supplements and Errata 1904).

87. Ellis, *A Study of British Genius;* Havelock Ellis, "The Study of the Criminal," *British Journal of Psychiatry* 36, no. 152 (1890): 1–15. For a general account of theories of degeneration, see Daniel Pick, *Faces of Degeneration: A European Disorder, c.1848–c.1918* (Cambridge: Cambridge University Press, 1989).

7

"Genius Must Do the Scullery Work of the World": New Women, Feminists, and Genius, circa 1880–1920

Lucy Delap

Genius in its nineteenth- and twentieth-century formations has powerful connotations of elitism, and is likely to have boundaries that exclude the socially marginalized or disempowered. It was a common assumption in Victorian and Edwardian Britain that women were by nature unlikely to display genius. Nonetheless, "genius" proved a captivating and, on occasion, workable concept for late nineteenth- and early twentieth-century feminists. The significance of creative, prophetic, and "superbest" individuals fascinated many within the women's movement, despite unpromising late Victorian scientific formulations of genius. This chapter examines the lives and writings of two feminist figures that theorized genius and attempted to enact it in their own lives. The British writer Edith Ellis and the South African Olive Schreiner were both born in the mid nineteenth century, but their writings stretch into the twentieth century. This chronological span serves to demonstrate the changing uses of "genius" in a rapidly changing sociocultural context. Though both Ellis and Schreiner were best known as novelists, this chapter will examine the correspondences, memoirs, lectures, and photographs produced by these two writers. Not only are these ephemera sources much less well known, but they also display very direct engagement with concepts of "genius." These sources enable a closer examination of both change over time and the visual lexicon of genius than the much smaller numbers of novels that each wrote.

One might have expected feminists to be critical of the idea of genius, which had so long worked to exclude women from creative or scientific realms. But from Mary Wollstonecraft onward, genius had proved fascinating and useful for politically active women. Many found the unsettling of conventions associated with genius a helpful means of giving their own projects license and traction. As Andrew Elfenbein has elaborated, genius in eighteenth-century Britain was understood as potentially open to all, without limits of education or income.[1] Radicals invested in the idea of "natural genius" because it seemed democratic, not only in terms of class status but also vis à vis gender. It was unclear whether genius was exercised by men who displayed feminine characteristics, or whether it was open to women in various forms, or indeed whether it made inapplicable the categories of sex and gender. But these uncertainties aside, genius was a quality that dignified the unconventional, and this made it useful to many thinkers.

Genius, however, acquired quite different connotations during the century that separated Wollstonecraft and the late nineteenth-century Ellis and Schreiner. It became a more secular, individualized category associated with suffering and delirium as well as exceptionality. Existing historical accounts of the uses of genius argue for a triumph of misogynistic late nineteenth-century science over earlier traditions of egalitarian liberalism and Enlightenment thought. Flavia Alaya and Susan Casteras, for example, identify the British sexologist Havelock Ellis as a litmus figure for this change. He started his career apparently open-minded about women's capacities, but ended it with a focus on genius that excluded women. Ellis's "polar dispositions of...mind," Alaya argues, and his painful experiences of attachment to articulate, activist women, left him convinced by what we might term the "Darwin-Galton" version of genius. The work of eugenicist and scientist Francis Galton, founded on methodologically dubious surveys of "great" men and women, is argued to have brought in a conception of "massive, vigorous, capable looking" genius figures, displacing the more open-ended romantic genius.[2] Others have also commented on the percolation of ideas that linked normalcy, insanity, and genius, particularly in the work of John Ferguson Nisbet and Cesare Lombroso.[3] The late nineteenth century witnessed an apparent closing down of the cultural space given to women's aspirations to political, intellectual, and creative forms of expression. Instead, as historians have argued, scientists, social scientists, and journalists preferred to offer universalistic, biologistic explanations to account for why the highest forms of human achievement were limited to males, often drawing on notions of the cultural and biological complementarity of the sexes to support this thesis.

This historical characterization, however, is ultimately too reductive, and deploys categories of genius and traditions of political and scientific thought in ways that are too sharply defined as opposed. Biological thinking, for example, is counterposed to liberalism, in a manner that fails to see their coproduction. Most historians persist in understanding genius as a concept that was imposed upon feminist thinkers. Alaya, for example, perceived feminists as "obliged" to argue for equality using debates about exceptionality, and neglects the appeal that the exceptional had for activist women. In practice, some fin de siècle feminists were ready to use these concepts, and found them productive.

This is particularly evident in the ideas of a small group of "advanced" or heterodox Anglo-American feminists in the early twentieth century, who drew on political thinkers such as Nietzsche and Max Stirner to explore the idea of the "superwoman."[4] These women were among the first to use the term "feminism" to describe their beliefs, in an attempt to distance themselves from the conventionality of the Edwardian suffrage movement. Feminism, a political formation normally understood as focused on claims about equality and the extension of citizenship, was formulated at this historical moment in ways that seem unfamiliar to twenty-first-century eyes—as a set of claims about the originality and creativity of elite figures. As one British feminist claimed, "We consider that only those women who are gifted to the extent of genius can be Freewomen, and all the rest must be Bondwomen, i.e., followers, servants."[5] This was a polemical statement that opened the pages of the extraordinary *Freewoman* periodical—the first to term itself a "feminist review" in the English-speaking world. Its British and American contributors went on to outline their faith in the evolution of the "superwoman" as that which would dissolve morality and usher in new modes of experimental living.

The cultivation of genius seems a curious goal for progressive or radical thinkers of the early twentieth century, at a time when there was also a widely shared expectation that citizenship rights, education, and other resources would be increasingly available to the many rather than the few. It seems an unpromising moment for genius to be a useful social, intellectual, or political category for any except the die-hard opponents of change. Nonetheless, genius remained the common currency of a certain set of literary figures, who used it to navigate the literary marketplace and to fashion their sense of self. *The Freewoman* contributors were influenced by, and influential upon, the early elements of modernist literary culture; their uses of genius went with a commitment to iconoclasm and rupture from the past.[6] However, it was not simply avant-garde figures who found genius a useful category. This chapter evaluates how persistent the use of genius by progressive thinkers was. It explores whether this was the last gasp of an essentially nineteenth-century category, or whether versions of "genius" continued to be politically and discursively significant and relevant into the mid-twentieth century.

In asking these questions, it is useful to extend our analysis beyond a history of ideas approach. Though "genius" might be termed a discourse, it was not just a category to think with or understood as a disembodied vital force. It could also be a set of practices and, in some cases, a form of embodiment. Genius might be performed, incorporated into self-identity, and read onto the body. The imagined body of the genius varied historically, but there were many attempts to discern its physiognomy and physical effects. There was a well-developed literature on the diseases of genius—gout and consumption had been associated with genius by Havelock Ellis, for example.[7] Ralph Waldo Emerson's influential account of genius stressed the physical qualities of the genius-orator.[8] Genius was often recognized through what Olive Schreiner termed the "bright eyes of genius"; she also linked its qualities to head-shape and facial characteristics.[9] The gendered or sexed qualities of the embodied genius, however, were rarely discussed. In this period, women's bodies became widely portrayed in the popular and periodical press as inducements to consumption, and activists (ranging from dress reformers to suffragists) deployed women's bodies as political terrain. It is no surprise that fin de siècle attributions of genius were disrupted by tensions around how women might perform or physically inhabit this subject position.

Olive Schreiner: Genius as suffering and joy

My first case study is of the long career of the celebrated South African writer Olive Schreiner, who spent her life between Britain and South Africa.[10] After moving to Britain in 1880, she published, to enormous acclaim, *The Story of an African Farm* in 1883. This novel depicted the "new woman as genius" figure that had been characteristic of the "new woman" literature of this period. Novelists of the 1890s such as Mona Caird and Sarah Grand produced heroines consciously identified as geniuses.[11] Schreiner's heroine, Lyndall, was a characteristic precocious yet childlike rebel. She was portrayed as "elfin-like," with a "wonderful yearning light" in her eyes, a preternaturally wise, yet innocent, child.[12]

Schreiner explored the idea of genius in many of her literary works, but it is also a recurrent reference point in her wide-ranging and influential personal and political correspondence, particularly within her close friendships with scientific or medical thinkers such as Karl Pearson and Havelock Ellis—those very figures blamed by Alaya for their misogynous versions of genius. Schreiner designated many of her contacts and acquaintances men or women of genius, ranging from military men to musicians. Her own version of genius was often a temporary rather than an ontological quality—her letters talk of touches or moments of genius. This enabled a broad "throw" to genius, a quality that Schreiner perceived among those she termed kaffirs and natives as much as among educated Europeans.

Schreiner repeated as a truism the idea that "genius has no sex," but also robustly defended the specific qualities of women's genius. Indeed, she believed that genius was more prevalent among women than men.[13] However, following conventional opinion, Schreiner divided genius into different, gendered forms. She conceded that women often lacked the "powerful reason and massive strength" needed to do justice to genius.[14] An early letter from Schreiner to the British scientist Karl Pearson allowed that women had weaker analytic skills than men, but argued that this was because "her narrower life has allowed of less development."[15] She resisted Pearson's tendency to biologise factors that she saw as social, yet nonetheless sometimes adopted from Havelock Ellis and others a scientifically framed and biologically based account of genius. She wrote, for example, to Ellis in 1889: "People of genius are those individuals in whom the sympathetic or instinctive nervous system is particularly well developed, or, rather, combined with that intellectual cerebro-spinal system peculiar to the higher vertebrate." Her letter went on in this fashion, yet she clearly felt that her attempts to use biological theories to convey what she thought of genius were insufficient. She may have been influenced by Ellis's own language in their correspondence, yet they were clearly intimate enough for her to develop her own approach to this topic they both felt strongly about. Indeed, Schreiner became increasingly skeptical of Ellis's scientific approach. Later in the same year, 1889, she commented to Ellis that "I don't think over much of your theories about genius—though they are true so far as they go."[16] It was in this year that Schreiner moved from Britain back to South Africa, where she lived until 1913.

Rather than engage with scientific versions of genius, Schreiner offered Havelock Ellis a curious parable to convey her views. The genre of the "parable" is not easily categorized, but it is in keeping with Schreiner's use of dreams and allegories to convey ideas in her creative writing. She recounted to Ellis: "Once God Almighty said 'I will produce a self-working automatic machinery for enduring suffering, which shall be capable of the largest amount of suffering in a given space,' & he made woman; but he wasn't satisfied that he reached the highest point of perfection so he made a man of genius; he was[n't] satisfied yet, so he combined the two—& made a woman of genius—& he was satisfied! That's the real theory.—But in the end he sold himself because the machinery he'd constructed, to endure suffering could enjoy bliss too."[17] Women's genius was to be able to combine suffering and creativity, and link this to pleasure and joy.

What are we to make of this rather opaque reflection? Schreiner was clearly drawing on James Hinton's influential work of some 30 years earlier in linking genius, femininity, pleasure, and suffering. Hinton (1822–1875) was (like Havelock Ellis) a medical doctor and progressive thinker. He had published on popular science and ethics from the 1850s and was famous for arguing that the power of nature was experienced by the genius as a form of possession or mediumship. Genius, in his view, was the point of least resistance to nature. It could thus be understood as a (creative) form of weakness, as well as an intoxicating instinct for lawbreaking. The ancient Greeks epitomized this life unhampered by convention and open to passion, a world lost by the coming of Christianity, though Christ himself, Hinton believed, was a genius. Hinton's work tended to drift between a refusal of the significance of gender, to a conventional gendered scheme where women were intuitive and natural. He wrote, for example: "genius has the woman's way of seeing (intuition) on a wider subject...men of genius are the women of the race."[18]

Theoretically open to both sexes, Hinton's genius was akin to sexual passion. He was known for sexual dissidence and, through his proposals for non-monogamous marriage, lacked respectability among his peers.[19] Schreiner was reading Hinton's *Life in Nature* in 1884, several years before she wrote her parable; she and Havelock Ellis corresponded about his ideas. She declared in a letter to Ellis that Hinton's value lay in his powers of stimulation. "He makes all thoughts live & throb which is the work of true genius."[20] Hinton clearly influenced Schreiner's attention to the powers of nature and to ideas of life force, though she was always cautious about his sexual morality. As in her parable, Hinton had argued that genius was about the combination of pleasure and pain. The bliss that Schreiner believed the woman of genius was capable of feeling may have been mental and creative, or may have been sexual or physical. Schreiner, however, distrusted sexual dissidence, and she rejected the exploration of diverse sexual passions found in avant-garde publications, such as *The Freewoman*, as "the tone of the brutal self-indulgent selfish male."[21]

Alongside Hinton, Schreiner was influenced by Emerson's rejection of the conventional and the embrace of spontaneity and intuition, which Emerson described as "the essence of genius."[22] Drawing on the romantic repertoire, she associated genius with a close relationship to nature—and this, of course, was a relatively conventional attribute of womanhood. She also stressed its link to the divine, again making genius associable with the perceived spiritual energies of women.

Schreiner saw genius as fairly commonplace among the artists and authors of the 1880s and 1890s; for her, it was a much used term of cultural approbation. It was also a term widely applied by others to Schreiner's own work. George Meredith had described her as a "new genius" when he read *The Story of an African Farm*, as she proudly reported to her husband. Schreiner clearly self-identified as a genius; she bluntly noted in a letter to Havelock Ellis: "How beautiful genius is, Harry! And it takes genius to understand genius."[23] She claimed to have the powers of observation of a child, in seeing the world with fresh eyes and problematizing the taken for granted: "men of genius are always childlike," she commented to Ellis. "A child sees everything, looks straight at it, examines it without any preconceived idea; most people after they are about eleven or twelve quite lose this power, they see everything through a few pre-conceived ideas which hang like a veil between them & the outer world." She herself, she noted, had long practiced the cultivation of this power of childlike perception. It had been honed during the uninspiring church services of her youth, and she advised Ellis to experiment for himself: "Listen to people talking as though you didn't understand what the words meant, or that the sound came from human voices. Listen to it just as a noise striking the ear."[24] She went on to discuss her own mystical allegories, which she described as written "with joy"; there is a hint of the idea of possession or mediumship in her writing.

Genius as tragedy

There is much here that is familiar to the romantic tradition of thinking about genius as childlike, and often tragic. Like many new woman novelists, Schreiner envisaged her unconventional genius figures, both male and female, as coming to bad ends; they mostly die tragic deaths. Literary historian Ann Heilmann has described this as the "double bind" of late nineteenth century genius.[25] Genius was a quality that, for women at least, seemed to entail being misunderstood and misrecognized, and was often only recognized posthumously. Schreiner outlined in an 1896 letter to the aristocratic British suffragist Constance Lytton her belief that female genius created a tragic conundrum for gifted women: "There is a great tragedy in the lives of modern women that women of the old style perhaps know nothing of: It is the tragedy which arises when a man cannot really love a woman *because she is too much his superior*; intellectually and emotionally she moves in a higher world than that in which he *can* move. It would kill him to live always in her atmosphere. A sparrow *cannot* live up in the air where an eagle breathes easily!"[26] The genius-woman could only exist in lonely isolation.

However, we should not take this romantic vision of the lonely artist, in touch with nature and her inner child, entirely at face value. Schreiner as a "cultural entrepreneur" was also deliberately cultivating an image that would sell in the literary marketplace.[27] Though she resented the commercial apparatus of celebrity and sometimes challenged its genres, Schreiner deliberately adopted forms of self presentation that might enhance her literary reputation. As Clare Gill has shown, this was particularly evident in the posted photographs that she had taken, which reveal a mannered unconventionality.[28] At the time of Schreiner's early writing career, the cult of the literary celebrity was gathering speed. With the advent of cheaper photoreproduction, writers would issue portraits of themselves, often in domestic settings. The new journalism was beginning to make familiar the diet of gossip, "tit bits," and interviews that came to characterize the celebrity culture of the 1880s and 1890s.[29] Schreiner criticized this trend for its commercial-mindedness and lack of seriousness, but she also sought to control her image. Her long correspondence with the editor and journalist W. T. Stead shows clearly her attempts to publicize her work, shape her career, and present a particular face to her audiences. Gill has explored the ways in which Schreiner fed Stead and other publishers with photographs, including some of her life in South Africa portraying her in remote veld settings. This represented an unsettling of the "writer at home" genre and a means to claim a distinctively South African identity. For all her frustration with the celebrity status of authors, Schreiner utilized her role as a "representative genius" of her nation, and was referred to by Stead as the only genius South Africa had produced.[30]

Nonetheless, Schreiner often found this a difficult process to manage. She was, for example, extremely concerned to limit the circulation of a particular portrait that she disliked. She had instructed the studio to destroy the negatives, but was very angry when what she called the "caricature" resurfaced in W. T. Stead's 1897 book *Notables of Britain* (figure 7.1).

The portrait perhaps seemed too prosaic, too weighty, to fit with her preferred identity as a literary genius, which she had likened to being an eagle, or childlike, open to bliss as well as pain. Schreiner was sensitive about her appearance as she aged—she wrote to a friend in 1908 that acquaintances no longer recognized her, despite, she claimed, her hair remaining "thicker and longer than ever, and hardly any grey ones."[31] Though portrait photography seemed to offer opportunities to display and perform genius, it proved a contradictory and far from workable identity to inhabit in a physical sense. Schreiner clearly felt the contradictions of female genius when it came to presenting herself to the world as a literary celebrity.

MISS
OLIVE SCHREINER
(Mrs. Cronwright).

Figure 7.1   Olive Schreiner's portrait in *Notables of Britain*.

Edith Ellis and the laughing genius

Olive Schreiner was friends with Edith Ellis (née Lees), a British writer who, like Schreiner, sought to both account for and enact genius. Schreiner had been having an intense and possibly sexual relationship with Havelock Ellis in the mid 1880s, but they did not formalize their relationship, which was largely conducted through letters. Ellis met Edith Lees in 1887, and they were married in 1891. Edith Ellis is a figure who can suggest both continuities and change in how it was possible to "think with" and "live with" genius. Edith had met Havelock through the Fellowship of the New Life, a group of British radicals who formed a utopian community and socialist political grouping in the 1890s.[32] From this group came the future leading lights of the Labour Party, the Fabian Society, and many other influential figures. Edith Ellis was the group's secretary and participated in its efforts to promote communal and simple living.[33] The fellowship sought a balance between the qualities of "solidarity" and "personality" (revealingly characterized by one member as "the two sexes" of democracy).[34] Its members were convinced that the distribution of resources in society must be made much more democratic and equitable, but also expected social change to happen through the contributions of the exceptional few; their goal was "the cultivation of perfect character in all" or "true individualism."[35] Like so many of their age, these socialists equivocated between elitism and democracy.

Edith Ellis was sexually attracted to women, while Havelock suffered from sexual impotence, and their marriage was probably never consummated. Alaya has described Edith's marriage to Havelock as so traumatizing that he turned against his feminist commitments and became skeptical of women's capacity for genius. They mostly lived separately, and Edith wrote of the benefits of "semi-detached marriage." She also controversially argued for periods of trial marriage in order to determine suitability. She wrote fiction, lectured in Britain and United States, and farmed in Cornwall. She died in her 50s, in 1916. She has certainly not been remembered as a genius, and her fictional and political writings are rarely read today. Her lectures were popular, reaching an educated audience, but not the intelligentsia, who responded somewhat superciliously. One reviewer commented in the *Observer* in 1921 that Mrs. Ellis was an "eminently sane" writer who "does not reach profundity but...opens her mind eagerly and seizes truth as it goes by."[36] Sanity, for this reviewer, clearly counted against Edith's genius potential. But Edith's work does help us understand something of the formulation of genius, and how it might have been enacted in a life and presented to a middlebrow audience.

Like Schreiner, Havelock Ellis had been very influenced by reading James Hinton as a young man, and had undertaken to edit some of his manuscripts after Hinton's death. This project did not lead to any publication, but it was taken over by Edith Ellis. She published a collection of her lectures on "modern seers" in 1910, in which she set Hinton alongside Nietzsche and Edward Carpenter, the latter a prominent British homosexual who was also a member of the Fellowship of the New Life. She later published *James Hinton: A Sketch*, which came out in 1918, after her death. Both these texts dwell on genius and argue that Hinton and the other figures all saw "a striving towards perfection of individual character as the chief factor in social progress."[37]

Edith Ellis offered an account of genius that disrupted the gender-complementarity model still evident in Olive Schreiner's work. She did not believe that men and women were necessarily complementary in creative, practical, or spiritual terms. Finding her own deepest friendships and passions with other women, she was disposed to think beyond the man/woman dyad. Both Hinton and Edith Ellis allowed that women might be geniuses, but they believed that genius expressed the universal, humanity, rather than the gendered self.

Influenced by Edward Carpenter's work on the third sex, Edith linked genius to inversion, or homosexuality, rather than conventional gender categories. Both geniuses and inverts, in her view, tended "to belong to the neurotic group" but had an important role to play in "the evolution of the world." Both conditions might be "menaces" but might also be empowering. "The abnormal person" or, sometimes, "the peculiar people" served her as a description of geniuses and inverts, and she believed them to have a vital contribution to make to "the race." Not just inversion, but a wide range of sexual preferences were included in her version of "peculiar." Her writings thus linked work on genius to the more progressive celebration of sexual diversity that can be seen in some versions of early sexology.[38] An anti-romanticism also emerges in Edith's commitment to training and self-cultivation. Rather than seeing genius as divine possession or a gift, she felt that it was a dimension of human experience that needed "prior training and control." This, she believed, applied to sexual passion as much as other creative passions and underlay her demand for democratic sex education.

What physical characteristics did Edith Ellis's toiling genius have? She understood the physiognomy of genius as distinctive, and wrote of "the strange head and mouth and eyes of Hinton" himself, noting "the strong mouth of genius, and the laugh in its eyes."[39] In similar terms, she described the "brown, dog-like eyes of [Edward] Carpenter's [which] pierce through appearances, and he sees jewels where most of us see only bottle glass."[40] It was in describing the physical characteristics of genius that Edith's own claims to genius can be discerned. Edward Carpenter provided a preface to her posthumously published essays *The New Horizon in Love and Life*, in which he noted the timbre of her voice as well as her "feverish energy," which gave her work, though hastily done, a "gem-like brilliance." For Carpenter, she was "democratic yet dominating...feminine and masculine all in one. The Woman and the Man (and indeed also the Child) were closely united in her; and this it was perhaps which gave her such prophetic insight."[41] More viscerally, an American journalist commented that "women in England have told me that when Edith Ellis entered a room the very air in the room seemed to change, to expand suddenly, to be different and more oxygenated...She saw with an internal and prophetic vision; knew often more by intuition than by material knowledge, and had at moments a quite uncanny gift of divination."[42]

Friends and those who attended her lectures commented on a sense of Edith being possessed by life force beyond the capacity of her body to contain. Edith's eyes were also widely commented on—one friend dwelt on her "extraordinary eyes," and Edith herself consciously emphasized her intense gaze in the portraits she circulated to publicize her lectures and books. A member of her literary set, Mrs. Clifford Bax, commented on Edith's "amazing blue eyes...I have never seen eyes so startlingly, so suggestively blue."[43] Her posed portraits offer a traditional romantic iconography of intense, serious, and even tragic genius.

Edith's queer or "peculiar" subjectivity emerges in an anecdote told by a friend about her transgression of physical taboos, particularly around female bodies. In a collection of personal reminiscences published after Edith's early death, one friend remembered: "One day I found her waiting for me in the hall of the Lyceum Club. She greeted me with sparkling eyes: 'Kiss my forehead, it's pure sweat: I've been on a committee!' I surveyed her heated person and . . . I elaborately groomed her beaded brow, tidied her mane with my finger combs and lifting her face, kissed her on the mouth, with an eye to the several 'starchy' persons present . . . We fell to laughing."[44] This is a strikingly unconventional memorialization, conveying a sexual charge that, for those who knew the code, signaled Edith's inverted or "lesbian-like" identity.

However, the anecdote also captured an important element of how Edith understood genius. Alongside the childlike genius, she was also very attracted to the idea of the "divine jester, who is able to express the subtle connection between the anguish and gaiety which lie at the heart of things." The idea of the ability to laugh as a mark of special giftedness was repeatedly stressed; Edith wrote of the "sense of humour" that "is a veritable gift from the gods."[45] This was clearly a defining feature of the genius-role that she performed and identified with. Havelock Ellis noted after her death that, to her friends, Edith "sometimes referred to herself as the Jester."[46] She had advised her readers that they should see themselves as "rollicking children of the Infinite" and apply their sense of humor widely—even to the "seers" who had done so much to shape her ideas of genius: "Nietzsche is a tonic, and wise women read him with an open mind, though, possibly, with the suspicion of a smile."[47] Her writings represented a down-to-earth version of genius, less tortured and tragic than Schreiner's; Edith's account of genius celebrated in the same breath the passion and courage of women in childbirth alongside the philosopher who could encounter the "Oversoul." The genius was not to turn aside from worldly affairs, but must, Ellis believed, engage in social service, and must "move in and out of crowds in order to minister to the spiritually deaf and dumb and blind." This seems to hark back to Emersonian genius but offers an account that is unusually attentive to women's realms and experiences. In a provocative gendered juxtaposition, Ellis argued that the genius "must do the scullery work of the world down to its most sordid details."[48] Her genius was rooted in socially degraded settings. Edith Ellis was not the first to stress service as a component of genius. James Hinton's, Ralph Waldo Emerson's, and Walt Whitman's accounts of genius had also noted it. Her distinctive contribution was to anchor this sense of the service owed by the genius to much more mundane, humble, and feminized settings—to the scullery, portraying the genius as charwoman. This serious commitment to social service was combined with the disorderly, subversive forces of humor and desire—a version of genius that was uniquely oriented to Edith's late nineteenth- and early twentieth-century feminist and socialist milieu.

Twentieth-century genius

These distinctive formulations of genius, produced by the literary marketplace and the turn toward utopian and radical thought at the fin de siècle, did not always resonate with the new concerns of the World War I years and subsequent decades. Havelock Ellis was well aware that James Hinton's work seemed of the nineteenth- rather than the twentieth century, lacking a connection to what he described as "a world re-oriented by Einstein." Nonetheless, he believed Hinton still had relevance, and in the 1930s asserted that "men of scientific training and distinction... are putting forth conceptions which Hinton would have greeted with joy."[49] Schreiner also welcomed the growth of technologically sophisticated or practical expressions of genius. She had moved back to Europe in 1913 and still wrote regularly to Havelock Ellis and other friends, becoming deeply involved in pacifist activism. Her correspondence stretched into the post-World War I years and provides evidence of her characteristic fin de siècle mystical, literary account of genius being reoriented toward the new prominence of science and technology. During the early years of World War I she wrote to a friend: "I don't know whether to laugh or cry when I hear of you or any man however great his genius putting it into 'literary' form." Schreiner retained her Hintonian focus on nature as a source of inspiration. She noted that genius was still "the cry of wild nature... as if the rocks & trees, & the very earth itself, & all the primitive human instincts for once found voice & cried out—*even the earth itself.*"[50] But she became convinced that it was not poets but scientists who could best express this: "The world is full of great men of genius and ability now... the *ability* of the age goes into science, into medicine, chemistry, etc; art and fine writing are in this age secondary. If Michael Angelo lived now he would *not* paint pictures or make statues. The great genius gives voice to the great wants of his age."[51] Despite her opposition to the world war, she welcomed and termed as an expression of genius a friend's invention of a new naval weapon.[52]

Alongside scientists, Schreiner also foregrounded political revolutionaries and theorists, writing of the political genius of Lenin, Marx, Keynes, Lloyd George, and Eleanor Aveling.[53] Her geniuses seemed practical, or politically minded, rather than the childlike, tender figures she described in the 1880s. During and after the war, Schreiner became more vocal in her rejection of Hinton's sexual politics, seeing him as advocating reckless "gratification of the sex instinct." Retreating from the modern sex radicals of Edwardian feminism, she preferred sexual emotions to be governed by reason and a sense of duty, though she recognized that this might make her work seem old-fashioned.[54] In particular, she regarded Hinton's influence on Edith Ellis as malign; when Edith was dying of diabetes in 1916, Schreiner commented to Havelock: "I looked at her & heard her raving, I thought: 'another wreck of Hintonism... Her poor weak brain & character couldn't stand it.'"[55]

Edith Ellis had always celebrated sexual diversity and did not share Schreiner's prurience. But she also recognized the need to update her concept of genius—mediated by the continuing influence of Hinton—to meet the concerns of a new century. She began to foreground a more concrete focus on the material circumstances that governed women's lives, and their ability to develop their potential. The influence of early twentieth century feminism and socialism is particularly clear in her sketch of Hinton, published in 1918, which noted critically, "Hinton never...really laid stress on the vital truth that woman will always remain a possession of man until she is economically free of him. No sex problem can be solved till economic conditions are perfectly equal."[56] Hinton's theory of genius still seemed relevant to the age, but Edith Ellis perceived that an individual's ability to channel the "life force" was rooted in the economic and material spaces she or he inhabited. Genius had become provisional rather than a surging creativity that could not be contained.

Edith Ellis represented a twentieth-century shift toward a more available, democratic, and socialist version of genius. This potentially provided a more hospitable intellectual space for feminist deployment, compared to nineteenth-century romanticism or the Nietszchean-influenced, self-consciously elitist visions of the aloof genius that flourished among Edwardians. Ellis's formulation was more "average," more mundane. In one of her lectures, she noted that "the characteristics of genius in modern life do not stand so apart from those of us who are average in brain and heart as they did thirty years ago...It is in fact growing more common to find amongst both men and women a mingling of the practical and the mystical." Having witnessed Edward Carpenter darning his socks, she noted, "There is no real difference in the arts of love, music, stocking-making, or redeeming." We might term this a "middlebrow" genius, which incorporated laughter into what had been a more tragic, narcissistic, and serious mode of selfhood. Ellis concluded that "in this age of Materialism, as we are fond of calling it, we need a prophet whose humor is keen."[57]

Conclusions

For those working on the period spanning the 1890s–1930s, there is a strong temptation to view the period through the lenses of "modernity," characterized by rejection of the literary, artistic, or intellectual frames of the nineteenth century. Talk within the women's movement at the fin de siècle of the "new woman" and "the superwoman," and references to Nietzsche or the work of sexologists, can be read as a dismissal of the sentimental and unconventional literary genius of the nineteenth century. But this chapter has suggested that there was more continuity in the uses of the term "genius," with no clear rejection of a nineteenth-century frame among feminists and intellectuals. A mid-nineteenth-century author, James Hinton, was persistently influential on the writers assessed here, and through them he continued to influence twentieth-century versions of genius. As so often is the case in intellectual history, there is no singular chronology to trace in questions of intellectual influence, but rather a complex movement back and forth, drawing on older resources and revisioning them for use in alternative contexts. The work of Schreiner and Edith Ellis is suggestive of hybrid or competing languages of genius, capable of taking on diverse connotations within the lives and ideas of these two feminist and socialist writers.

Schreiner continued to be heavily influenced by her mystical sense of genius as possessed by nature's "life force," though she moved away from literary vehicles for this in the years during and after World War I until her death in December 1920. Her difficulties with managing her self-presentation as a "woman of genius" may be due to the clash between her tragic, childlike version of genius, her contentious political interventions over South African affairs, and her public self-presentation as a national icon, the genius of South Africa. She may also have found her ageing body and rather solid features increasingly hard to reconcile with her vision of the physically waif-like genius. Furthermore, she was clearly uncomfortable at the connotations of sexual dissidence that genius seemed to be taking on. Nonetheless, genius continued to resonate as a major concern of Schreiner's into the twentieth century in helping to think through the significance of the turn toward democracy and mass society. It provided ways of talking about leadership and individuality within the context of consumer culture, mass housing, and mass readerships—the "vulgar herd," as Schreiner referred to them, though perhaps with irony.[58]

For Edith Ellis, ideas of genius similarly allowed her to celebrate the individualist within democracy and to reconcile the two. Edith Ellis's version of genius, which scripted her own life and self presentation, was unusually attentive to laughter and labor. Genius could be used in ways to represent subjects or performances that were less exceptional and pathological, and more oriented to the mundane and everyday. For Ellis, genius was interwoven with forms of social service, or indicated by the leavening powers of sexual passion or humor—qualities and experiences to which *all* potentially had access.

Several scholars have written of the persistent power of genius in its nineteenth- and early twentieth-century formations to create space for eccentric, peculiar, or queer subject positions. Schreiner, more concerned with acting as a representative genius or prophetess for her country, argued for women's inclusion but retained a fairly conventional sense of what the genius was. Edith Ellis, in contrast, delighted in her peculiarity and sexual transgression. As Victoria Olwell and Gustave Stadler have argued, genius proved a workable category for feminists and other kinds of dissidents.[59] In particular, Olwell has argued that popular culture and literature proved a hospitable space for an "eccentric" politics of women's genius, where more "highbrow" or philosophical discourses did not. I would extend this to the category of the "middlebrow," a readership at which Edith Ellis's chatty lectures and pen-portraits were aimed at. While Schreiner's talk of the great politicians and technical engineers of World War I and after seemed to close down possibilities for women's genius, Edith Ellis's memorable portrayal of the genius as "heaven's jester or heaven's charwoman" indicates the renewal of a more workable, queer, materially rooted, feminist, and democratic vision of genius.[60]

Notes

1. A. Elfenbein, *Romantic Genius: The Prehistory of a Homosexual Role* (New York: Columbia University Press, 1999).

2. F. Alaya, "Victorian Science and the Genius of Women," *Journal of the History of Ideas* 38 (1977): 267; Susan P Casteras, "Excluding Women: The Cult of the Male Genius in Victorian Painting," in *Rewriting the Victorians: Theory, History, and the Politics of Gender*, ed. Linda M. Shires (London: Routledge, 1992).
3. Anne Stiles, "Literature in Mind: H. G. Wells and the Evolution of the Mad Scientist," *Journal of the History of Ideas* 70 (2009): 317–39.
4. Lucy Delap, "The Superwoman: Theories of Gender and Genius in Edwardian Britain," *The Historical Journal* 47 (2004): 101–26.
5. Dora Marsden, *The Freewoman*, November 30, 1911, 21.
6. B. Clarke, *Dora Marsden and Early Modernism* (Ann Arbor: University of Michigan Press, 1996); Elizabeth Francis, *The Secret Treachery of Words: Feminism and Modernism in America* (Minneapolis: University of Minnesota Press, 2002).
7. Havelock Ellis, *A Study of British Genius* (London: Hurst and Blackett, 1904; 1901), 182.
8. Ralph Waldo Emerson, Ronald A. Bosco, and Joel Myerson, *The Selected Lectures of Ralph Waldo Emerson* (Athens: University of Georgia Press, 2005), 67–81.
9. Schreiner to Havelock Ellis, September 4, 1885, Harry Ransom Research Center, University of Texas at Austin; Schreiner to Alice Greene, December 24, 1904, UCT Manuscripts and Archives, Olive Schreiner Letters Project [henceforth OSLP] transcriptions.
10. Olive Schreiner, *The Story of an African Farm* (London: Virago, 1989 [1883]).
11. Ann Heilmann discusses the recurrent and irresolvable question of women's genius in "new woman" novels. Sarah Grand's 1897 novel *The Beth Book* was subtitled "a study from the life of Elizabeth Caldwell Maclure, a woman of genius"; Mona Caird depicted Hadria, a woman of frustrated creative genius, in the 1894 *Daughters of Danaus*. Ann Heilmann, *New Woman Strategies: Sarah Grand, Olive Schreiner, Mona Caird* (Manchester: Manchester University Press, 2004), 6.
12. Schreiner, *The Story of an African Farm*, 20, 265.
13. Schreiner to Anna Purcell née Cambier Faure, November 29, 1902, NLSA Cape Town, Special Collections, OSLP transcription.
14. Schreiner to Havelock Ellis, May 26, 1889, NLSA Cape Town, Special Collections, OSLP transcription.
15. Schreiner to Karl Pearson, May 10, 1886, University College London Library, Special Collections, UCL, London, OSLP transcription.
16. Schreiner to Havelock Ellis, February 5, 1889, NLSA Cape Town, Special Collections, Schreiner to Havelock Ellis, 1888, Harry Ransom Research Center, University of Texas at Austin, Olive Schreiner Letters Project transcription, OSLP transcriptions.
17. Schreiner to Havelock Ellis, 1888, Harry Ransom Research Center, University of Texas at Austin, OSLP transcription.
18. J. Hinton, *Selections from Manuscripts*, vol. I (London: Theo Johnson, 1856), 46.
19. Susan Morgan, *A Passion for Purity: Ellice Hopkins and the Politics of Gender in the Late-Victorian Church* (Bristol: Centre for Comparative Studies in Religion and Gender, 1999), 50–51.
20. Schreiner to Havelock Ellis, July 8, 1885, Harry Ransom Research Center, University of Texas at Austin, OSLP transcription.
21. Schreiner to Havelock Ellis, July 23, 1884, Harry Ransom Research Center, University of Texas at Austin; Schreiner to Havelock Ellis, August 7, 1912, NLSA Cape Town, Special Collections, OSLP transcriptions.
22. Emerson, quoted in Carolyn Burdett, *Olive Schreiner and the Progress of Feminism: Evolution, Gender, Empire* (Basingstoke: Palgrave Macmillan, 2001), 41.
23. Schreiner to Havelock Ellis, February 24, 1890, NLSA Cape Town, Special Collections, OSLP transcription.
24. Schreiner to Havelock Ellis, July 19, 1884, National English Literary Museum, Grahamstown, OSLP transcription.
25. Heilmann, *New Woman Strategies*, 6.
26. Schreiner to Constance Lytton, December 1896, Lytton Family Papers, Knebworth, OSLP transcription.

27. Liz Stanley, Andrea Salter, and Helen Dampier, "Olive Schreiner, Epistolary Practices and Microhistories: A Cultural Entrepreneur in a Historical Landscape," *Cultural and Social History* 10 (2013): 577–97.
28. James Hinton, *Life in Nature* (London: G Allen & Unwin, 1932); Clare Gill, "'I'm Really Going to Kill Him This Time': Olive Schreiner, W. T. Stead, and the Politics of Publicity in the Review of Reviews," *Victorian Periodicals Review* 46, no. 2 (2013): 184–210
29. Richard Salmon, "'A Simulacrum of Power': Intimacy and Abstraction in the Rhetoric of the New Journalism," *Victorian Periodicals Review* 30 (1997): 41–52; Alexis Easley, *Literary Celebrity, Gender, and Victorian Authorship, 1850–1914* (Newark: University of Delaware Press, 2011).
30. Gill, "Olive Schreiner, W. T. Stead, and the Politics of Publicity."
31. Schreiner to Robert Franklin ("Bob") Muirhead, November 16, 1908, MacFarlane Collection, OSLP transcription.
32. Kevin Manton, "The Fellowship of the New Life: English Ethical Socialism Reconsidered," *History of Political Thought* 24 (2003): 282–304.
33. Jo-Ann Wallace, "The Case of Edith Ellis," in *Modernist Sexualities*, ed. Hugh Stevens and Caroline Howlett (Manchester: Manchester University Press, 2000).
34. Henry Binns, *A Modern Humanist* (1900), quoted in Manton, "Fellowship of the New Life," 290.
35. Herbert Rix, "Individualism or Socialism?," in *Sermons and Addresses* (1907) quoted in Ibid., 291.
36. *Observer*, April 24, 1921.
37. Edith Ellis, *Three Modern Seers* (London: Stanley Paul, 1910), 7.
38. Heike Bauer, "Theorizing Female Inversion: Sexology, Discipline, and Gender at the Fin de Siècle," *Journal of the History of Sexuality* 18 (2009): 84–102.
39. Edith Ellis, *James Hinton: A Sketch* (London: Paul, 1918), 251, 203.
40. Edith Ellis, *Personal Impressions of Edward Carpenter* (Berkeley Heights, NJ: Free Spirit Press, 1922), 9.
41. Edith Ellis, *The New Horizon in Love and Life* (London: A. & C. Black, 1921), xi.
42. Ibid., xxviii.
43. Ellis Ellis, *Stories and Essays* (Berkeley Heights, NJ: Free Spirit Press, 1924), ix.
44. Ibid., xiii.
45. Ellis, *New Horizon*, 64, 71, 186, 85.
46. Ellis, *Stories and Essays*, xvii.
47. Ellis, *Three Modern Seers*, 185.
48. Ellis, *New Horizon,* 190–91.
49. Havelock, Ellis introduction to James Hinton, *Life in Nature* (London: George Allen & Unwin, 1932), xxv–xxvi.
50. Schreiner to John Hodgson, October 1914, Harry Ransom Research Center, University of Texas at Austin, OSLP transcription.
51. Schreiner to Havelock Ellis, 1919, NLSA Cape Town, Special Collections, OSLP transcription.
52. Schreiner to John Hodgson, March 1915, Harry Ransom Research Center, University of Texas at Austin, OSLP transcription.
53. Schreiner to Havelock Ellis, 1919, NLSA Cape Town, Special Collections; Schreiner to Karl Pearson, March 8, 1886, University College London Library, Special Collections, UCL, London; Schreiner to William Philip ("Will") Schreiner, August 18, 1914, UCT Manuscripts & Archives, OSLP transcriptions.
54. Schreiner to Havelock Ellis, July 4, 1916, Harry Ransom Research Center, University of Texas at Austin, OSLP transcription. Schreiner recognized that her morals made her seem out of touch—she commented to a friend in 1913 that "I am quite out of the fashion now—no one wants to have anything to do with me." Schreiner to Anna Purcell née Cambier Faure, December 1914, NLSA Cape Town, Special Collections, OSLP transcription.
55. Schreiner to Havelock Ellis, April 24, 1916, Harry Ransom Research Center, University of Texas at Austin, OSLP transcription. Schreiner had liked Edith Ellis's work on Edward

Carpenter, but "detested" her views on Hinton, "and the other fellow," as she referred to Nietzsche, with whose work she was clearly unfamiliar. Olive Schreiner to Edward Carpenter, January 31, 1911, Sheffield Libraries, Archives & Information, OSLP transcription.

56. Ellis, *James Hinton, a Sketch*, 247.
57. Ellis, *Personal Impressions of Edward Carpenter*, 8, 12, 15.
58. Olive Schreiner to Havelock Ellis, June 29, 1916, Harry Ransom Research Center, University of Texas at Austin, OSLP transcription.
59. Gustavus Stadler, "Louisa May Alcott's Queer Geniuses," *American Literature* 71 (1999): 657–77; Victoria Olwell, "'It Spoke Itself': Women's Genius and Eccentric Politics," *American Literature* 77 (2005): 33–63.
60. Ellis, *James Hinton, a Sketch*, 202.

8

The Cult of the Genius in Germany and Austria at the Dawn of the Twentieth Century

Julia Barbara Köhne

In his 1918 monograph *Die Geniereligion* ("The Religion of Genius"), Edgar Zilsel, a philosopher of the history of science and a lecturer in adult education in Vienna, observed the following of his Austrian and German contemporaries:

> [O]ur audience does not believe that there is anything wrong with admiring genius, in fact it seems to them to be the obvious thing to do. We do not see a problem in the notion of genius, our literature and our *Zeitgeist* has completely appropriated it. There is not the slightest hint of alienation, let alone rejection. [...] Although we ourselves seem only partially aware of the extent of our admiration for genius, our notion of genius is of relevance to cultural historians; the full significance of such semi-conscious guiding concepts will only truly come to light with the benefit of time.[1]

Zilsel, who was sympathetic to socialism, was concerned by what he described as "genius enthusiasm" and the "genius enthusiasts" who preached it (figure 8.1).

Part of the community of contemporary writers and intellectuals, he affirmed, had become willing victims of the cult of the individual personality and the "glory ideal," which they peddled in their works in a far from disinterested way. By declaring themselves connoisseurs of "genius" and awarding the title to specific historical figures, these writers vaunted their own importance. Zilsel mocked the pretensions of these petty "genius priests," who were in truth nothing but second-rate schoolmasters:

> Here comes the modern minister of genius, a measure of merit ["Wertmaßstab"] in his hands, like a schoolmaster; anyone who can "discern" is a "genius," who gives priority to the mysteries of knowledge, a

Verlag von **Ernst Hofmann & Co.** in **Berlin** SW. 46, Hedemannstr. 2.

Geisteshelden.

Eine Sammlung von Biographieen.

1. **Walther v. d. Vogelweide.** 2. Aufl. Von Prof. A. E. Schönbach.
2/3. **Hölderlin. ✻ Reuter.** 2. Aufl. Von Dr. Ad. Wilbrandt.
4. **Anzengruber.** 2. Aufl. Von Dr. Anton Bettelheim.
5. **Columbus.** Von Prof. Dr. Sophus Ruge.
6. **Carlyle.** 2. Aufl. Von Prof. Dr. G. v. Schulze-Gaevernitz.
7. **Jahn.** Von Dr. F. G. Schultheiß. **Preisgekrönt.**
8. **Shakspere.** Von Prof. Dr. Alois Brandl.
9. **Spinoza.** Von Prof. Dr. Wilhelm Bolin.
10/11. 37/38. **Moltke,** 3 Bde. Von Oberstleutnant Dr. M. Jähns.
12. **Stein.** Von Dr. Fr. Neubauer. **Preisgekrönt.**
13/15. **Goethe.** Von Privatdoz. Dr. Rich. M. Meyer. **Preisgekrönt.**
16/17. 27. **Luther.** I. II,1. Von Prof. Dr. Arn. E. Berger.
18. **Cotta.** Von Minister Dr. Albert Schäffle.
19. **Darwin.** Von Prof. Dr. Wilhelm Preyer †.
20. **Montesquieu.** Von Prof. Dr. Alb. Sorel.
21. **Dante.** Von Pfarrer Dr. Joh. Andr. Scartazzini.
22. **Kepler. ✻ Galilei.** Von Prof. Dr. S. Günther.
23. **Görres.** Von Prof. Dr. J. N. Sepp.
24. **Stanley.** Von Paul Reichard.
25/26. **Schopenhauer.** Von Konsul Dr. Ed. Grisebach.
28/29. **Schiller.** Von Prof. Dr. Otto Harnack.
30/31. **Peter der Grosse.** Von Dr. K. Waliszewski.
32. **Tennyson.** Von Prof. Dr. Emil Koeppel.
33. **Mozart.** Von Prof. Dr. O. Fleischer.
34/35. **Lessing.** Von Privatdozent Dr. K. Borinski.
36. **Tizian.** Von Dr. Georg Gronau.
39. **A. v. Humboldt. ✻ L. v. Buch.** Von Prof. Dr. S. Günther.

Preis jedes Bandes: Geheftet Mk. 2,40; Leinenbd. 3,20; Halbfranzbd. 3,80.

☞ In Vorbereitung: **Richard Wagner,** von Prof. Dr. Max Koch.

Figure 8.1 *"Geistesheldenbiographien"*—list of genius biographies from 1900. Robert Saitchick, Genie und Charakter. Shakespeare, Lessing, Goethe, Schiller, Schopenhauer, Wagner (Berlin: Hofmann, 1900).

profound person ["tiefe Persönlichkeit"]; in contrast the remaining thinkers are relegated to the back seats in the philosophical classroom like mediocre pupils ["Dutzendmenschen"].[2]

Yet genius-enthusiasm was not only fodder for Zilsel's ironic humor and an annoying aspect of the times, but also dangerous. The "religion-like nature"[3] of the cult of genius, Zilsel asserted, fostered alienation, contempt of the masses, and the exclusion of the "Other."[4] Toward the end of *Die Geniereligion*, Zilsel cautioned that "ignorance and strong prejudices" of the kind demonstrated by such contemporary admirers of genius as Houston Stewart Chamberlain would be "paid for with the happiness and blood of fellow men."[5] The dominance of the "notion of the genius personality and of profundity" indicated a "severe danger"[6] for the age. Indeed, the racist, antifeminist, and anti-Semitic tendencies of the greater part of the writings of the time dealing with the question of genius can be interpreted as *one* foundational component for a range of political programs fostering violence. Radical National Socialists, among others, would seize upon these tendencies and put them into effect.

The object of Zilsel's critical analysis—the figure of the genius—was virulently and obsessively discussed in the late nineteenth and early twentieth centuries. That is the theme of this chapter, which focuses on genius research and literature, published in particular between 1890 and 1920, that conceptualized the "genius" as a controversial figure of knowledge and representation, employing the category of genius as what Zilsel described as a "semiconscious guiding concept" ("halb unbewusste Leitidee"). Although the cultural-historical discourse of genius can be traced back much earlier, the "genius" was increasingly conceived as a self-conscious object of modern epistemic interest and cultural and scientific inquiry from the middle of the nineteenth century, as the well-known work of such influential writers as Thomas Carlyle and Ralph Waldo Emerson makes clear. Moreover, genius reflection and the research that blossomed around it was not cultivated as a single discipline, but rather found its way into diverse and quite extensive fields of knowledge and university departments, some of which were newly constituted or recently reformed at the time. These included religious studies, sociology, anthropology, psychology, psychoanalysis and psychobiography, psychiatry/neurology/pathography, philosophy, literary criticism, sexual science, evolutionary theory, phrenology, craniometry, biology, and race-theory (including eugenics). In this chapter, the following questions will be traced from a constructivist and interdisciplinary perspective: what was "genius" and who earned this ennobling distinction? how was the "genius," who was most often investigated only *post mortem*, conceptualized, represented, and interpreted? which strategic and political functions did this legitimizing heroic figure serve? and what role did the concept play with regard to the conditions of possibility and the self-image of the authors, literatures, cultures, and disciplines that negotiated its characteristics with such passion?

In responding to these questions, I will develop the thesis that invoking the abstract notion of genius had a twofold discursive and strategic function, serving the interests of those scholars and scientists who undertook genius research, while at the same time impacting the wider political and cultural sphere. On the one hand, there was a group of genius researchers who believed in the "genius" as a godlike savior, a redeemer of society, and a creator of culture. They included, among others, Hans Blüher, Houston Stewart Chamberlain, Ernst Kretschmer, and Otto Weininger, and they invariably imagined the genius as white, male, and of European descent— singular, original, creative, inventive, self-taught as well as self-generating, autonomous, and either inspired by the divine or godlike creatures themselves. Despite—or perhaps precisely because of—secularization, these authors believed in the "genius" as a redeemer and liberator of society, as Edgar Zilsel observed. Yet the characteristics attributed to genius reveal more about the visions of the authors themselves than about their putative topic of inquiry. The "genius" was imagined not just as the subject of inventive creativity—a view already common in various aesthetic perspectives around 1800—but the genius researcher now tried to figuratively blend or "bleed" into his research object.[7] In some of the texts, the genius figure helped fragile and newly constituted or reformed academic disciplines construct their professional identity, legitimize their (often cross-disciplinary) methodologies, and reassure themselves of their own rational, intellectual, and creative powers by association with the qualities of so-called "great men of history" ("große Männer der Geschichte"), "eminences" ("Eminenzen"), "superlatives of mankind" ("Superlative der Menschheit"), "exceptional individuals" ("Ausnahmemenschen"), "intellectual leaders" ("geistige Führer"), "male heroes" ("Männerhelden"), and the like.

This is especially interesting because the "genius," long seen as a cultic, mythic, and quasi-religious figure, had been demystified and debased in certain respects in the course of the nineteenth century by writers such as Moreau de Tours or Cesare Lombroso,[8] who, in the light of the new medical and psychological sciences, had associated "genius" with mental instability, unworldliness, loneliness, melancholy, degeneration, and insanity. Some of the latter characteristics had, on a structural-symbolic level, a de-potentiating or feminizing effect on the imagined male gender of the "genius," as manliness traditionally had been associated with intelligence and thereby mental stability, independence, assertiveness, and virility. The genius literature around 1900 ran counter to those sources that feminized the "genius" by combining it with degenerative decline. Instead, it re-masculinized the "genius" and reinvigorated its discursive potency as a leading figure.

On the other hand, a handful of thinkers, including Walter Benjamin, Jakob Wassermann, and Edgar Zilsel—all, not coincidentally, of Jewish heritage—described and criticized the "genius" in the context of wider sociocultural problems, insecurities, and utopian beliefs. In their eyes, the genius knowledge of the time and the artificial "geniusification" of individuals were connected to mechanisms of exclusion and extremist ideologies of race and gender. Contemporary writings on genius, these authors observed, expounded antifeminist and anti-Semitic tendencies that from the 1900s onward merged more and more with ideologies of "Aryan" heredity and "racial hygiene" ("Rassenhygiene," "Volkshygiene")—for example, in the writings of Houston Stewart Chamberlain, Ottokar Matura, Alfred Rosenberg, and Richard Wagner—and became increasingly entangled with intelligence research and fantasies of human breeding of the "highly gifted" of the "German Empire." By the turn of the century, women and Jews were considered to be the "Others" in the prevailing Western genius formula, which emphasized the inherent superiority of white males.

Yet, on the whole, authors such as Benjamin, Zilsel, and Wassermann were a distinct minority. It was much more common to idolize and adore "geniuses" than to critically evaluate the rhetorical and biographical narratives related to them or to deconstruct the phenomenon of genius-admiration. Indeed, the overall atmosphere of the times was thick with "genius-fever," which was fed by competition between multiple disciplines of knowledge, with each attempting to describe, define, interpret, and instrumentalize this miraculous figure as precisely as it could. At the same time, hundreds of biographies of "geniuses," and high-circulation science publications on the problem of "genius," impressed themselves on large sections of society.[9] Most of these texts only dealt with surface matters—matters of biography and personality and *not* the genius' achievements, artefacts, or writings. And while they alternatively admired and idealized, mystified and pathologized—resulting in varied, and sometimes contradictory, ascriptions—the overall effect of this diverse body of writing was to enhance the aura of genius and the genius figure.

The problem that the genius transcended

Apart from its specific role within the academic and intellectual constellation, the cult of the genius was a response to dramatic and wide-ranging historical changes and urgent sociocultural problems evident at the turn of the century. These included secularization and the corresponding tendency of re-sacralization amidst specters of social decline; democratization and the weakening of aristocracy; the impact of Darwinian and social Darwinian thought; the rise of male associations ("Männerbünde");[10] the so-called *Frauenfrage*, the first wave of the women's movement and the erosion of gender as a category of knowledge; anti-Semitism; and the nationalistic question of breeding excellent offspring.[11] The genius figure provided a way to overcome or transcend these problems by means of what has been described as a "god-trick."[12] That is, the genius was imagined and instrumentalized by genius-enthusiasts as a being in possession of infinite vision and omniscient perspective—a being objective and transcendent, patriarchal and authoritarian, like god. Associated symbolically with the rational, objective, neutral, and "asexual" ("Geschlechtslosigkeit"),[13] and imagined as pure, superior, transcendent, and divine, the "genius" transcended social fissures and problems. This was true regardless of whether the genius was conceived as a self-generating hyper-individual (*sui generis* and self-made) initiating a line of descent of his own; as the "Aryan" new "son of humanity" ("Menschensohn")[14] who negates everything considered "Jewish and feminine"; a quasi-god who, by his creative work and his intelligence, surpasses corporeality and mortality; or as a model for an imagined "Aryan-Christian" charismatic leader. The "genius" in all these conceptions could be hailed as a being who towered above social problems, and who was said to be capable alone of providing blueprints for a better future. The genius figure, in short, operated conceptually as an invulnerable and transcendent player, who symbolized the desire to gain control of the trajectory of an increasingly complex society. As such, it was a secular substitute for suppressed religious feelings and a collective fantasy of the possibility of overcoming and finding solutions to contemporary problems through creative and intellectual vision. "Genius," in this context, incarnated the possibility of salvation, and the very word possessed a kind of mystical attraction. It served as what the philosopher of science and physician Ludwik Fleck described in the 1930s as a "thought-charm" ("eigentümlicher Denkzauber"), charged with sacramental power.[15]

"Genius," as a scientific and literary-philosophical term, could not be contained by its rational-logical explanations, for the word and concept served a further symbolic function, suggesting an imagined ideal image of intellectual authority and at the same time of magic. Members of the scientific community and literary scene identified with and mirrored themselves in its self-made characteristics. The genius-word-charm ("Wortzauber") helped, in this way, to constitute what Fleck described as a confined "thought-collective" ("Denkkollektiv"), which united participants in a particular "thought-style" ("Denkstil"), based on shared education, training, and traditions. Such thought-collectives were the product of "the circulation of ideas and social practices," and rested on a certain unconscious conditioning of the scientists' style of perception, thinking, and acting.[16] In contrast to other "thought-collectives,"[17] which had their own criteria to detect what counted as true knowledge or an exceptional idea, the genius thought-collective imagined itself as excellent, exclusive, and brilliant by virtue of its recognition of and participation in "genius." Because the quasi-magical genius knowledge transcended disciplinary boundaries, it united theories of science, literature, and culture and bridged the gaps between different forms of knowledge. Those who succumbed to the "thought-charm" of the genius-notion were unified by a "collective mood"[18] ("Kollektivstimmung," "Stimmungskameradschaft") that created a certain "intra-group mental solidarity" and helped to enhance the cohesion and promote the professionalization of research institutions. With Fleck, it is possible to appreciate the unconscious, subliminal messages guiding humanistic and literary practices. And this, in turn, allows us to better observe the cultish tendencies, the self-idealization, and limitations of those scholars and scientists participating in the study and worship of genius.

By referring to the "great men of history," researchers tended to view themselves as ingenious. This was due to a process of "coloring" and transference of feelings ("Abfärben der Gefühle")[19] that had long been a part of the history of constructing the genius ideal, as Zilsel observed in 1918. Something of the "genius" seemed to rub off on those who studied and at the same time admired "genius," taking on the shape of psychological or religious feelings like fear, respect, and awe. This phenomenon reached into the deepest layers of consciousness, manifesting itself in a particular kind of suggestive mood ("suggestive Stimmung") that Zilsel compared invidiously to reasonable thinking:[20]

Nothing is more opposed to this fuzzy transfer of feelings ["unscharfe Gefühlsübertragung"] than reason, which has its goals in precision, and in the clear separation of everything that does not belong together. The "Abfärben" of feelings must thus disappear the more admiration is rationalized and replaced by value judgments. When we now want to start examining the genius ideal, we cannot allow ourselves an admiration that can "abfärben," but will have to talk about values, that are no longer permitted to "abfärben," and for which the artist and his work, enthusiasm and its goal are distinguished carefully from each other.[21]

As the passage intimates, those who in their own estimation best understood what "genius" was about—revealing its secrets and identifying its formulas—made pretensions to similar qualities themselves in what may be described as a process of self-invention or "self-geniusification." In this way, researchers in the many disciplines that studied genius presented themselves as at once traditional and serious, innovative and original, free and independent, universal and at the same time compatible with particular social norms. They became "free riders" on the successful bandwagon of the "genius." The coupling with the genius concept, in short, accelerated the social acceptance of research in the disciplines that studied it, which, in turn, gave greater credence to the political implications that attended the genius discourse.

Stellar genius: Natural metaphors

In his seminal 1957 essay, "Licht als Metapher der Wahrheit" ("Light as a Metaphor for Truth"),[22] Hans Blumenberg pointed to the nexus between light metaphors and the semantics of truth in Christian and Gnostic knowledge. According to Blumenberg, the metaphor helped to give form to understanding, recasting what were originally aesthetic-sensuous perceptions as theological propositions. The move, which transformed nonconceptual ("absolute") metaphors into consolidating *termini technici*, entailed a considerable loss of complexity, clearness, and substance. This is exactly what happened to the language of genius. The notion of genius took on a particular semantic "coloring" that opened up discursive perspectives and spaces, shedding former layers of meaning while retaining and adopting others.[23]

The transformation of the concept of genius around the end of the seventeenth century, from a quality that one possessed to something one was, marked the historical turning point at which human beings began to see themselves as self-luminous, possessing a luminosity of the mind that radiated charisma and impact in the world: "[Man] becomes, himself, the principle of a structural formation that emanates from within him," Blumenberg observed. "And by realizing himself as *sapiens*, he gains that emanative and world-moving force: self-realization becomes a condition for world-realization."[24] In scientific and literary narratives from around 1900, the "genius" was associated repeatedly with metaphors from the realm of nature and cosmic space. This had the effect of naturalizing, essentializing, and ontologically verifying the particular content that the object of research, the "genius," was supposed to embody. The "genius" *was* like a volcano that erupted at irregular intervals or continually spewed forth. As the psychologist Johannes G. Thöne pointed out in the 1920s:

> Geniuses can be compared to volcanoes. Just as some volcanoes are "burnt out" after one single eruption, *some geniuses also suffer a similar "burnout" after one singular achievement.* [...] Other geniuses, like more active volcanoes, continue to produce results for a second or third time, and there are even a few (such as Goethe, Beethoven, Bismarck) who *continue producing great results for most of their lives.*[25]

The image of the volcano combines the two elements, fire and earth. Through the use of this metaphor, certain periods of achievement in the life of a "genius" and corresponding age-groups of "geniuses" can be determined and explained. Just as volcanoes become inactive, geniuses can "burn out" ("verglühen").[26] By orienting "geniuses" rhetorically with nature, authors insisted on the naturalness of their power without feeling the need to explicate this proposition in further detail. The "soft" semiotics of genius metaphors and their openness to interpretation could thus be transformed into "hard" stable knowledge about the "genius" and his specific characteristics.

The amalgamation of the "genius" with unspoiled nature was further reinforced via astral metaphors, along with metaphors of light and fire. In the metaphorology of genius research, the "genius" was often a figure who revealed human longing for transcendence and who initiated a rhetorical connection to the stars. In numerous texts, the "genius" was imagined as global and universal and as providing sunlight and the light of stars to humankind. Via metaphorization, the "genius" opened up an infinite and inapprehensible stellar "potential space." The Germanophile racist writer Chamberlain pictured the "genius" as a "personality in its highest potentiality."[27] Elsewhere, he employed the Promothean metaphor of a torch:

> In recent years it has been discovered that in the depths of the ocean, to which the sunlight does not penetrate, there are fishes which light up this world of darkness electrically; even thus is the dark night of human knowledge lighted up by the torch of genius. Goethe lit a torch with his *Faust*, Kant another with his conception of the transcendental ideality of time and space: both were creators of great imaginative power, both were men of genius.[28]

Similarly, from the time of the foundation of the "Reich" (*Reichsgründung*) and well into the twentieth century, Otto von Bismarck was celebrated in the German-speaking world as the "lodestar" or "guiding star" ("Leitstern").[29] The association of light and "genius" was ubiquitous and long-lived. In a text from 1927, for example, the Austrian author Stefan Zweig employed astral metaphors in connection with his "heroic" view of history:

> But if a genius arises in art, he outlives his times; if such a critical moment occurs in the world, it is decisive for decades and centuries. Just as the

electricity of the whole atmosphere is concentrated in the tip of a lightning rod, an immeasurable number of events then come together in the narrowest span of time ("Sternstunde der Menschheit").

Such dramatically concentrated, such fateful moments, in which a decision that transcends its own time is compressed into a single date, a single hour, and often only a minute, are rare in the life of an individual, and rare in the course of history. I have attempted here to call to mind a few such starry moments—I have called them that because, like glowing and immutable stars, they shine through the night of transitoriness—from the most diverse times and places.[30]

The "genius" represented a light source and a source of illumination, who made visible the hidden and unseen, while simultaneously, as Thomas Macho explains, laying claim to metaphysical enlightenment himself.[31] Or, to invoke the work of Mitchell Ash, one can speak of the genius concept as a "metaphorical sealant" ("metaphorischer Kitt"), a kind of cement that ensures all knowledge connected and bound to him is verified, naturalized, and displayed as "uniquely thinkable" ("einzig denkmöglich").[32]

Sexualized genius: Reproductive and familial metaphors

One of the core aspects of genius discourse was the rhetorical dimension of gender and sexualization. With deep roots in the history of the genius concept, which from Classical times had been associated with notions of male begetting and birth (the very word "genius" derives from the Latin *gignere, generare* or *genere*, meaning to father, beget, or give birth), this dimension was closely connected to ideas of male procreation, "spiritual begetting" ("geistiges Zeugen"),[33] and the strength to engender philosophical thoughts.[34] Rudolf Steiner wrote in 1900: "Genius is all about creating, producing and propagating...In essence, ingenuity is intellectual procreation."[35] "The artist's works are his children; they preserve his place in posterity," another author observed typically, presenting the "genius" as simultaneously barren and fecund.[36] In her 1939 doctoral thesis *Wahrsinn oder Wahnsinn des Genius?*, the medical scientist and cultural anthropologist Helga Baisch struck a similar note: "Ingenuity is paid for with vitality. Nature wants works from geniuses and not children...Extraordinary people...cannot produce both children and masterpieces."[37]

Even though in most contexts of the period around 1900, "genius" implied biological maleness by definition, "geniuses" could incarnate aspects of a mixed gender identity. Hence, "genius" seemed to provide a solution for the male crisis caused by eroding gender boundaries in the context of first-wave feminism: it was simultaneously hyper-male *and* a sexual hybrid. Thus, in a number of genius narratives concerning the question of gender—for example, in writings by Helga Baisch, Johannes Barolin, Johann Wilhelm Ritter, Jakob Wassermann, and Otto Weininger[38]—the self-procreating, and at the same time anti-familial, "genius" was depicted on a structural level as androgynous.

In this way, "genius" was represented as an autonomous vanishing point, which transgressed and unified the binary gender poles. Frequently, "genius" was associated with such contrasting features and characteristics as "hysteria," hermaphroditism, frigidity, hyper-virility, and impotence within the same narrative context.

Nevertheless, in numerous texts, the genius formula was constructed as purely male, in contrast to the idea of a blending of masculine and feminine parts in the single person of the "genius." Precisely because the nexus with femininity challenged the purely masculine position of the "genius" in the two-sex model and made its gender-specific classification porous, in parallel, it was reinforced even more resolutely. (The male-formula was the basis for its separation from the "feminine" and the "Jewish," aiming at a sociopolitical exclusion of real persons, women and Jews, from the community of potential "geniuses" and broader intellectual circles.) Symptomatic of the conceptual and political exclusion of the "feminine" was a rhetoric laden with reproductive and familial metaphors. Authors invoked intellectual (in-)fertility,[39] "mental pregnancy," "spiritual creation," and "spiritual children" while writing of men as "pregnant with knowledge."[40] Walter Benjamin diagnosed these gendering metaphors as a sexualization and eroticization of the spiritual (Vergeschlechtlichung des Geistigen). Ironically, the excluded "feminine" enabled the "resur-/erection" of ingenuity and intellectual powers. The semantics of genius adhered to a rhetorical—and in the bisexualization of the "genius," to some extent also a conceptual—inclusion, but a factual exclusion of the "feminine" and those associated with it. In his early writings, Benjamin acknowledged that the excluded "female," by its very existence as a discursive marker embodying sexuality, materiality, and finiteness, served as a guarantor for the "asexuality of the spiritual" ("Geschlechtslosigkeit des Geistigen").[41]

The symptomatic manifestation of the excluded "feminine" in language must be seen in the context of a much older repression. The etymological origins of the word *genius*, to repeat, are sexually coded, deriving from a family of words that refer to sexual or phylogenetic procreation, production, generation, creation, and the act of giving birth. The semantic connection between genus, genealogy, genesis, and genius, not surprisingly, manifests itself in gendering metaphors. In his 1916 essay "Sokrates," Benjamin criticized this phenomenon in the course of his reinterpretation of the monologues of the Platonic Socrates in terms of the "terrible domination of sexual views in the spiritual."[42] Benjamin read Socrates against the grain and emphasized— instead of the maieutic talents that were traditionally associated with this character—his male "know-it-all" attitude that, according to Benjamin, presented itself as an "erection of knowledge"[43] ("Erektion des Wissens") and left no space for spiritual "conception" (geistiges "Empfangen"). Benjamin used the "genius" as a figure in order to criticize gendered discourse and culture more broadly. He reformulated the commonly male-coded concept of genius (associated with penetration, procreation, and power) by stressing its feminine reproductive attributes such as receptivity, passivity, and silence. "Just as immaculate conception is for the woman, the rapturous notion of purity, so conception without pregnancy is most profoundly the spiritual mark of the male genius."[44] Even if Benjamin substituted one gesture of sexualization with another—by speaking of an "erection of knowledge" in reference to Socrates' methods of interrogating his partners in dialogue—he succeeded in rewriting the former genius conception by feminizing it and repressing the male dogma.

The religion of genius

With Friedrich Nietzsche, Blumenberg, and René Girard, one can argue that the gradual disappearance of god and the divine in a secularized modernity prompted, in turn, a heightened need for religion.[45] In Blumenberg's eyes, secularization meant a *"reassignment (Umbesetzung)* of a position that had become vacant, but could not be eliminated as such."[46] Sacred elements in a community that now understood itself as secularized were no longer interpreted as signs of continuity and certainty but were given "reassigned functions" in a system of meaning ("umbesetzte Systemfunktionen") in the "process of epochal change" ("Prozeß des Epochenwandels").[47] At the same time, allegedly secular discussions still often referred to Christian or other religious concepts, such as angels, demigods, and religiously inspired leaders. And so the already well-established symbolic and rhetorical linkage of the concept of genius to religious metaphors and imagery was revitalized and given new energy. The genius figure was described in a range of metaphors that touched on different aspects of the divine, ranging from images of Biblical salvation to visions of apocalypse. Scientific, belletristic, and biographical writings adopted the rhetoric of the sacred; and in an era of apparent godlessness, exceptional historical personalities were re-sacralized as secular apostles, prophets, and saints.

Part of the religious potential of the "genius," as one could derive from Blumenberg, is to aggrandize the re-sacralization of the profane. Secular religions practiced in scientific and literary arenas—such as the religion of genius—borrowed and transmuted central elements of monotheistic religions of the book, such as the longing for salvation and redemption, and the desire for life after death. The "genius" was addressed as a godlike being, a demiurge, or Christlike figure who, at the same time, labored in the pursuit of modern science and knowledge.

The creation of new gods to serve as descendants of more traditional gods and religious figures, or as replacements for aristocratic leaders, was criticized by Hirsch and Zilsel in their respective publications, *Die Genesis des Ruhmes* (1914) and *Die Geniereligion* (1918), which appeared one after the other immediately before and after World War I.[48] They are two of the most sensitive, skeptical, and critical responses to the exclusive notion of "genius" and genius-admiration written in the early twentieth century. With slightly differing tools and terms, their analyses referred to the sociological, empirical, and cultural-historical aspects of the cult of personality, for which Zilsel coined the term "Geniereligion."[49] Allegedly scholarly examinations and biographical descriptions of the "genius," he argued, explicitly and implicitly referred to religious and metaphysical categories. For example, the genius literature repeatedly alluded to the fraternization of dead "geniuses," who in the afterlife met in a celestial community,[50] linked only by the posthumously conferred identification of "genius." Frequently, these were men who had gone unrecognized and underappreciated in life, working in loneliness and sacrifice, yet who served in death as paragons of earthly existence. "After all," Zilsel declared, "posterity does not recognize an already existing significance but first *creates* it itself."[51] He added that "[t]here is a certain connection between the irrational genius-cult's belief in posterity and the rational and enlightened idea of progress: both interpret progress in time as an increase in value; one has the impression that the passage of time enriches the culture and amends the verdict on the deceased."[52] And he was insightful about the process by which fame—a sort of secular canonization—was manufactured retrospectively to serve the uses of the present:

> In the genesis of posthumous fame [...] numerous, totally accidental circumstances play a significant role, including serendipity, influential benefactors and enthusiastic disciples. [...] The personal idiosyncrasies, artistic and philosophical qualities of the famous and influential dead are the focus of posterity; they are mentioned in numerous texts, yet at the same time transformed and reinterpreted or distorted depending on the disposition of posterity.[53]

According to Zilsel, the discursive existence of the "genius" functioned on the basis of religious-dogmatic conditions and the postulated belief, admiration, and enthusiasm of the idolizing group. Zilsel described the "Geniereligion" as a response to de-sacralizing trends, as at once a conscious and unconscious (textual) strategy, created mostly by male scholars and researchers, to justify anti-egalitarian politics and metaphysics. Zilsel was opposed to the latter, favoring principles of rationality, practicality, and objectivity. Yet in some ways these same principles prevented him from grasping the typical characteristics of the cult of the genius: its sentimentality and subjectivity as well as the need of its followers to evaluate (and give value to) the surrounding world ("*Wertungsbedürfnis*").[54]

   Hirsch and Zilsel, just like successors such as Wilhelm Lange-Eichbaum and Axel Gehring, treated the deification of historical personalities as a serious sociocultural and pedagogical problem of great political relevance. The cultural, political, and literary instrumentalization of the cult of genius, they believed, was irrational and dangerous. In their opinion, human beings relinquished their agency in surrendering themselves to genius admiration, lowered their self-esteem, and relegated themselves to serving as mere reflections of the genius' glory.

Collective genius: Race and gender

Increasingly in the 1920s and 1930s, certain aspects of the genius formula merged with the racist and bio-political imperatives of social exclusion and control, including demarcations based on classification and typification. In the first part of his 1903 monograph *Geschlecht und Charakter* (*Sex and Character: An Investigation of Fundamental Principles*),[55] Otto Weininger assumed that every human being, male or female, was born as a "bisexual" (potentially with parts from both sexes). In this way did he seem to soften the strictly polar biological matrix of the two-sex model and transform it into a model of "intermediate forms" ("Zwischenformen"). However, he cast the "feminine" and the "masculine" into the "corset" of ideal principles (via abstraction, he immunized himself against objections in terms of the real-politic "game of the sexes"), and only the "male" was granted a positive image. In the second part of his book, moreover, Weininger revised his only ostensibly progressive idea on the bisexual nature of the sexes, referring to psychological and characterological criteria in order to determine who was "male" and who was "female." In his misogynistic investigation, the "feminine" merged on the symbolic level with the "Jewish" and both were harshly discredited.

Weininger's cult of the (male) genius was born on the back of others, namely, women and Jews, whom he deemed representative of the whole "irreligious saeculum" and charged with a deficit in belief. Both were placed at the bottom of Weininger's schematic pyramid that was built to give orientation regarding superiors and inferiors in society. At its top, Weininger located Jesus of Nazareth, who in narrative terms had been depicted as a "genius" in numerous biographies of the time.[56] Weininger saw in Jesus an ideal individual, who had progressed several steps up the pyramid scale and who succeeded in overcoming his own Jewishness in order to become the independent founder of a religion ("Religionsstifter"). "Metaphysically, the only purpose of the Jewish character is to serve as a pedestal for the founder of a religion."[57] The latter represented a special kind of being who, in Weininger's genius-metaphysics, even transcended the category of the ordinary "genius."

> [T]*he founder of a religion is the greatest genius.* He has achieved what the most profound thinkers of humankind have only presented as a possibility, with hesitation, in order to preserve their ethical outlook and to avoid having to abandon the *freedom of choice: the complete rebirth of the human being*, his "regeneration," the total reversal of the will.[58]

Elsewhere, Weininger employs a light metaphor in reference to the "founder of a religion": "He ascends from the night to the light, and his most ghastly horror is that of the night in which he has so far lived blindly and comfortably."[59]

In addition, Weininger projected the genius-figure onto a collective image of a "new humankind" ("neue Menschheit") of defeminized, desexualized, and disembodied men, in which not only the individual but also the whole nation should evolve into an extraordinary collective subject, a great collective "genius." Similarly, in the wider political arena, the vision of the male "Aryan-Christian" genius was not limited to single individuals. From at least the time of the publication of Chamberlain's 1898–99 monograph *Die Grundlagen des 19. Jahrhunderts* (*The Foundations of the Nineteenth Century*) and Weininger's *Geschlecht und Charakter* (1903), genius discourse was bound up with fantasies of human breeding, which became more and more relevant for the conceptualization of the German collective body. Even though this ran contrary to its popular contemporary encoding, the genius formula, originally based on singularity, rarity, and exclusiveness, was gradually applied to the ideal of an "Aryan" body of the German people ("Volkskörper") that, in turn, ought to be held up by singular "geniuses." According to Chamberlain, the "right" race, namely the "Aryan," could transform a "man of pure origin" ("edelgezüchteter Mensch") into a "genius" who surmounted the whole of humankind:[60]

> Race lifts a man above himself: it endows him with extraordinary—I might almost say supernatural—powers, so entirely does it distinguish him from the individual who springs from the chaotic jumble of peoples drawn from all parts of the world: and should this man of pure origin be perchance gifted above his fellows, then the fact of Race strengthens and elevates him on every hand, and he becomes a genius towering over the rest of mankind, [...] because he soars heavenward like some strong and stately tree, nourished by thousands and thousands of roots—no solitary individual, but the living sum of untold souls striving for the same goal.[61]

The chemist and Nobel laureate Wilhelm Ostwald discussed the problem of scientific creativity in his 1909 study of geniuses in the sciences, *Große Männer*. He asked how "geniuses" could be bred and cultivated, and how parents could be preconditioned to be able "to procreate a genius." Universities should serve as "breeding institutions" ("Züchtungsanstalten") for geniuses to come.[62]

Such literature urged that particularly valuable individuals—those with a potential for "genius"—should be invested in for the benefit of the community. The idea of promoting highly talented German offspring, by means of selecting gifted young people to breed "geniuses," found its expression in texts like Albert Reibmayr's *Die Entwicklungsgeschichte des Talentes und Genies* (1908), Flügge's *Rassenhygiene und Sexualethik* (1924), Kretschmer's *Geniale Menschen* (1929), and Matura's *Das Deutsche Genie* (1941).[63] Invoking the intellectual potency or capacity of unborn children would protect society from the decay it feared. Evident in this literature was a major fear of pathological anomalies and concerns about the extinction of "German geniuses."[64]

Theorists were fascinated by the prospect of racial- and social-hygienic pro-
gramming, which culminated in the chimera of a race of genius, predicated
on the demographic control of "racial mixing." And though some authors
continued to subscribe to the nineteenth-century view that individual genius
was a form of pathology—a view evident in Flügge's writings, among others—the "genius" could also represent the idea of a healthy, "Aryan" creative
German people ("Volk"). The "genius" descended from its pantheon to serve,
in German educational establishments, as a model of normality. The spiritual
fertility that was named "genius" would protect the German nation from disease and any other dysfunction.

This newly inflamed striving for genius and ingenuity lent itself well to
a fascist human armament program that was optimized in terms of racial
heredity ("Reinrassigkeit"). In alignment with National Socialism, moreover, genius discourse fused with the *Führer*-principle, criticized so incisively
by Max Weber in his writings on "charismatic authority" ("charismatische
Herrschaft"). The sociologist Theodor Geiger analyzed this emphatic genius
discourse in his "Führer und Genie" ("Führer and Genius") of 1926–1927 as
a response to the scientific objectivation of the world.[65] The public cherished
personalities whose history and achievements were structured by popular
myths and legends, not reason and science. They did not want to be led *by* the
great man but *to* the great man.[66] Genius concepts in the Weimar Republic
were conducive to the pursuit of "self-incapacitation,"[67] ceding power to
political authorities and "genius leaders."

At the same time that the exceptional "genius" was exalted, the so-called
normal humans ("Normalmenschen," "Menschen der Mitte") were deval-
ued.[68] The categories of the "Jewish" and "feminine" counted as "non-gen-
ius," and the genius discourse helped to present this as a natural fact. Alfred
Rosenberg, who adopted Chamberlain's concept of the dominance of the
"Nordic-Atlantic race" over the "Jewish-Semitic" peoples, was convinced that
Jews were not able to create valuable artistic artefacts or to found a state. He
was interested in creating a "pure race" ("reine Rasse") that would be superior, "folkish" ("völkisch"), healthy, and culturally pristine. Rosenberg associated the idea of an ingenious German people with the support of talents
and "great men," while extinguishing everything identifiable as "Jewish."
The Nazi Party platform, published in 1920, was edited and introduced by
Rosenberg in this 1943 version:

> Great men are the most valuable asset of the "Volk" or nation. When such
> talents are unable to flourish, it shows that conditions are extremely unfa-
> vorable [volksfeindlichsten] (unless the nation is totally incapable of pro-
> ducing great men). No nation can do without its leading minds [führende
> völkische Intelligenz] without ceasing to exist as a "Volk." Such men are
> the bloom of the nation, the [...] embodiment of what is called the soul
> of the people. Nurturing this mental power [geistigen Energien] should be
> a self-evident duty of the state. [H]owever, certain conditions need to be
> in place to make this development possible. After the termination of the

domestic political battle, the complete elimination of the Jewish elements in all cultural institutions, schools, universities, academies etc. needs to be demanded. [...] The German state will support the advancement of intellectual powers and character attributes in every way possible [...] insofar as they are healthy.[69]

Under National Socialism, talent could only be located in "non-Jewish" males, who should strive to become "great men" or "geniuses" if possible, furthering folkish intelligence ("völkische Intelligenz") and the "German renaissance" ("deutsche Wiedergeburt").[70]

Conclusion

As an object of knowledge and inquiry around the turn of the twentieth century, the genius project was impossible to complete, for the category was not bounded by its own characteristics; the "genius" was never a discrete figure. Rather, "genius" inserted itself into the formation of late modernity as a complex phenomenon of overlapping processes, such as the differentiation and profiling of academic disciplines, and the interdependence of (pseudo-) religion, culture, science, power, and politics. This chapter has focused on the question of why researchers from various disciplinary perspectives, as well as nonacademic researchers, writers, and, intellectuals of the period, debated the question of genius in long and elaborate texts. Why, in short, was "genius" a favorite theme? The answer is as broad as it is intricate. The "genius" was an important figure of reference not only on the sociocultural level but also on the scientific level. Genius served to legitimize the thought, intelligence, and *esprit* of authors who gave it scholarly and scientific significance, while helping to build up certain academic disciplines and research institutions in the way that a figurehead does. Those undertaking new forms of research and investigation employed genius discourse as a means to reassure themselves of their own intellectual prowess and creative capacities. The genius figure was a device used to guard against institutional insecurities that accompanied disciplines and their researchers in the process of self-construction.

The epistemological characteristic of the genius theme was that the "genius" as an object of empirical research could not be accessed directly, but only in terms of the genius' *œuvre*, (auto-)biographies, letters and personal testimonies, photographs, and the like. This was due to the fact that, in most cases, fame was a *posthumous* phenomenon and the incidence of "genius" only occurred rarely. Therefore, genius research most often worked with dead "geniuses," who had lived their lives in the past. Individual researchers worshipped their own favorite "ensemble of geniuses." "Genius" was an abstract term, a virtual and theoretical invention, whose existence, characteristics, and behavior were assumed hypothetically in order to explain certain extraordinary empirical observations or to indulge wishful thinking. In other words, the "genius" was resurrected and brought back to life in the cultural-historical present, created or revitalized by writing and talking about him. Dead "geniuses" were animated, for example, through multiple biographies, which transformed them into living memories promising revelation and truth.

The genius figure occupied what was virtually a magic or cultic point in a relationship of tension between modernization, secularization, formal rationalization, cultural differentiation, and humanistic and literary profiling. Each new context of knowledge or appropriation of genius discourse resulted in another metamorphosis of the genius figure, who could appear as a dignified, celebrated, glorified, and admired super-individual, but who could also go unrecognized, misjudged, or despised. As a bisexual or pathological figure, the "genius" embodied the "Other" of science, while simultaneously confirming its maleness, objectivity, independence, purity, asexuality, and transcendence. Wishes, myths, and ideals, along with fantasies and fears were anthropomorphized in the "genius."

The popularization and legitimation of the genius formula had powerful political effects, serving to justify and facilitate strategies of exclusion aimed particularly at women and Jews, while enhancing the prospect of rule by extraordinary or charismatic authority. As such, the genius discourse of the early twentieth century must be analyzed as a manipulative and ideological tool of power and a catalyst for growing racial-political power structures in the context of German and Austrian fascist tendencies. It simultaneously reflected the frictions between an older literary-aesthetic (romantic) discourse of genius, national myths, fantasies of universalization, the constitution of new scientific and cultural knowledge, and the attempt to guide the "higher" development of human civilization through population policy. This may have increased the production of knowledge around the question of genius and enabled intellectual and cultural self-affirmation, but it also raised the danger of hubris, political asymmetries, and hastened what Zilsel described 96 years ago as society's "delivery" or "discharge into inhumanity" ("Entladung in Unmenschlichkeit").[71]

Notes

1. Edgar Zilsel, *Die Geniereligion. Ein kritischer Versuch über das moderne Persönlichkeitsideal, mit einer historischen Begründung*, ed. and intro. Johann Dvořak (Frankfurt: Suhrkamp, 1990 [1918]), 51–53. Unless otherwise stated, all translations from the German are my own.
2. Edgar Zilsel, *Die Entstehung des Geniebegriffes. Ein Beitrag zur Ideengeschichte der Antike und des Frühkapitalismus* (Tübingen: J. C. B. Mohr (Paul Siebeck), 1926), 232.
3. Zilsel, *Die Geniereligion*, 53.
4. Ibid., 51.
5. Ibid., 233.
6. Ibid.
7. The cult of the genius in the early twentieth century differs from the well-known genius aesthetics of the *Sturm-und-Drang* period and the Romantic era of the early 1800s. See Ina Schabert, ed., *Autorschaft. Genus und Genie in der Zeit um 1800* (Berlin: Schmidt, 1994); Günter Peters, *Der zerrissene Engel. Genieästhetik und literarische Selbstdarstellung im*

achtzehnten Jahrhundert (Stuttgart: Metzler, 1982 [1981]); Christina Juliane Fleck, *Genie und Wahrheit. Der Geniegedanke im Sturm und Drang* (Marburg: Tectum, 2006). The romantic universal genius ["Universalgenie"] around 1800, in literature, poetics and philosophy was associated with such keywords as nature, the mystical, spirituality, sovereignty, authorship, autonomy, obsession, emotion, imagination, individuality, sensitivity, and androgyny.

8. Cesare Lombroso, *Genio et follia. Prelezione ai corsi di antropologia e clinica psichiatrica presso la R. Universita di Pavia* (Milano: Tip. e Libreria di Giuseppe Chiusi, 1864); Cesare Lombroso, "Genius and Degeneration," *Psychological Review* 2, no. 3 (1895 [1894]): 288–90; Jacques-Joseph Moreau de Tours, *La Psychologie morbide dans ses rapports avec la philosophie de l'histoire, ou De l'influence des névropathies sur le dynamisme intellectuel* (Paris: Victor Masson, 1859).

9. Central writings of the genius research of the era that enjoyed an extremely high circulation include Otto Weininger, *Geschlecht und Charakter. Eine prinzipielle Untersuchung* (Munich: Matthes & Seitz, 1997 [1903]) [Rep., 1st edition: Vienna: Braumüller. K. u. K. Hof- und Universitäts-Buchhändler]; Houston Stewart Chamberlain, *Die Grundlagen des 19. Jahrhunderts.* Jubiläumsausgabe (Munich, 1940 [1898]); Ernst Kretschmer, *Geniale Menschen. Mit einer Portraitsammlung* (Berlin: Julius Springer, 1931 [1929]).

10. Hans Blüher, *Die deutsche Wandervogelbewegung als erotisches Phänomen. Ein Beitrag zur Erkenntnis der sexuellen Inversion* (Berlin-Tempelhof: Weise, 1912). Cf. Julia Barbara Köhne, *Geniekult in Geisteswissenschaften und Literaturen um 1900 und seine filmischen Adaptionen* (Vienna/Cologne/Weimar: Böhlau, 2014), esp. ch. 2, sect. 1: "Religiosität und Genie bei Hans Blüher," 134–86.

11. I treat each of these themes in detail in Köhne, *Geniekult*, esp. 361–400.

12. Donna Haraway has coined the term "god-trick" in another context to describe the illusion of infinite vision, of an objective-transcendent perspective that claims truth in the sciences, a patriarchal-authoritarian, hierarchical point of view when looking at research objects, which she describes as "seeing everything from nowhere." See Donna Haraway, "The Persistence of Vision," in *The Visual Culture Reader*, ed. Nicholas Mirzoeff (London: Routledge, 2002; 2nd edition), 678–84, here 678.

13. Walter Benjamin, "Socrates" [1916], in *Selected Writings*, vol. 1: *1913–1926, Walter Benjamin*, ed. Marcus Bullock and Michael W. Jennings (Cambridge, MA and London: Harvard University Press 2002 [1996]), 52–54, here 53.

14. Hans Blüher, *Die Aristie des Jesus von Nazareth. Philosophische Grundlegung der Lehre und der Erscheinung Christi* (Prien: Kampmann & Schnabel, 1922 [1921]), 80.

15. Ludwik Fleck, "The Problem of Epistemology" [1936], in *Cognition and Fact. Materials on Ludwik Fleck*, ed. Robert S. Cohen and Thomas Schnelle (Dordrecht, Boston et al.: D. Reidel Publishing, 1986), 79–112, here 99–100, see also 80, 81: "We lack the possibility of formulating the intellectual personality of old thinkers: in the history textbooks they are geniuses, but when reading their own works we often find primitive thinking, unsettled views and naive theories."

16. Cf. also Sylwia Werner and Claus Zittel, "Einleitung: Denkstile und Tatsachen," in Ludwik Fleck, *Denkstile und Tatsachen. Gesammelte Schriften und Zeugnisse*, ed. Sylwia Werner and Claus Zittel (Frankfurt: Suhrkamp, 2011), 9–38, here 18–19.

17. Fleck: "The Problem of Epistemology," 81: "What truth (or 'lofty truth') is for one of them, is a 'base invention' (or naive illusion) for the other."

18. Fleck, "The Problem of Epistemology," 89, 101: "The force which maintains the collective and unites its members is derived from the community of the collective mood. This mood produces the readiness for an identically directed perception, evaluation and use of what is perceived, i.e. a common thought-style."

19. Zilsel, *Die Geniereligion*, 106.

20. Ibid., 105, 107.

21. Ibid., 107.

22. Hans Blumenberg, "Light as a Metaphor for Truth: At the Preliminary Stage of Philosophical Concept Formation," in *Modernity and the Hegemony of Vision*, ed.

David Michael Levin; trans. Joel Anderson (Berkeley: University of California, 1993), 30–62.

23. Cf. Hans Blumenberg, *Paradigmen zu einer Metaphorologie* (Frankfurt: Suhrkamp, 1997 [1960]).

24. Blumenberg, "Light as a Metaphor for Truth," 51.

25. Johannes G. Thöne, *Menschen, wie sie sind. Versuch einer modernen Charakterkunde* (Hamburg: Alster, 1925), 151–52.

26. Alexander Bartl, "Vom Dienstmann zum Popstar. Zur Darstellung Mozarts bei Karl Hartl und Milos Forman," in *Genie und Leidenschaft. Künstlerleben im Film*, ed. Jürgen Felix (St. Augustin: Gardez!, 2000), 129.

27. Houston Stewart Chamberlain, *Foundations of the Nineteenth Century*, 2 vols., trans. John Lees (New York: John Lane, 1912) [*Die Grundlagen des 19. Jahrhunderts*, 1898–99], II, 434.

28. Ibid., I, xc.

29. Hans Schleier, "Überlegungen zur historischen Biographie um die Jahrhundertwende in Deutschland," in *Historiographiegeschichte als Methodologiegeschichte. Zum 80. Geburtstag von Ernst Engelberg*, ed. Wolfgang Küttler and Karl-Heinz Noack (Berlin: Akademie, 1991), 81–87, here 81.

30. Stefan Zweig, *Decisive Moments in History: Twelve Historical Miniatures*, trans. Lowell A. Bangerter (Riverside, CA: Ariadne Press, 1999), 5–6.

31. Thomas Macho, *Vorbilder* (Munich: Fink, 2011), 213–14, 223.

32. Mitchell G. Ash, "Die Wissenschaften in der Geschichte der Moderne." Antrittsvorlesung, Vienna, April 2, 1998, in *Österreichische Zeitschrift für Geschichtswissenschaften* 10 (1999): 105–29, here 113.

33. Ludwig Flügge, *Rassenhygiene und Sexualethik. Psychoanalyse und hysterophiles Genie—Das Interesse des Staats an der Sexualethik—Rassenbiologie und Sport* (Berlin: Deutsches Literarisches Institut, 1924), 17; Weininger, *Geschlecht und Charakter*, 423.

34. Concerning the cultural-historical linkage between biological procreation and intellectual creation, see Christian Begemann and David E. Wellbery, ed., *Kunst—Zeugung—Geburt. Theorien und Metaphern ästhetischer Produktion in der Neuzeit* (Freiburg: Rombach, 2003).

35. Rudolf Steiner, "Der geniale Mensch," *Magazin für Literatur* 69, no. 19–20 (May 12 and 19, 1900): 422–32.

36. Georg Lomer, "Vom Doppelgeschlecht des künstlerischen Menschen," in *Jahrbuch für sexuelle Zwischenstufen mit besonderer Berücksichtigung der Homosexualität* XIII(4), ed. Magnus Hirschfeld (Leipzig: Max Spohr, 1913), 378–506, here 484–85 [first published in *Gegenwart*, January 8, 1912].

37. Helga Baisch, *Wahrsinn oder Wahnsinn des Genius? Sinn und Grenzen der pathographischen und psychographischen Methodik in der Anthropologie des Genius* (Leipzig: Johann Ambrosius, 1939), 47, 49.

38. Cf. for example: Johannes C. Barolin, *Inspiration und Genialität* (Vienna and Leipzig: Wilhelm Braumüller and Universitäts-Verlagsbuchhandlung, 1927), 22, 11; Jakob Wassermann, *Mein Weg als Deutscher und Jude* (Munich: dtv, 1994 [1921]), 64; Johann Wilhelm Ritter, ed., *Fragmente aus dem Nachlasse eines jungen Physikers*. Re-edited by Friedrich von der Leyen (Leipzig: Insel, 1946 [1810]), fragment 495, 55; Otto Weininger, *Sex and Character: An Investigation of Fundamental Principles*, ed. Daniel Steuer with Laura Marcus; trans. Ladislaus Löb (Indiana: Indiana University Press, 2005), 199: "Earthly fatherhood is as deficient in value as motherhood. It is immoral [...].''; Jakob Wassermann, *Mein Weg als Deutscher und Jude* (Munich: dtv, 1994 [1921]), 64.

39. Kretschmer, *Geniale Menschen*, 111.

40. Benjamin, "Socrates," 53.

41. Ibid.: "In a society of males, there would be no genius; genius lives through the existence of the feminine. It is true: the existence of the feminine guarantees the asexuality of the spiritual in the world [...W]herever this knowledge concerning the feminine prevails in the world, that which belongs to genius is born. [...] How the mere exist-

ence of the female guarantees the asexuality of the spiritual remains the greatest secret."

42. Benjamin, "Socrates," 54.
43. Ibid., 53.
44. Ibid.
45. Friedrich Nietzsche, "125. Aphorismus: Der tolle Mensch," in *Kritische Studienausgabe*, ed. Giorgio Colli and Mazzino Montinari (Munich: de Gruyter, 1999 [1882]), 481ff; Réne Girard, "The Founding Murder in the Philosophy of Nietzsche," in *Violence and Truth. On the Work of René Girard*, ed. Paul Dumouchel; trans. Mark R. Anspach (Stanford: Stanford University Press, 1988 [1985]), 227–46.
46. Hans Blumenberg, "'Säkularisation.' Kritik einer Kategorie historischer Illegitimität," in *Die Philosophie und die Frage nach dem Fortschritt*, ed. Franz Wiedmann and Helmut Kuhn (Munich: Pustet, 1964 [1962]), 240–65, here 241.
47. Hans Blumenberg, *Die Legitimität der Neuzeit* (Frankfurt: Suhrkamp, 1988 [1974]), 88.
48. Julian Hirsch, *Die Genesis des Ruhmes. Ein Beitrag zur Methodenlehre der Geschichte* (Leipzig: Johann Ambrosius Barth, 1914). See also Zilsel, *Die Entstehung des Geniebegriffes*.
49. Cf. Darrin M. McMahon, *Divine Fury: A History of Genius* (New York: Basic Books, 2013), 189–227.
50. Zilsel, *Die Entstehung des Geniebegriffes*, 83–92.
51. Zilsel, *Die Geniereligion*, 74.
52. Ibid., 70, 72.
53. Ibid., 75.
54. Ibid., 195.
55. Weininger, *Sex and Character*.
56. Cf. Köhne, *Geniekult*, ch. 1: "Biographisieren: Genie—Leben—Schreiben," 58–113.
57. Weininger, *Sex and Character*, 299.
58. Ibid., 297.
59. Ibid., 421.
60. Jochen Schmidt, *Die Geschichte des Genie-Gedankens in der deutschen Literatur, Philosophie und Politik 1750–1945*, vol. 2: *Von der Romantik bis zum Ende des Dritten Reiches* (Darmstadt: Wissenschaftliche Buchgesellschaft, 1985 [2. Auflage 1988, 3. verbesserte Auflage 2004]), 213–15, 225. Cf. Chamberlain, *Die Grundlagen des 19. Jahrhunderts*, 320 or: Chamberlain, *Foundations of the Nineteenth Century*, 269.
61. Chamberlain, *Foundations of the Nineteenth Century*, 269.
62. Wilhelm Ostwald, *Große Männer. Studien zur Biologie des Geistes* (Leipzig: Akademische, 1909), 324, 412–15.
63. Albert Reibmayr, *Die Entwicklungsgeschichte des Talentes und Genies* (München: J. F. Lehmann, 1908).
64. Ottokar Matura, *Das Deutsche Genie. Neue grundlegende Forschungsergebnisse über Zahl, Vorkommen und Artenreichtum genialer Menschen im völkischen Staat* (Vienna: Österreichischer Landesverlag, 1941).
65. Theodor Geiger, "Führer und Genie," *Kölner Vierteljahreshefte für Sozialwissenschaften* 6 (1926/27): 232–47.
66. Ibid., 244.
67. Schmidt, *Die Geschichte des Genie-Gedankens*, vol. 2, 195–198.
68. In the following passage of Fleck's "The Problem of Epistemology," 103, he describes the phenomenon of contrasting the crowd with the élite (or the genius, one might add): "[I]n those communities in which the position of the crowd is weaker than that of the élite, the latter tends to maintain distance and becomes isolated. It stresses the supranatural origin of the ideas it represents, and its significance requires obedience and docility. The criterion of truth and acceptance is found in some single master, often a mythical one. In such communities, ceremonials and dogma develop. They are more or less precisely limited and conservative: their ideal lies in the past [...] Examples of such a community are the majority of religious communities."

69. Alfred Rosenberg, ed. and intro., *Das Parteiprogramm. Wesen, Grundsätze und Ziele der NSDAP* (Munich: Zentralverlag der NSDAP, 1943; 25th edition), 34. By 1943, the program was already in its 25th edition, and had been printed over a million times. The word "Volk" specifically refers to the German interpretation of *Volk* from the "völkisch" movement, with both its romantic focus on national identity and folklore and its stress on the "unpolluted race."
70. Ernst Piper, *Alfred Rosenberg. Hitlers Chefideologe* (Munich: Blessing, 2005), esp. 179–212, 202.
71. Zilsel, *Die Geniereligion*, 233.

9
Cultivating Genius in a Bolshevik Country

*Irina Sirotkina**

Fyodor Dostoevsky was arguably the first to examine the dilemma of genius and equality in the Russian context. In his novel, *The Possessed*, Petr Verkhovensky and Nikolai Stavrogin discuss a quasi-socialist doctrine by someone called Shigalov (or Shigaliov):

> Shigalov is a man of genius! Do you know he is a genius like Fourier, but bolder than Fourier; stronger. I'll look after him. He's discovered "equality"! [...] He suggests a system of spying. Every member of the society spies on the others, and it's his duty to inform against them. Every one belongs to all and all to every one. All are slaves and equal in their slavery. [...] To begin with, the level of education, science, and talents is lowered. A high level of education and science is only possible for great intellects, and they are not wanted. The great intellects have always seized the power and been despots. Great intellects cannot help being despots and they've always done more harm than good. They will be banished or put to death. Cicero will have his tongue cut out, Copernicus will have his eyes put out, Shakespeare will be stoned—that's Shigalovism.[1]

In the name of Shigalovism, Dostoevsky wrote a parody of early socialist thinkers, of whom he himself had been a follower in his youth and for which he paid so dearly. Yet, even in his young years, the writer was not an adept of the proposed socialist way of living. In the words of a contemporary, he once said that life in an Icarian commune or phalanstery seemed to him more terrible and repugnant than any prison. Dostoevsky also spoke of the "relentless necessity of Fourierism in his deposition," and his like-minded friend, "when called in for questioning, expatiated on the lack of privacy in the phalanstery and compared life there to living in an army barracks."[2] It was a bitter irony that Dostoevsky's own worst suffering in prison was from the lack of privacy: as a prisoner, he was never left alone.

The ideological origins of Shigalovism could be found in the *Programme of Revolutionary Activities* by Sergei Nechaev (Nechayev).[3] After Nechaev's attempt to found a secret society and to seal the bonds between the members by a group murder of one of them, nearly all fellow revolutionaries distanced themselves from him. Critical of Nechayevshchina/Nechayevism, Karl Marx coined the term "barracks communism" to refer to a crude, authoritarian, forced collectivism and communism, where all aspects of life are bureaucratically regimented and communal. "What a wonderful example of barracks-communism!" he wrote. "Everything is here: common pots and dormitories, control commissioners and comptoirs, the regulation of education and consumption—in one word, of all social activity; and at the top, our Committee, anonymous and unknown, as the Supreme direction."[4]

Dostoevsky wanted to show how, starting from unlimited freedom, Shigaliov (and his protagonist Nechaev) arrived at unlimited despotism, or barrack communism, to use Marx's term. Both terms, Nechayevshchina and Shigalovschina, could be used as synonyms. While Soviet Marxists termed the forced communism of Mao Zedong "Nechayevshchina," the poet Boris Pasternak called Stalin's repression "Shigalovschina."[5] During the repressions carried out in the name of equality, the whole class of old professionals—especially scientists and engineers—was labelled "bourgeois specialist" and, together with intellectuals, repressed. To be precise, the politics of the Soviet government toward the intelligentsia varied: it alternated between exterminating the old intelligentsia and "winning it over," that is, using their capacities. At the same time, an effort was made to form a new intelligentsia, the "red professors" and young Soviet specialists.[6] The effort included bringing part of the new intelligentsia into the party-state establishment and offering them social protection benefits. This was the context in which it became viable to speak about genius and talent and to suggest a kind of eugenic project in connection with persons of outstanding ability—geniuses.

The project came as the personal initiative of a medical doctor and artist, G. V. Segalin.[7] It can be viewed as part of eugenic movement widespread in Russia as well as in other countries in the first decades of the twentieth century. In general, eugenics refers to demographic policies applied to individuals for the sake of improving the hereditary qualities of the population. In conception, eugenics is an application of animal breeding practices to the human species. Two approaches are possible: negative and positive eugenics. The former consists of either exterminating or excluding from procreation individuals with negative qualities, like hereditary mental illnesses. The latter encourages procreation of individuals with positive or valued qualities.

The same year the Russian revolutionaries drew up a plan for a new social order and tried to implement it, Francis Galton in Britain published a book, *Hereditary Genius*,[8] in which he demonstrated, to his satisfaction, the hereditary nature of talent in general, and he went on to suggest improving society by encouraging talented persons to procreate. Galton had followers in Russia. Segalin was one of them, and he suggested a eugenic policy for protecting persons of genius and ensuring their productivity for the sake of the entire country. His plan included both a research institution to deal with all aspects of genius and creativity and a social welfare system for geniuses. Though the project never materialized, such ideas were characteristic of the very beginning of the Soviet era, when the wildest human and social experiments seemed possible. We will examine the motivation behind Segalin's project and the turn it took during the first Soviet decades.

Segalin

Girsh (Grigorii Vladimirovich) Segalin (1878–1960) was the son of a wealthy Jewish manufacturer, an owner of a factory in Moscow. The family subsequently moved to Kazan' (now the capital of Tatarstan). In Kazan', he studied painting with Nikolai Fechin (1881–1955), subsequently a famous Tatar-Russian-American artist. In the 1920s Fechin left Russia and moved to the United States; later he settled in California, opened a studio in Pasadena, and eventually died in Santa-Monica. He was especially famous for his portraits; like him, Segalin specialized in portrait painting. After having studied with Fechin in Kazan', he went to an art school in Berlin. Although he was already 25, his father's capital allowed him to take another degree, now in medicine. From 1904 till 1909, Segalin studied at the University of Jena, then worked on a dissertation at Halle.[9]

In the last decades of the nineteenth century, Jena gained a reputation as a "citadel of Social Darwinism" owing to Ernst Haeckel and his followers. In 1898 the Jena historian, Ottokar Lorenz, published a book on genealogy relating his approach to Weismann's concept of the ancestral *germplasm*—an early concept of genes.[10] In 1904, the year when Segalin arrived there, Jena hosted a competition for the best essay on the application of the laws of evolution to society, which stimulated a variety of socio-biological projects. The same year, the Jena psychiatrist Wilhelm Strohmeyer launched a research program for psychopathology based on statistical genealogy, an idea soon enthusiastically developed by Ernst Rüdin. The Nietzschean aphorism, "the way forward led from being a species to a superspecies," stimulated Alfred Ploetz to write the first monograph on racial hygiene. It also inspired a cult of geniuses, which penetrated medicine and biology with the help of such authors as Max Nordau and Otto Weininger.[11] In 1905, the same year when the racial hygiene movement established itself, Haeckel founded his Monist League with the goal to reform life, art, and psychology on a biological basis. Segalin became enthusiastic about the eugenic idea of cultivating scientific and artistic geniuses.

He started working as an intern specializing in psychiatry—a discipline he had chosen probably because it was closer than other medical disciplines to his interests as a portrait painter. Yet, in 1914, the war pushed him out of Germany. Back in Kazan', he converted his German medical degree in order to qualify for Russian state employment. Immediately thereafter, Segalin was sent to the front where he served four years in a psychoneurological hospital of the Russian Red Cross located in Kiev. After the Bolsheviks had taken over the Ukraine, Segalin worked in the Red Army medical commission organized to fight the typhus epidemic. Demobilized, he settled in Ekaterinburg, a town in the Urals (renamed Sverdlovsk after 1925), where he helped organize a medical school at the new University of the Urals. He taught psychiatry and neurology there and founded a laboratory of psychotechnics at the Polytechnic College. He was also active in the public sphere as a member of the local government commission on minor criminals, as an expert in political trials, so frequent during the Stalin years, and as a consultant to a variety of institutions from the Institute of Occupational Hygiene to the Opera Theater.

"A weedy long-haired and sociable man in large glasses," Doctor Segalin "appeared in a shapeless Tolstoy-shirt, with a case full of manuscripts, drawings, and proofs."[12] To his townsmen, he appeared "a mad original, bearing some fantastic ideas," yet an observant contemporary found him "though not without oddities, a most interesting person."[13] Segalin was in correspondence with many celebrities, including Maxim Gorky who collected such interesting and odd people. Having become part of the Soviet medical establishment, Segalin did not give up his artistic interests. His most successful painting was an epic tableau, "Madhouse, or Victims of the War." It was allegedly painted directly in a hospital and invoked consultations with the patients. In the center, there was a full-size figure of the "prophet," with his head giving out light. The prophet was surrounded by various groups of people, some of whom met his preaching enthusiastically while others rejected it aggressively. The painting caused much talk in town. During World War II, Segalin founded a portrait gallery of local celebrities and veterans and he himself painted several portraits. He also wrote journalistic sketches and even was, in a sign of the highest official recognition, elected to the National Writers Union. Unfortunately, many of Segalin's paintings and the biggest part of his literary archive were lost after the war when he moved from the Urals. His last medical work on "pre-cancer syndrome" is dated 1948.[14]

The institute of genius

In the early twentieth century, Russia was ready for change. The intellectuals almost univocally welcomed it, though different groups envisaged different ways by which the alterations would come. The methods of modernization varied from a revolution and reforms to the improvement of human nature. In contrast with political and social changes, the latter measures focused on the individual and the biological. A new cohort of experts in the human sciences aspired to achieve moral and mental perfection of humankind through eugenics, mental hygiene, and psychology. They positioned themselves as a new technocracy.[15] After the Revolution, these experts gained the chance to implement their plans for the betterment of humankind on a scale unseen before.

In Russia, after the Bolshevik Revolution, a group of left-wing psychiatrists developed an ambitious plan to transform mental health care by making it preventive. The plan was for creating a network of outpatient units modeled on French dispensaries and, with their help, monitoring the entire population. The proposed health care system had an ambivalent character as it potentially turned everybody into a patient for the dispensaries. In a similar way, Segalin planned dispensaries for geniuses, where these otherwise "socially ill-adapted" people would receive professional help and care.

In this case, the clash between the ideas—of genius as an embodiment of human excellence, on one hand, and of institutions of a welfare state such as social medicine, on the other—is particularly striking. Although Segalin's project followed in Francis Galton's steps of positive eugenics, it did not repeat it. The Russian experts suggested their own ways combining experiments on human nature with social reforms. Like many eugenic and para-eugenic projects, Segalin's was not implemented. Yet, its development and, especially, its end reveal the fate of the hope for improving society through perfecting human nature in a dictatorship like the Soviet Union under Stalin.

Segalin proposed to take care of talented people who were often exploited and abused in the past. "Who does not know the sad pages from great people's biographies," he rhetorically asked, and listed these pages himself:

> Complete misunderstanding of new ideas of a talented person by his contemporaries; prosecution of any creative innovation if it contradicts the tastes and wishes of the powerful; incredible exploitation of artists' work by editors, re-sellers, agents of different kinds; abuse of *wunderkinds*; talented people living in poverty and dying early as a result of inability to adapt to social and economic conditions, to be servile and please their patrons, to advertise themselves and sell their souls; their abuse by the corrupt media; or the opposite—when talented people have to serve the vulgar tastes of the petty bourgeoisie, produce pseudo-art, prostitute art, literature, science, theater, when they clown, pose, arrogantly advertise themselves. All this in order not to starve.[16]

Though socialism should eliminate the conditions that made abuse of geniuses possible, the author assumed that the situation would not improve automatically. Geniuses, he argued, owing to their individualistic, asocial nature and frequent ailments, find adjustment to any society difficult. Asocial by nature, they easily fall victim to society and may be incarcerated in asylums and prisons. If, however, they are cured of their illnesses and socialized on a par with everybody else, they may loose their creative abilities. The author suggested that a special branch of medicine—aesthetic medicine—should protect geniuses from routine abuse and increase the output of their work.

Only in a socialist society, where protection of the weak is state policy, could aesthetic medicine become a reality. Alongside general departments of social welfare, the state should establish special institutions for geniuses: dispensaries and "departments of social welfare for mad geniuses" (*sobez genial'nogo bezumtsa*; *sobez* is an accepted abbreviation for a social welfare department). The institutions would assist in protecting talented people from hostile environments and in placing them in favorable conditions for the completion of socially valuable work. The plan for institutions for geniuses was designed to take care of children—both *wunderkinds* and those who appear mentally retarded at school but nevertheless grow up as talented people—within this framework. It suggested that children should be either directed to special schools or provided with individual developmental counseling.

In fact, some measures for which Segalin aspired were indeed implemented in Russia with the introduction of the New Economic Policy in 1921. About the same time, the Bolshevik government changed from attacking the old intelligentsia—the so-called bourgeois specialists, a category that included scientists and engineers—to "winning them over." This lead to the establishment of the Central Commission on Improving the Life of Scholars and other forms of state support and privileges for scientists, including upgraded food rations and medical care. Likewise, tests were introduced in schools to classify pupils according to their intellect and to select those who promised high achievement level.

Segalin's project went beyond welfare institutions for geniuses; on top of it, there was to be a program of research coordinated by the Special Institute of Genius: "Since a talented person's brain and body have not yet been objects of systematic study," Segalin wrote, "the Institute is to decree the compulsory dissection of brains of all outstanding people without exception, and, if necessary, also a post-mortem on the corpse, which then will be kept in the anatomical theater for subsequent study."[17] Other tasks assigned to the institute included experimenting with the conditions that are known to produce creative states of mind (including stimulating substances) and even fulfilling the functions of the art critique. Segalin claimed that contemporary art was degenerating into "almost hysterical forms" ("pochti sploshnoe klikushestvo"; *klikushestvo* is a Russian term for a particular form of hysteria that affected peasant women). His ambition was to assist art experts in museums and galleries to distinguish a genuine work of art inspired by a "real creative illness" from a fake made by a pretended "mad artist." Parallel to the work of a forensic psychiatrist, a specialist in aesthetic medicine would provide expertise to the courts in questions of pornography and "antisocial" art in general.[18] This was relevant in the circumstances when, in 1922, the party-state readjusted its policies toward literature and art and established new institutions of censorship, including *Glavlit*—the Main Administration for Literary and Publishing Affairs.

The project for aesthetic medicine was a continuation of psychiatric ambitions to control artists and art education. Thus, a proponent of mental hygiene in Russia prior to the Revolution, Grigorii Rossolimo (1860–1928), labeled some contemporary artists as insane and their art as a danger to the mental health of the population. Rossolimo worked on child neurology, psychiatry, and psychology; he founded a neurological clinic for children, the first in Russia, and composed psychological tests for diagnosing mental development. He was the key person who helped Segalin arrange the presentation of his projects in the Institute of Child Neurology in Moscow. Rossolimo was also instrumental in establishing a government commission to oversee the work on the project—the commission, which he headed, included the painter Vassily Kandinsky, the literary critic Yulii Aikhenval'd, the psychologist Nikolai Rybnikov, and the psychoanalyst Ivan Ermakov.[19] This commission, however, never functioned.

In spite of acquiring influence locally and beyond, Segalin had difficulties in promoting his project. An obstacle could have been his focus on associating talent with mental illness. In Germany, as I have already mentioned, he was exposed to the cult of genius and the ideas of race hygiene. He read the authors who elevated genius above the average healthy person and believed that mediocrity rather than disease is the cause of degeneration. These authors thought that geniuses, whether ill or healthy, showed the road to a progressive evolution of the human species.[20] Inspired by Nietzsche and Haeckel, Russian intellectuals shared this belief. In the entry on genius in the *Soviet Medical Encyclopedia*, the psychologist L. S. Vygotsky and the psychiatrist P. M. Zinov'ev defined genius, referring to the work of the Italian psychiatrist Enrico Morselli, as "an evolving, progressive variation of the human type."[21] Segalin suggested that by examining, analyzing, protecting, and stimulating geniuses, the human species could cultivate itself and rise to as yet unknown heights. He argued for the divide between the normal and abnormal be abandoned because "nature...knows only one division—between repetitive and creative work." The distinction, he argued, should lie not between illness and health, but between productive and unproductive illness. Segalin compared creative illness with birth. He could have had in mind the common image of Russia as a woman giving birth, as the country lay in ruins and awaited regeneration. This was also a motive for Russian biologists and medical scientists, such as Nikolai Kol'tsov, Yurii Filipchenko, Sergei Davidenkov, or Aleksandr Serebrovsky, to establish the Russian Eugenic Society in 1920.[22]

Many believed, however, that revival was impossible without sacrifices, and that the country would have to pay a heavy cost for its communist rebirth. In 1926, a fellow-psychiatrist, Pavel Karpov, wrote: "in the course of human development some individuals are ahead of others, and because of that they are unstable and vulnerable to mental diseases...Humanity makes sacrifices, leaving in its path of development individuals who fall down in a disordered state."[23] At the newly established Academy of Art Sciences, Karpov founded and headed the Commission for Studying Creative Work of the Mentally Ill (1924–1929). The ideas of humanity's progeneration and the sacrifices it has to make on the way echo the Russian proverb, "when you chop wood, chips fly." Incidentally, Stalin made the proverb a slogan of the day in order to justify the repression. Using the same metaphor, Segalin compared human evolution to a gigantic building site where pathology—"the chips"—are the inevitable cost of progeneration, the process opposite to the dreaded degeneration of humankind. His own project aimed at minimizing the amount of "chips"—the number of geniuses who perish in this process.

The reason why his project remained unfulfilled did not lie in its unreality. It was hardly odder than Professor I. I. Ivanov's experiments in crossbreeding apes with humans,[24] or indeed the hereditary data-banks created by German psychiatrists, and a great deal more innocent than the sterilization of the mentally ill in some Scandinavian countries. In fact, Segalin's idea to collect outstanding people's brains in the Institute of Genius anticipated V. M. Bekhterev's idea of a "Pantheon of Brain." In 1926, Segalin's journal published an article by A. A. Kapustin who reported on his dissections of the brains of the famous physicians, S. S. Korsakov, A. Ia. Kozhevnikov, and P. I. Bakmet'ev, which were kept in the collection of Rossolimo's Neurological Institute.[25] But, unlike the academician Bekhterev—a physician to many notables, including the last tsar, Lenin, and Stalin—Segalin was an eccentric provincial who, as a result of many years abroad, had not sufficiently established himself in Russia. Though the presentation of his project in Moscow went well, he failed to maintain the interest of those with access to power. He therefore reoriented his project toward a journal, which he launched in the provinces in 1925 and published almost single-handedly, financed from his personal budget.

In the center of Segalin's project was the assumption that scientific and medical experts would take control over "geniuses" and their work. The project sent therefore ambiguous signals to the authorities. On one hand, the Bolsheviks deeply mistrusted the old intelligentsia and tried to control it—in this way, the project might have appeared attractive. On the other hand, they wanted to do it themselves rather than passing the control functions over to what is now called the "technocracy."[26] What was the role of experts, including Segalin? If they were unable to be, in sociologist Zigmunt Baumann's terms, legislators of culture, they could still be its interpreters.[27] The interpretation of genius as mad became a brand mark of Segalin's journal.

The Journal

The journal had a long and loud title: *Clinical Archive of Genius and Talent (of Europathology), Dedicated to the Questions of Pathology of Gifted Personality As Well As of Creative Work with Any Psychopathological Bias.*[28] For the opening and subsequent issues, Segalin arranged contributions from the Swiss psychiatrist Auguste Forel and the Germans Wilhelm Lange and Walther Riese. The journal consisted of two main divisions: a theory section, filled mainly with Segalin's own writings, and a pathography section. In the first theoretical article, Segalin announced the creation of a new academic discipline that he termed, interchangeably, "ingeniology"(the study of creative work of any origin, "healthy" as well as "pathological") and "europathology" (the study of the effect of mental illness on creative work). The latter term was derived in part from the Greek word, "Eureka" (from which "heuristic" also originates), but it also resembled such neologisms of the time as "eugenics" or "eurythmie"—a name for both Émile Jacques-Delcroze's gymnastic and Rudolf Steiner's anthroposophic dance. Whatever the name, the new discipline was to study creative people, from children to mad geniuses, under a variety of conditions, and from normal states to bouts of momentary madness. As one of his purposes, Segalin mentioned the construction of creativity tests, so-called schemes for "practical semiotics and diagnostics," in order to distinguish, for instance, "the inspirations of an epileptic" from those of a hysterical person. Armed with these tests and schemes, a psychiatrist would be able to diagnose the disease "as easily as a chemist detects the composition of minerals in the sun by its spectrum," just by looking at a person's artistic style.[29]

In the atmosphere of early Soviet iconoclasm, previously sacred names were reconsidered. The old culture found itself cast into purgatory by proletarian critics. The literary associations, the Futurists, and *Proletkult*, who were the first to declare themselves on the side of the new regime, launched a nihilist attack on the past, threatening to "throw Pushkin and Dostoevsky overboard the ship of modernity."[30] As before the Revolution, the new cultural criticism readily found support in psychiatry. If Pushkin was a model poet for prerevolutionary critics and an example of perfect mental health for psychiatrists, after the revolution the literary young Turks denounced the classics, and psychiatrists of the younger generation questioned Pushkin's mental health. Zinov'ev wrote that "in order to understand Pushkin...correctly, it is necessary to accept that from the psychiatric point of view he was, though a highly valuable person, yet a psychopath."[31] Similarly, Rozenshtein assumed that Pushkin was a cycloid, according to Kretschmer's classification of character, and that Pushkin's famous irony resulted from his occasional "hypomaniac states."[32] Another psychiatrist argued from the position of a fashionable endocrinology theory, according to which individual differences are a function of glands. He classified Pushkin as an erotoman with hypertrophied gonads, and Gogol as a "hypogonadial type" accompanied, in his case, by schizophrenia.[33]

Psychiatrists of the younger generation found "absolutely unjustified" their predecessors' unwillingness, out of respect for the writers' suffering, to speak about the writers' mental illnesses. One of the departments of Segalin's Institute of Genius was to rewrite old-fashioned biographies, which avoided exposing the weaknesses and illnesses of outstanding people, and to stress the role of illness in talent. He also encouraged contributors to the *Clinical Archive* to write pathographies of outstanding figures—a suggestion that they eagerly followed up. A psychiatrist, N. A. Iurman, insisted on a thorough examination of Dostoevsky's "shadowy as well as bright sides,"[34] which was soon undertaken by a psychoanalytically oriented author, Tatiana Rozental', who interpreted Dostoevsky's disease as hysterical epilepsy.[35] Segalin agreed with her that Dostoevsky's epilepsy was not genuine but "affective," that is, caused by traumatic influences.[36]

Alongside the ongoing reevaluation of the past, the revolution initiated extravagant literary experiments, and in the atmosphere of relative political freedom, literary and artistic movements and groups proliferated. The symbolists' successors, the Akmeists, coexisted with the militant Futurists, the visionary Imaginists, the peasant poets fearful of growing urbanism, and the proletarian writers, who glorified industrialization and argued that the new culture should be based not on art but on science and technology.

The communist leaders recognized the existence of non-proletarian writers as "fellow-travelers," but they wanted either to reform or break the authors labeled as "bourgeois." Not coincidentally, these poets became objects of psychiatric attention. Referring to a literary critic who argued that Alexander Blok's poetry was "ill" and his romanticism "unhealthy," a Moscow psychiatrist diagnosed Blok as epileptic.[37] His colleague from the town of Smolensk, V. S. Grinevich, quoted the prerevolutionary view, repeated by proletarian critics, that symbolism and decadence are an escape from reality. Grinevich diagnosed as a "psychopath" the poet Nikolai Tikhonov, a member of the "fellow-travelers" group, "The Serapion Brothers," because he "quarreled with the commissars in the Cheka" (the security police, "Emergency Commission").[38] Grinevich, who presented himself as an "objective psychopathologist," concluded that the unstable, pessimistic, doubting, and schizophrenic "bourgeois" poets should give way to healthy proletarian writers. He died from consumption at the age of 24, the same year when his paper was published.

Responding to Segalin's invitation to rewrite biographies as pathographies, a young Moscow psychiatrist reassessed even Jesus Christ.[39] Pathographies of religious figures were not a new phenomenon, but psychiatrists felt especially encouraged to write them when atheism became state policy. The psychiatrist Ia. V. Mints diagnosed paranoia in Jesus Christ and attributed it to his week "asthenic" constitution. Exercising Marxist analysis, Mints concluded that the founder of Christianity, who originated from a craftsman's family, had a "petty bourgeois" social background.

Writers with established reputations were not excused from pathographies either. Gorky's mental health was questioned on the grounds that, when he was 18, the writer made a suicide attempt.[40] Tolstoy, Dostoevsky, Nekrasov, Byron, Balzac, and Nietzsche underwent the same scrutiny.[41] Segalin diagnosed Tolstoy's "affective epilepsy," discovering traces of the disease in the "epileptic intensity" of his literature as well as in the writer's supposed conservatism.[42] He followed the radical critics who had earlier reproached Tolstoy, writing that in his struggle with tsarism he did not go far enough—up to revolution. Segalin's article persuaded his colleague from Baku, V. I. Rudnev, who reported that it "clarified for me both Tolstoy's world-view and his sudden change [in the late 1870s] which took all of us by surprise." Rudnev wrote that he had found further evidence of Tolstoy's epilepsy in his *Memoirs of a Madman*,[43] which only confirmed Segalin's diagnosis.[44]

Written in the year of Tolstoy' jubilee, Segalin's articles might have been the last drop that finally brought the journal to an end. (Another reason could be the lack of funds: Segalin, as we have mentioned, published the journal privately with his own means). By the late 1920s, the nihilist spirit and wild experiments that followed the Revolution were already tamed, and the Soviet literary establishment had returned to the classics. Both Tolstoy and Dostoevsky were—successfully though not without controversy—accepted into the Soviet literary pantheon. The leading critic of the 1920s, A. K. Voronskii, planned "to limit Dostoevsky's pessimism with Tolstoy and to adjust Tolstoy's optimism with Dostoevsky."[45] Though he viciously attacked

Tolstoy's philosophy of nonresistance, Lenin respected his unique stature in Russian culture and preferred him to the new Soviet writers. He supported the publication of the unprecedented 90-volume collection of Tolstoy's work. Tolstoy's centenary in 1928 was the first large-scale government-sponsored event celebrating a prerevolutionary writer. It included a seven-hour celebration at the Bolshoi Theater, with the keynote address by the minister of education, Lunacharsky.[46]

The Tolstoy issue of the *Clinical Archive* had become its last volume (the following issue, though announced, never came out). Following the pattern of Stalinist political campaigns, the journal's end was prepared and was then followed by a series of critical articles written not by political leaders but by psychiatrists. Thus, a psychiatrist from the provinces, N. I. Balaban, published a critical review of Segalin's article in the official organ of the Society of Psychoneurologist-Materialists, *Soviet Psychoneurology* (*Sovetskaia psikhonevrologiia*). He argued that Segalin's diagnosis of Tolstoy would confuse the reader familiar with the writer's international reputation. Lenin's and Lunacharsky's view of Tolstoy as a sober realist stood in sharp contrast to the image of a hallucinating writer created by Segalin. The latter had argued that Tolstoy, before he was 50, was at a "manic stage" and that later his "affective epilepsy" switched to a "depressive stage." In Balaban's view, Segalin repeated the outdated cliché about Tolstoy's "sudden crisis," which had already been rejected by literary historians. Balaban insisted that Tolstoy's changes should not be explained by illness, and he criticized Segalin for reproducing suspicious Lombrosian views (from the Italian theorist Cesare Lombroso) without enriching medical knowledge.[47]

Balaban's article only confirmed the end of Segalin's initiatives. Yet, at that time Segalin still believed that the Institute of Genius stood a chance. His hopes revived when he had heard that "some psychological circles" in Moscow discussed an idea for a "eurological institute." He also learned about the Academy of Sciences' decision to establish a "central organ" superintending the conditions of scientists' life and work. Further, the success of neuropsychiatric dispensaries encouraged Segalin to raise the question of "special dispensaries for creative people." The ambitions of social hygienists had indeed grown, and they campaigned to place all medical institutions under the "united dispensary." Their objectives were to screen the population, to introduce health passports for every worker, "to calculate the coefficient of work capacity," and to provide "timely prophylactic, curative, sanitary and social aid."[48] Similarly, in Segalin's project, dispensaries for geniuses were to control "abnormal and asocial art" and stimulate "unproductive euroneurotics" with the help of "eurotherapy."[49] Yet, together with the Institute of Genius and aesthetic medicine, the plan had to be abandoned in circumstances unfavorable for the early Soviet project of preventive mental health care.

In the 1930s, the Narkomzdrav was in crisis. It lacked both the funds and the strategy to cope with the consequences of brutal industrialization and collectivization. The welfare services did not match the needs of the growing urban population—a result of the disastrous famine. Although the strategy for preventive health care was widely publicized and had already attracted the attention of socialist-oriented physicians in the West, the gap between the ambitions of social medicine and the reality was blatant. In 1931 a government decree indicated the grim situation in the understaffed and undersupplied mental hospitals, where the number of patients many times exceeded the intended population.[50] The decree also ordered that no other institutions of preventive psychiatry were to be founded. The dispensary campaign slowed down, and its main proponents disappeared from the stage. In 1930 the patron of social hygiene, N. A. Semashko, was removed from his post as Commissar of Public Health. The new Narkomzdrav strategy was more class-oriented and concentrated on establishing medical facilities for workers at their workplaces.[51]

Segalin's marginal position as a provincial psychiatrist protected him from physical repression, yet his europathology was destroyed in embryo. Its association with eugenics, which in the West had by that time acquired racial connotations, made it especially vulnerable. In 1928, both the German Society of Mental Hygiene and the Eugenic Society in London initiated a campaign for sterilization as a preventive measure against mental illnesses. Three years later, National Socialists in the Reichstag petitioned for the sterilization of hereditary criminals. The founding father of German racial hygiene, Alfred Ploetz, as the historian Paul Weindling remarked, "metamorphosed from being an admirer of Kautsky to a supporter of Hitler."[52] In the Soviet Union, these developments were ideologically unacceptable, and they endangered the position of eugenics in this country. In 1930, the Russian Eugenics Society was disbanded and its journal terminated, almost simultaneously with Segalin's journal. Segalin wisely closed down his europathology project and retreated to general medicine.

The Great Break—Stalin's name for the sharp turn toward industrialization and collectivization—directly affected theories that linked the biological and the social, including eugenics and the idea of mad genius. First, in the new political climate, psychiatrists could no longer claim scientific neutrality. When Lombroso's contemporaries reproached him for "compromising" genius by his theories, he wrote in his defense: "but has not nature caused to grow from similar germs, and on the same clod of earth, the nettle and the jasmine, the aconite and the rose? The botanist cannot be blamed for these coincidences."[53] In the 1930s, it was no longer possible to argue that the psychiatrist studies mental illness as the botanist examines a flower—the myth of politically neutral psychiatry ceased to work. It was arguably one of very few positive outcomes of state control over scholarship exercised in the 1930s—an early example of political correctness.

Yet, political censorship over these matters also had negative consequences. With the end of eugenic research, the concept of genius also went out of fashion. To reiterate the paradox of genius and equality in *The Possessed*, Petr Verkhovensky announces Shigalov "a man of genius" because "he's discovered

'equality.'" Shigalov's own "genius" was to deny genius. "To level the mountains is a fine idea, not an absurd one," Verkhovensky claims:

> I am for Shigalov. Down with culture. We've had enough science! Without
> science we have material enough to go on for a thousand years, but one
> must have discipline. The one thing wanting in the world is discipline.
> The thirst for culture is an aristocratic thirst. The moment you have fam-
> ily ties or love you get the desire for property. We will destroy that desire;
> we'll make use of drunkenness, slander, spying; we'll make use of incred-
> ible corruption; we'll stifle every genius in its infancy. We'll reduce all to a
> common denominator! Complete equality![54]

When Dostoevsky published *The Possessed*, his contemporaries saw the
novel as a political pamphlet, not a prophecy. Yet, half a century later, the
country's intellectual elite perished in the purges and was replaced by the
undereducated and mediocre. Shigalov's prospect for total levelling won
over Segalin's project of cultivating genius; the crude notion of equality
finally won over exceptionality. Yet, while paying lip service to equality, the
country was, in fact, building a highly controlled hierarchical society—a
dictatorship. The only genius was thereby the man who topped the hierarchy—the dictator himself. For several decades to come, scientific studies
of creativity stopped, and the very concept of "genius" was excluded from
academic discourse.

Notes

* I thank Kirill Rossiianov and Roger Smith for reading the draft of this essay.

1. Fyodor Dostoevsky, *The Possessed*, trans. Constance Garnett, any edition, chapter 2.8,
   "Ivan the Tsarevitch." Quoted in The Project Gutenberg EBook of The Possessed, by Fyodor
   Dostoevsky http://www.gutenberg.org/files/8117/8117-h/8117-h.htm#2HCH0013.
2. Joseph Frank, *The Seed of Revolt, 1821–1849* (Princeton, NJ: Princeton University Press,
   1976), 254.
3. "Programma revolutsionnykh deistvii" was written by Nechaev together with Petr Tkachev
   in 1868, see Joseph Frank, *Dostoevsky: The Miraculous Years, 1865–1871* (Princeton, NJ:
   Princeton University Press, 1997), 450. See also James Goodwin, *Confronting Dostoevsky's
   Demons: Anarchism and the Specter of Bakunin in Twentieth-Century Russia* (New York: Peter
   Lang, 2010).
4. Quoted in Christopher G. A. Bryant, *Sociology in Action (Routledge Revivals): A Critique of
   Selected Conceptions of the Social Role of the Sociologist* (London: Routledge, 2013), 186.
5. A. K. Gladkov quoted in E. Pastenak and M. Feinberg, eds., *Vospominaniia o Borise
   Pasternake* (Moscow: Slovo, 1993), 323.
6. See Michael David-Fox, *Revolution of the Mind: Higher Learning Among the Bolsheviks, 1918–
   1929* (Ithaca, NY: Cornell University Press, 1997).
7. See Irina Sirotkina, *Diagnosing Literary Genius: A Cultural History of Psychiatry in Russia,
   1880–1930* (Baltimore, MD: Johns Hopkins University Press, 2002).
8. Francis Galton, *Hereditary Genius* (London: Macmillan, 1869).
9. See Iurii Sorkin, "Polivalentnyi chelovek [A Polyvalent person]," *Nauka Urala* 12 (1992):
   4–5; Yu. E. Sorkin, "G. V. Segalin i ego *Klinicheskii arkhiv genial'nosti i odarennosti* [G. V.
   Segalin and His *Clinical Archive of Genius and Talent*]," in *Institut genial'nosti* [Institute for
   Genius Studies], ed. Yu. E. Sorkin (Ekaterinburg: Ural'skii Universitet, 1992), 5–10.

10. Paul Weindling, *Health, Race, and German Politics between National Unification and Nazism 1870–1945* (Cambridge: Cambridge University Press, 1989), 231.
11. Ibid., 141–54.
12. Evgenii Petriaev, quoted in A. P. Kormushkin, "Introduction," in *Klinicheskii arkhiv genial'nosti i odarennosti*, accessed July 12, 2014, http://www.pathographia.narod.ru/klinic2/str1.htm.
13. Sorkin, "Polivalentnyi chelovek," 4.
14. Ibid., 5.
15. See Daniel Beer, *Renovating Russia: The Human Sciences and the Fate of Liberal Modernity, 1880–1930* (Ithaca, NY: Cornell University Press, 2008).
16. G. V. Segalin, "Institut genial'nogo tvorchestva [Institute of Creative Genius]," *Klinicheskii arkhiv genial'nosti i odarennosti* [further—*KA*] 1 (1928): 53–59.
17. Ibid., 54.
18. Ibid., 57–58.
19. B. Ia. Vol'fson, "'Panteon mozga' Bekhtereva i 'Insitut genial'nogo tvorchestva' Segalina [Bekhterev's *Pantheon of Brain* and Segalin's *Institute for Creative Genius*]," *KA* 1 (1928): 52–53.
20. T. I. Iudin, "Review of *Norm und Entartung der Menschen*, by Kurt Hildebrandt," *Russkii evgenicheskii zhurnal* 1 (1924): 72.
21. L. S. Vygotsky and P. M. Zinov'ev, "Genial'nost' [Genius]," in *Bol'shaia meditsinskaia entsiklopediia* [Great Soviet Encyclopaedia], ed. N. A. Semashko (Moscow: Sovetskaia entsiklopediia, 1929), VI, 612.
22. Mark B. Adams, "Eugenics in Russia," in *The Well–Born Science: Eugenics in Germany, France, Brazil and Russia*, ed. Mark B. Adams (Oxford: Oxford University Press, 1990), 153–216.
23. P. I. Karpov, *Tvorchestvo dushevnobol'nykh i ego vliianie na razvitie nauki, iskusstva i tekhniki* [Creativity of the Mentally Ill and Its Impact on the Development of Science, Art, and Technology] (Moscow: GIZ, 1926), 7.
24. K. O. Rossiianov, "Beyond Species: Ilya Ivanov and His Experiments on Cross-Breeding Humans with Anthropoid Apes," *Science in Context* 15 (2002): 277–316.
25. A. A. Kapustin, "O mozge uchenykh v sviazi s problemoi vzaimootnosheniia mezhdu velichinoi mozga i odarennost'iu [On the Brain of Scientists in Relation to the Problem of Brain Volume and Giftedness]," *KA* 2 (1926): 107–14; Monika Spivak, *Posmertnaia diagnostika genial'nosti* [Postmortem Diagnostics of Geniuses] (Moscow: Agraf, 2001).
26. Adams, "Eugenics in Russia," 153–216.
27. Zigmunt Baumann, *Legislators and Interpreters: On Modernity, Post-Modernity, Intellectuals* (Ithaca, NY: Cornell University Press, 1987).
28. There is a recent re-edition of the journal's issues by A. N. Kormushkin, a psychologist from Saint Petersburg (see note 13).
29. Segalin, "Institut genial'nogo," 55.
30. Gleb Struve, *Russian Literature Under Lenin and Stalin, 1917–1953* (Norman: University of Oklahoma Press, 1971), 14.
31. P. M. Zinov'ev, "O zadachakh patograficheskoi raboty [On the objective of pathographical work]," in *Pamiati P. B. Gannushkina* [In Memoriam P. B. Gannushkin], ed. A. O. Edel'shtein (Moscow and Leningrad: GIZ, 1935), 411–13.
32. L. M. Rozenshtein, "Psikhopatologiia myshleniia pri maniakal'no-depressivnom psikhoze i osobye paralogicheskie formy maniakal'nogo sostoianiia [Psychopathology of Thinking in Manic-depression Psychosis and Peculiar Paralogial Forms of the Manic State]," *Zhurnal nevropatologii i psikhiatrii imeni S. S. Korsakova* 7 (1926): 5–28.
33. I. B. Galant, "Evroendokrinologiia velikikh russkikh pisatelei i poetov [Euroendocrinology of Great Russian Writers and Poets]," *KA* 1 (1927): 50.
34. N. A. Iurman, "Bolezn' Dostoevskogo [Dostoevsky's illness]," *KA* 1 (1928): 62.
35. T. K. Rozental', "Stradanie i tvorchestvo Dostoevskogo (psikhoanaliticheskoe issledovanie) [Dostoevsky's Suffering and Creative Writing (A Psychoanalytical Study)]," *Voprosy izucheniia i vospitaniia lichnosti* 1 (1919): 88–107.

36. G. V. Segalin, "Evropatologiia genial'nykh epileptikov [Europathology of Persons of Genius Attained by Epilepsy]," *KA* 3 (1926): 143–87.
37. Ia. V. Mints, "Alexander Blok (patograficheskii ocherk) [Alexander Blok: A Pathographical Essay]," *KA* 3 (1928): 53.
38. V. S. Grinevich, "Iskusstvo sovremennoi epokhi v svete patologii [Contemporary Art in the Light of Pathology]," *KA* 1 (1928): 49.
39. Ia. V. Mints, "Iisus Khristos—kak tip dushevnobol'nogo [Jesus Christ as a Type of a Mentally Ill Person]," *KA* 3 (1927): 243–52.
40. I. B. Galant, "O suitsidomanii Maksima Gor'kogo. Lichnost' M. Gor'kogo v svete sovershennogo im v dekabre 1887 goda pokusheniia na samoubiistvo [On Maxim Gorky's Suicidal Mania: M. Gorky's Personality in the Light of His Attempt at a Suicide in December 1887]," *KA* 3 (1925): 93–109.
41. G. V. Segalin, "Obshchaia simptomatologiia evro-aktivnykh (tvorcheskikh) pristupov [General Symptomatic of Euro-Active (Creative) Attacks]," *KA* 1 (1926): 3–78.
42. G. V. Segalin, "Evropatologiia lichnosti i tvorchestva L'va Tolstogo [Europathology of Lev Tolstoy's Personality and Creativity]," *KA* 3–4 (1929): 5–148.
43. V. I. Rudnev, "*Zapiski sumasshedshego* L. Tolstogo [L. Tolstoy's *Memoirs of a Madman*]," *KA* 1 (1929): 69.
44. G. V. Segalin, "*Zapiski sumasshedshego* L'va Tolstogo kak patograficheskii document [Lev Tolstoy's *Memoirs of a Madman* as a Pathographical Document]," *KA* 1 (1929): 73–78.
45. R. A. Maguire, *Red Virgin Soil: Soviet Literature in the 1920s* (Princeton, NJ: Princeton University Press, 1968), 280–81.
46. S. L. Frank, "Tolstoi i bol'shevism [Tolstoy and the Bolshevism]," in *Russkoe mirovozzrenie*, ed. A. A. Ermichev (Saint-Petersburg: Nauka, 1996), 454–59.
47. N. I. Balaban, "O patologicheskom v lichnosti L'va Tolstogo. Kriticheskii ocherk [On the Pathological in Lev Tolstoy's Personality]," *Sovetskaia psikhonevrologiia* 3 (1933): 108–11.
48. V. I. Smirnov, ed., *Sotsialisticheskaia rekonstruktsiia zdravookhranenia* [Socialist Reconstruction of Public Health Care] (Moscow and Leningrad: GIZ, 1930), 5.
49. G. V. Segalin, "Izobretateli kak tvorcheskie nevrotiki (evronevrotiki) [Inventors as Creative Neurotics (Euroneurotics)]," *KA* 2 (1929): 70–72.
50. Irina Sirotkina, Marina Kokorina, "The Dialectics of Labour in a Psychiatric Ward: Work Therapy in the Kaschenko Hospital," in *Psychiatry in Communist Europe*, ed. Sarah Marks, Mat Savelli (New York: Palgrave Macmillan, 2015): 27–49.
51. *Zdravookhranenie v gody vosstanovleniia i sotsialisticheskoi rekonstruktsii narodnogo khoziaistva SSSR, 1925–1940* [Health Care System in the Years of Socialist Reconstruction of People's Economy, 1925–1940] (Moscow: Meditsina, 1973), 174–76.
52. Weindling, *Health, Race*, 451–52; Karl Kautsky (1854–1938)—a socialist, at one time close to Marx, and a leader of the Second International.
53. Cesare Lombroso, *The Man of Genius* (London: Walter Scott Publishing, 1910), ix.
54. Dostoevsky, *The Possessed*.

10
Insight in the Age of Automation
David Bates

There is a dominant movement in contemporary cognitive science that stresses the unconscious automaticity of much (if not all) of our thought processes. Whatever minimal functions consciousness might perform, it has been demonstrated over and over again how judgment and reasoning can take place automatically with very little influence from what we usually call the self, or consciousness. Even the highest forms of intellectual expertise are, to borrow the words of Malcolm Gladwell, "thinking without thinking."[1] The model of a "cognitive unconscious" constituted a new explanatory frame for understanding how creative and innovative ideas emerge from our minds.[2] "The creative process is characterized by flashes of insight that arise from unconscious reservoirs of the mind and brain."[3] Those moments of insight, when one experiences, like Archimedes did in his bath, that "Aha!" feeling of suddenly solving an intractable problem, have been shown to be preceded by unconscious cognitive activities traceable by sophisticated brain imaging techniques.[4] And so, for many cognitive scientists today, the mental feats of the genius can still be described as visitations from some otherworldly realm. Creativity, insight, intuition, judgment, intelligence—all of these mental capacities can now be studied as emanations from the unconscious, a world that we can glimpse only as it is revealed within the controlled conditions of psychological experimentation and brain scanning. As one researcher puts it: "The conscious you—the *I* that flickers to life when you wake up in the morning—is the smallest bit of what's transpiring in your brain."[5]

What has been called the "new unconscious" has very little to do with the Freudian version that has defined the term for much of the past century. This is because the new unconscious is a *cognitive* unconscious, capable, that is, of systematic, rational, and coherent thinking, whereas the psychoanalytic one is driven by more primal, irrational desires. To help explain the model of complex unconscious thought, cognitive science often draws on technological models of computation and processing developed in computer science and artificial intelligence (AI) research. Since it is true that various forms of machinic "thinking" can mimic even the most advanced cognition, such as symbolic manipulation, logic, heuristic searching, statistical predictions, and calculation, and since these machine processes are, of course, resolutely unconscious, the implication is that we can understand the human mind in a similar fashion. High-speed unconscious cognitive processes are always running in the background, so to speak. As the editors of a recent collection note: "The computer metaphor legitimized complex theories about unobservable processes while apparently avoiding the sins of anthropomorphizing."[6]

Crucial to the model of unconscious cognition is the assumption of automatic operation. "Experiments on automaticity are important because they indicate that a great deal of complex cognitive activity can go on outside of conscious awareness... as long as these processes are automated."[7] The result is that more and more cognitive capacities are relegated to the "colossal operating system"[8] that is the unconscious. The kind of creative thinking characteristic of the intellectual genius—the sudden discovery of some radically new idea—is readily assimilated to this new unconscious, because the sudden appearance of an inspired thought implies that it was produced outside of consciousness altogether. As Douglas Hofstadter has written, "intelligence emerges out of the interactions of many thousands of parallel processes that take place within milliseconds and are inaccessible to introspection."[9]

Whatever the explanatory value of research on the cognitive unconscious, in the process, human beings are becoming more and more alienated from the thing that marks them as human, namely, their intelligent minds. And especially the technologization of even creative thought contributes to what has been called (with only some irony) "the unbearable automaticity of being."[10] The functioning of our minds seems as opaque and distant from us as the mysterious inner functioning of our own computers.

How did we get to this point? Obviously, this particular vision of the unconscious mind can be traced back to the emergence of modern computing in the middle of the twentieth century. Indeed, the origins of cognitive science can be traced to the effort of early psychologists such as George Miller, Donald Broadbent, and Ulric Neisser to explain perception and cognition as examples of complex information processing.[11] But, in fact, this is part of a far longer story, a story of how the mind has become entangled with many different forms of technology since at least the Scientific Revolution in the seventeenth century. This is not at all a story of progressive *reduction* of the special capacities of the human mind to the grim automaticity of modern industrial machinery. Instead, we can say that the understanding of intelligence and creative thinking in the modern era has been facilitated by analyses of the human being itself as an organized system. Technological exemplars provided the foundation for these analyses. And yet, the continuing interest in human creativity has always challenged any simple model of automaticity and mechanization. A critique of some of the more extreme theorizations of human cognition as a largely automatic (and hence unconscious) activity can therefore be generated through a critical history of mental automaticity itself.

Cognitive systems in the age of reason

The rise of mechanistic theory in the seventeenth century opened up for the first time the possibility of a *comprehensive* conceptualization of the human body as a machine. Of course, the place of intellectual activity in that material context remained highly problematic. For some thinkers, such as Robert Boyle, the exceptional status of the human mind—its capacity for creative insight, and especially scientific insight—was predicated on an analogy of thought with divine creation itself.[12] But for others, such as Thomas Hobbes, the mechanical philosophy was a challenge. Would it be possible to explain all human behavior, including reason itself, only by recourse to the physical nature of the body?

The status of the brain and nervous system was central to this problematic in the seventeenth century. The inquiry known as "psychology" changed radically: instead of accounting for all the Aristotelian categories of thought, it now meant the study of the mind as an embodied function.[13] Descartes himself, belying his reputation as a radical dualist, sought a deep understanding of all the operations of what might be called corporeal cognition. As he reported in a letter from 1632: "I am dissecting the heads of various animals, in order to explain what imagination, memory, etc. consists of."[14] In his physiological writings, Descartes would propose a sophisticated interpretation of the nervous system and brain as a material information system. His model for the body's organization was not the enclosed mechanism of the clock but instead the responsive machinery found in the grottoes of the royal gardens at Saint-Germain en Laye; Descartes was fascinated by the way automata would move when a visitor stepped on a special tile on the floor.[15] In the *Traité de l'homme* of 1630, he developed a detailed theory of corporeal cognition that explained perception, reflex action, memory, and the imaginative reorganization of acquired ideas. Instead of explaining the physical motions and reactions of physiological processes (as he did when discussing, say, digestion and circulation), he recognized that the sensory system functioned in a completely different way. The organs of sense were described as made up of extraordinarily sensitive tissue. When they were moved by motions in the environment, these organs transmitted the form, or pattern, of those movements through the nerves. For Descartes, the nerves were hollow tubes, filled with what he calls "animal spirits." Despite the use of an older Galenic term, Descartes' hypothesis was that these spirits were nothing more than the very finest particulate matter, so diffuse that it is like a wind. The patterns of sensory motion were carried through the animal spirits to the brain. Descartes in effect depicted an information machine, for what mattered in the nervous system was the pattern, a kind of wave, and not its material instantiation, that is, the animal spirits. These waves of information all flowed to the brain, where they were integrated in the infamous pineal gland.

In his early physiological work, we can see how for Descartes much of what we call cognition is in fact a thoroughly unconscious, and automatic, activity that took place completely within the body. The complexity of the cognitive response to the world flowed from the faculty of memory, which Descartes described as a function of animal spirits—as they flowed through the "soft and pliant" structure of the brain, they, in essence, carved pathways, so that, on future occasions, new sensory information could flow into these pathways and reawaken past experiences. Or, more precisely, past nervous responses. The point here is that the Cartesian soul, which sets itself up at the pineal gland, where all sensory information is coordinated, was capable of *consciously* experiencing the world only because it can inhabit, so to speak, the automatic cognitive activity of the body. Most of the *soul's* experience, then, is a doubling of the automaticity of the corporeal cognition of the body. Descartes also argues, as we know, that the soul could also intervene in this sphere—though how exactly remained somewhat mysterious. However, to judge, according to Descartes, is for the soul to "see" something in experience that is not marked by the body itself.

For Descartes, there was therefore no simple division between mind and body. There was, instead, a recognition that thought was at once embodied, material, unconscious, *and* a space for conscious invention, insight, and judgment. The difficulty was to distinguish between genuine acts of intellect and the automatic forms of mental organization. An example from the *Meditations* reveals the tension inherent in Descartes's distinction between intelligence and automaticity: "If I look out at my window and see men crossing the square, as I just happen to have done, I normally say that I see the men themselves...Yet do I see any more than hats and coats which could conceal automata?"[16]

In the wake of Descartes, Spinoza and Leibniz both made an effort to systematize the operations of the rational Cartesian mind, the pure intellect that always seemed to escape corporeal explication and, hence, any hint of automaticity. For these thinkers, the soul was not some exception to the lawful structure of the mechanical universe, as it seemed to be in Descartes's philosophy. The mind had its own coherent laws of operation—these laws were, in fact, the new object of psychology. For Spinoza and Leibniz, the soul was a kind of "spiritual automaton."[17] Leibniz explained it this way: "the functioning of spiritual automata, that is to say, minds (*âmes*) is not at all mechanical, but they share to a great degree what is beautiful in the mechanical."[18]

Instead of maintaining this formal, rigorous distinction between the insights of the mind and corporeal sensibility, Enlightenment thinkers examined how ideas and experiences naturally formed themselves into systems and organizations, even as they held out the possibility of a rational reorganization of these ideas. As Locke explained, "The Understanding is not taught to reason...it has a native Faculty to perceive the Coherence or Incoherence of its *Ideas*, and can range them right."[19] Hence, a space was preserved for something like the interventional cut of Descartes's pure intellect; however, it was now incorporated into the natural cognitive economy of the sensible body. Of course, Hume would radicalize the naturalization of reason, searching in vain for its extra-cognitive legitimation. In the end, for Hume, "reason is nothing but a wonderful and intelligible instinct in our souls, which carries us along a certain train of ideas."[20] Reason, in other words, is nothing more than a tendency internal to the dynamics of the cognitive system. As Gilles Deleuze pointed out in his study of Hume, the atomic elements of the mind, ideas, have certain tendencies of attraction, and these "give rise to *habits*." But ultimately, the thinking mind itself is just another tendency of the system— "We are habits, nothing but habits—the habit of saying 'I'."[21]

The formation of habits through associations of ideas would be explained, in the eighteenth century, as a function of the nerves. Locke admitted the ultimate importance of the nervous system for thinking; if impressions were made in sensory organs, he said, then the hypothesis that these "motions from thence continued to the brain may be conceived, and that these produce ideas in our minds, I am persuaded, but in a manner to me incomprehensible."[22] Similarly, Hume admitted, in the *Treatise*, that the dynamics of association in mental life were caused by nervous activity: "It would have been easy to have made an imaginary dissection of the brain, and have shewn, why, upon our conception of any idea, the animal spirits run into all the contiguous traces, and rouze up the other ideas that are related to it."[23] At its most radical, this associationist psychology would imply a largely material understanding of the mind's organizational logic. As Diderot once remarked, genius was really just "a certain conformation of the head and the viscera, a certain constitution of the humors."[24] In his treatise on psychology, Charles Bonnet allowed himself to entertain an extreme thought experiment—what if human beings were just automata? As Bonnet would go on to suggest, we should understand habit as a process of literally writing on the nerves and the brain. The original, primitive state of the nerve fibers would, he said, be materially transformed by "frequent repetition." The very molecules of organic matter were then given a "new order" in the process of social and intellectual training. As Bonnet would note, once we understand the original openness of the nervous material, we can see that "education is a second birth, which imprints on the brain new determinations." The mind, the self, the brain, they were all transformed by experience and education; they were just different aspects of this new, artificial being.[25]

However, the open brain that was susceptible to being determined from outside could also be imagined as simultaneously capable of acts of *self-determination*. "Voluntary and semi-voluntary powers of calling up ideas, of exciting and restraining affections, and of performing or suspending actions, arise from the mechanism of our natures," wrote David Hartley.[26] Diderot would express a similar view in his speculative treatise, the *Éléments de physiologie*. The brain, he explained there, was not just the material underpinning of mental activity. The brain was in fact an active writer and reader of its own transformations, a producer of its own automatisms, that is, and therefore always capable of surpassing them. For Diderot, and here he echoes Descartes' own *Treatise on Man*, the soft matter of the brain was like "a sensible and living wax, susceptible of all sorts of forms, but losing none of those that it has received, and by receiving ceaselessly new ones that it keeps."[27] The Humean system of habit becomes here a sign of both productivity and passivity, of creativity and automaticity at the very same time. This dynamic was the ground for human intelligence.

In the economy of the nervous system, the brain would function then as the site of both habitual regularity and its creative disruption. As the philosopher Maine de Biran argued in his book on habit, the brain is the site for habitual formation, but as the ground of this organization, it was also able to interrupt established knowledge and training. "Independently of all acquired determination, the organ of thought draws sometimes from its own foundations."[28] Both were dependent on the foundational openness of the nervous system. On the threshold of the nineteenth century, then, the distinction between mental automaticity and the kind of intellectual or aesthetic novelty, often ascribed to the genius, was not at all predicated on a radical dualism, one that opposed body and mind. Rather, the brain as a pliant organ emerged as the site for conceptualizing both the formation of cognitive automaticities and the transgressive powers of insight and discovery, which were made possible by forging new relations within a system of thinking, largely defined by learned associations.

Unconscious cognition and the nineteenth-century mind

In early nineteenth-century thinking, the interventional character of insight, its structure as a gift from outside the operations of the normal mind, was internalized, assigned to the murky, and irrational, domain of the unconscious. The "genius in the man of genius" is in fact the unconscious, as Coleridge once put it.[29] Romantic ideas of a powerful unconscious force aligned it with the instinctive powers of the body, as, for example, in Schopenhauer's influential theory, where freedom was equated with a separation of conscious thought from the unconscious realm. Indeed, for Schopenhauer, genius was defined as the self-isolation of the intellect from the world. The brain was a "parasite" on the vital body, and could lead its life separate from the physiological economy.[30] These ideas would lead, as Henri Ellenberger showed in his iconic history of the unconscious, to the theories of psychoanalysis.[31]

Yet, there was another trajectory of the unconscious in the nineteenth century, one that centered on its critical cognitive role. This new approach to the mind was produced from the intersection of new neurophysiological research and the associationist tradition of psychological theory kept alive by thinkers such as Thomas Reid and James Mill. By mid century, thinkers were developing what would be called "psychophysics," theories that would explain mental activity and experience as a direct consequence of nerve action. The discovery of reflex actions, and the distinction between afferent (sensory) and efferent (motor) nerves, revealed many systematic automatisms within the nervous system, and as research progressed, it was known that even within the brain itself automatic responses could be generated. As Herbert Spencer put it, in his influential treatise on psychology, the nervous system was a space of integration. The conscious mind was in a sense a complicated fiction constructed out of a limited set of sensory experiences. "Out of a great number of psychical action going on in the organism, only a part is woven into the thread of consciousness."[32] The *unconscious* activity of the nervous system was continually generating responses, integrating memories, and producing automatisms. And as evolutionary theories in the nineteenth century took hold, the nervous system could also be understood as the inheritor of a whole evolutionary history of learned responses. Reason, for Spencer, was explained as a gap in the series of automatic functions, a moment of interruption, that is, where these acquired ideas and memories, the evolutionary inheritance, this whole storehouse of automatisms, would be newly organized to help adjust the organism to its challenging environmental circumstances. Reason existed to bridge the difference between the "perfectly automatic" and the "imperfectly automatic."[33]

In this historical moment, then, the conscious thought was not reduced to its material base, nor was it wholly extricated from its vital bodily home. Rather, the conscious mind became a particular (perhaps even peculiar) function, just one aspect of a complex nervous system. This was the argument of the vastly popular (if relentlessly critiqued) bestseller, Eduard von Hartmann's *Philosophie des Unbewussten* (1869).[34] As such, consciousness had very limited access to the vast set operations taking place in the brain and the nerves. As such, the mind's intellectual capacity could not be mapped onto its nervous substrate. Thinking was therefore something that took place both unconsciously and consciously. The relationship was not antagonistic necessarily, but neither was it wholly harmonious. Intellectual insight came from both conscious attention and the interruptions from the automatic nervous system. William Carpenter would call these processes "unconscious cerebration," where the "mind may undergo modifications, sometimes of considerable importance, without being itself conscious of the process, until its results present themselves to consciousness, in the new ideas, or new combinations of ideas, which the process has evolved."[35]

The theory of unconscious cognition therefore implied a whole new way of understanding the inspirations of creative minds, or the productions of the genius. "But what is genius other than a reunion of cerebral conditions under the sole excitation of life, organic functions, and perceptions?"[36] The novelty of the insight, and its subsequent assimilation into memory as knowledge, were both located in the nervous system, often understood in the later nineteenth century as an electrified communication system.[37] If genius was "the power of forming novel adjustments to circumstances," these novel mental connections, noted one thinker, are produced by the nervous current flowing into "virgin soil" within the brain. Once this current "rearranges some of the molecules" of the brain, future current flows more easily—the path has been laid down and the thinking of this association becomes largely automatic, an updating of Descartes's earlier theory of animal spirits flowing in the open structure of the brain.[38] The distinction between conscious and unconscious was more or less a distinction between different kinds of nervous activity. As Joseph J. Murphy explained, the organs of thinking were located in the cerebral hemispheres. Such thought became conscious through a sympathetic awakening of the separate "nerves of consciousness," which were located in the sensory ganglia. This was in essence an incidental, if not sometimes accidental, relationship. At the very least, the logic of cognition was not at all located in the functions of consciousness itself. This is why the moments of insight appeared despite conscious effort and will: "Men of inventive minds say that their happiest thoughts have often come to them involuntary, almost unconsciously, unsought, they know not how."[39] Indeed, conscious thought was even believed to interfere at times with the automatic cognition of the brain: "The rapidity and success of conception, and the reaction of one conception upon another, are much affected by the state of this active but unconscious cerebral life: the poet is compelled to wait for the moment of inspiration; and the thinker, after great but fruitless pains, must often tarry until a more favourable disposition of mind."[40] For Maudsley, insight and creativity flowed from the novelty of association within a system of nervous organization. Genius, he says, is a result of some "unconscious development" that arrives in the conscious mind like a "grateful surprise."[41] The conscious mind could even be disparaged for its uselessness for intellectual understanding. "The more I have examined the workings of my own mind, the less respect I feel for the part played by consciousness. Sudden inspirations...are the natural outcome of what is known as genius, are undoubted products of unconscious cerebration. [Consciousness] appears to be that of helpless spectator of but a minute fraction of a huge amount of automatic brain work."[42] In 1784, Thomas Huxley would describe human beings as merely "conscious automata," carried along by automatic processes (physiological and cognitive) without any interference at all from the subjective mind. For Huxley, Descartes was on the right track in his theories of the animal nervous system as an automatic information processor; he just did not go far enough and explain all the operations of human intelligence with the exact same model. At any rate, there was no functional role ascribed to the conscious mind.[43]

These theories of unconscious (and automatic) cognition can be juxtaposed with the contemporary development of automatic thinking machines. The possibility of artificial cognition had already been raised as early as the seventeenth century, when both Pascal and Leibniz independently invented their own mechanical calculators. In a way, the subsequent Age of Enlightenment could be called the Age of Automata, as engineers and philosophers (and political figures) speculated about the intricate mechanisms of life and of thought.[44] At the threshold of the nineteenth century, the infamous Chess-playing Turk automaton, which was exhibited across Europe and then America, staged a powerful illusion of mechanical intelligence. Not long after, Charles Babbage demonstrated perhaps the very first completely automatic thinking technology—namely the Difference Engine, built in the 1840s. In the late 1860s, William Jevons constructed a "logic piano," an instrument that deployed new developments in symbolic logic for automatic deductive inferences. It is therefore not surprising that an analogy would be made between the automated, mechanized processes of these deductions and the operation of unconscious, automatic cognition. Commenting on the formal operation of logic, the American pragmatist Charles S. Peirce remarked:

"Since this performance is no more than a machine might go through, it has no essential relation to the circumstance that the machine happens to work by geared wheels, while a man happens to work by an ill-understood arrangement of brain-cells."[45] Peirce himself would go on to suggest that logic could be automatically performed by electrical circuits, inspiring the design for a completely electrical version of Jevons's logic piano.[46]

The psychological theory of unconscious cerebration was adopted by scientists and mathematicians in this period as a way of understanding the critical moment of insight that led to the discovery of new ideas, and the formation of novel scientific hypotheses. The German chemist August Kekulé, for example, famously discovered the structure of the benzene molecule while dozing in front of the fire; in a "flash of lightning" the circular solution appeared to him in the image of a snake devouring its own tail.[47] Helmholtz, who had developed an influential theory of the perceptual system as a series of "unconscious inferences," explained that the "sudden inspirations and insights" (*Zufälle und Einfälle*) of understanding were always unconsciously produced, and never the result of conscious intellectual labor.[48] The great mathematician Henri Poincaré famously recounted how the solution to an intractable problem might appear rather unexpectedly in some mundane moment, while waking up in the morning, or even exiting from a bus. The implication was that the serious mathematical work leading to the solution had been performed by the unconscious mind. Poincaré would therefore ascribe high intelligence to this unconscious mind, noting, in fact, that it "is not purely automatic; it is capable of discernment; it has tact, delicacy; it knows how to choose, to divine...It knows better how to divine than the conscious self, since it succeeds where that has failed. In a word, is not the subliminal self superior to the conscious self?"[49]

These largely anecdotal narratives of sudden insight and psychological conceptualizations of unconscious thinking were eventually synthesized by Graham Wallas in his book *The Art of Thought*, published first in 1926. Wallas explained how creative thought followed four distinct stages of development. First was "preparation," that is the setting up of the problem through conscious attention. Second was "incubation," a reference to the unconscious phase of cognition. Then came "illumination," when the new idea enters into consciousness. Finally, the new insight must go through a process of "verification."[50] Wallas's model was not entirely dependent on the idea of an *automatic* unconscious. Drawing on some of the latest neurophysiological research on the capacity of the brain to overcome injury through reorganization—in particular Karl Lashley's brain ablation experiments testing the persistence of animal memory[51]—Wallas made an analogy between the nervous system and the constitution of Britain. Both, he said, had "newer structures superposed upon older," both benefitted from overlapping functions, and both had a fundamental *elasticity*.[52] The site of creative cognition was a dynamic and complex system of activity.

Wallas was here alluding to a tradition of psychological and neurological theory that emphasized the importance of plasticity as a way of explaining both the production of habitual automation in the nervous system *and* its potential disruption in creative thinking. In 1879, William James wrote the essay "Are We Automata?" as a response to Huxley's bold thesis that humans were just conscious automata, opening up a new path for psychology by focusing on the important function of consciousness and attention. This was not, however, a return to some spiritual dualism. James was interested in how the conscious mind intervened actively in those moments when the automatic systems of the experimental psychologists *failed*. Drawing on contemporary neurological theories, James located both automaticity and its interruption within the brain. The lower animals, James explained, are governed by the "determinateness" of their nervous responses, and even higher animals preserve such automatic systems. In humans, however, "the most perfected parts of the brain are those whose action are least determinate. It is this very vagueness which constitutes their advantage."[53] The "instability" of the brain makes it both sensitive and liable to produce novel reactions.[54] As the great British neurologist John Hughlings Jackson put it, "if the highest centers were already organized, there could be no new organizations," therefore, "there would be no possibility for correct adjustments in new circumstances."[55] For Hughlings Jackson, the openness of the undetermined cortex was the very space where evolution was still at work. Human creativity in cognition was made possible by the absence of automaticity in the higher brain. James himself pointed to the "extraordinary degree of plasticity" characteristic of organic tissue in his theory of psychological habit. Humans became automata in a sense, but the ground of acquired automation was in fact *plasticity*. James would invoke that openness to explain the sensitivity and adaptability of the human mind in new or uncertain environments.[56]

Insight, in early twentieth-century psychology, was the term used to mark the appearance of a new solution to a problem that had no precedent, no learned behaviors that could respond. As the Gestalt psychologist Wolfgang Köhler demonstrated in his studies of apes during World War I, insight was the sudden realization of a path to an objective, a realization that required a complete reorganization of the situation.[57] Gestalt theory would probe the conditions of "productive thinking" as a function of both conscious attention and neurophysiological organization.[58] How that reorganization took place was somewhat mysterious. However, it is important to recognize that both the brain and the mind were understood to be capable of such reorganizations, in the first half of the twentieth century. Creative intelligence was a kind of interruption of the normal conditions of thinking. The insight therefore revealed something fundamentally indefinite about the processes of cognition, whether it was considered to be conscious or not.

Intelligence in the age of the computer

When Alan Turing imagined an automatic computing machine, in a paper from 1936 on mathematical logic, it was a rather strange object. It was at the same time the most determined of automatic devices, since its whole operation was governed by strict instruction tables, and the most *plastic* and undetermined, for it had no intrinsic organization of its own.[59] The Turing machine would function only once it had been, so to speak, *programmed* with instructions. After the war, when digital computers had been built in America and England, Turing speculated on the prospect of AI in his famous essay of 1950, "Computing machinery and intelligence."[60] The idea was that because the digital computer was such an open machine, it could be programmed to imitate any other discrete-state machine, in other words, any other entity that proceeded by predictable discrete steps. The idea that such a machine could successfully imitate a living human mind implied two related assumptions, namely, that the human thinking was a rule-governed, hence deterministic, process, and that the brain (the organ of thinking) was therefore also rule-governed. And so it seems that the discipline of AI was from the start linked with neurological and psychological theories that emphasized purely mechanistic models of the mind and the brain. At the threshold of the computer age, the "mathematical imagination, the hypothesis of the scientist, the inspiration of the poet, and the intuition of the everyday man,"[61] all were ascribed to an unconscious operation of the brain. However, that brain was no mere automatic mechanism. The challenge was to understand how the brain could produce from within itself intelligent deviation that led to discovery and insight.

Turing himself was in fact very interested in the theories of brain plasticity and intelligence that were prominent in the interwar period (not to mention his interest in psychoanalysis). In some striking reflections in the late 1940s, Turing argued that using the new computers to carry out specific instructions was akin to treating the machine like a "slave." For Turing, intelligence was something more than just following rules, because that would never lead to a creative or novel act. Of course, as a scientist, Turing was hesitant to hypothesize some kind of nonmaterial mental reality. Turing argued that the instruction tables that the computer executed should only have an interim status; they ought to be able to modify themselves, as Turing put it, "if good reason arose." This would then lead to some interesting, and entirely unforeseen, new computing operations. It was the *break* with its own instructions that constituted true intelligence. As Turing commented: "It would be like a pupil who had learnt much from his master, but had added much more by his own work. When this happens I feel that one is obliged to regard the machine as showing intelligence."[62] In a long report on "Intelligent machinery" from 1948, Turing developed an original theorization of both intelligence and machinery. As an example of intelligence, he pointed to the famous anecdote about the mathematician Gauss. When told as a youth to add up a long series of numbers, Gauss quickly came up with a novel solution. Instead of patiently following the rules by adding up each number in turn, he had the insight that a more efficient formula would allow him to evade the tedious calculations. This ability to deviate from the known rules and seek new methods was particularly crucial when facing those situations where routines had failed to make any progress, or when one encountered the "undecidable." Of course, an intelligent machine needed to have regular operations for normal conditions; but at the same time, it had to have the internal flexibility to deviate from its own norms in crisis situations. As one thinker explained in 1945, the phenomenon of insight, "the sudden grasp of a solution," is recounted in numerous narratives of scientific discoveries, yet the actual nervous mechanisms involved were significantly harder to understand. Since "much brain work precedes the imaginative flash," a theory of how "new functional connections" were made in the brain was needed if we were to understand these intellectual "leaps" that were made in "times of emergency or conflict."[63]

Turing realized that the truly intelligent machine had to rely on what was *not* present in the rules. His suggestion was to take advantage of the inherent indetermination of the computer, which was, after all, the very foundation of its endlessly flexible determination. So to create an intelligent machine, Turing says, we should "start with an unorganized machine and to try to bring both discipline and initiative into it at once." Here, Turing's model was the human brain itself. It was, according to him, a relatively open machine that became determined through extensive "interference" from outside. This was what we call education. Order comes after an initial disorder. He relied here on the science of the brain. "We believe then that there are large parts of the brain, chiefly in the cortex, whose function is largely indeterminate."[64] And so, once intelligence is defined by Turing as "a departure from the completely disciplined behavior involved in computation, but a rather slight one,"[65] we can see that an initial plasticity is preserved in the educated brain, providing the ground for such "deviation" from determination. As Turing remarked: "A large remnant of the random behavior of infancy remains in the adult" and it is this that grounds the possibility of internal disruption of the nonrandom rule-governed processes.

From the very beginning, work in AI recognized that creative thinking was essential to human cognition. As the pioneer AI researcher Marvin Minsky noted in 1959, "many people are hostile to an investigation of creativity, maintaining that creativity (or intelligence) is some kind of gift which simply cannot be understood or mechanized." The influential work undertaken by the team of Allen Newell and Herbert Simon, begun in the 1950s, aimed to model the general principles of human intelligence, which they understood as the capacity to solve problems. In an early paper, they borrowed the terminology of Wallas's *Art of Thought* to focus, in particular, on the processes of incubation and illumination. Their goal was to identify the "operational specifications" for creativity, then seek to demonstrate that a program based on these specifications "would exhibit the phenomena that commonly accompany creative thinking."[66] Yet, in this and their subsequent work, Newell and Simon made no distinction between conscious and unconscious processes. Given that "a human being is able to think because…he has acquired a program that is effective for guiding thought processes," the only issue was how to specify these programs precisely.[67]

As the philosopher Hubert Dreyfus repeatedly showed, this approach to AI was bound to fail (as it eventually did), because one could never specify all the knowledge that might be relevant in any one situation, or identify all the particular operations that a mind might perform on any one occasion. Human cognition had to be understood as flexible, embodied, and intuitive, not rule-bound, Dreyfus argued. Yet, those alternative approaches to AI that did make use of flexible, teachable nerve nets, or parallel distributed systems, were never able to model the high level cognitive processes of insight and discovery; they focused more on perceptual processes (like pattern recognition)[68] or kinesthetic actions.[69]

Working outside the major schools of AI, Douglas Hofstadter drew from both the representational symbolic approaches and the distributed model, arguing that intelligent thought was largely a function of the mind's unconscious organization of concepts as a response to novel situations. As he wrote in 1995:

> Frantic striving to be original will usually get you nowhere. Far better to relax and let your perceptual system and your category system work together unconsciously, occasionally coming up with unbidden connections. At that point you—the lucky owner of the mind in question—can seize the opportunity and follow out the proffered hint. This view of creativity has the conscious mind being quite passive, content to sit back and wait for the unconscious to do its remarkable broodings and brewings.[70]

In a series of computer programs developed in the 1980s, Hofstadter and his students focused their attention on how the mind can instantly perceive meaningful patterns and manipulate them to predict the future or to resolve challenging problems. This work culminated in the Copycat program, one designed to solve analogy problems. For Hofstadter, "genuine insight" comes from "strong analogies" between experiences.[71] This particular program was an effort to pinpoint the subterranean processes that allowed the bridging of meaning from one context to another. But these were not understood to be processes along the lines of Newell's and Simon's. Drawing on the older work of Oliver Selfridge and Ulric Neisser, Hofstadter showed how individual agents, deployed stochastically on a problem, could isolate and remark on certain features or characteristics. Aggregating these many individual forays, the program would build up an interpretation of the problem that would allow it to draw on its own set of stored representations.[72]

What Hofstadter was trying to show was that both creative thinking and rule-bound habitual thinking could be modeled in the same system if, as Turing was suggesting many years before, we think of established routine and established knowledge as being susceptible to internal deviation. Hofstadter's term for this was "slippage." Concepts in our unconscious mind were related to other concepts in specific ways; however, under pressure from a challenging situation, concepts can be brought closer together and others driven further apart, so that an analogical relationship could be established. Hofstadter defined intelligent thinking as *fluid*, because the genuine insight comes when the mind makes an analogical comparison of a novel situation with stored knowledge—which inevitably involves the slippage of that knowledge into a new context, into a new form. In an echo of Turing, Hofstadter explains that "nondeliberate yet nonaccidental slippage permeates our mental processes, and is the very crux of fluid thought."[73]

We can see from this brief history of insight and automaticity that a critique of contemporary models of unconscious cognition in cognitive science rests not on the rejection of unconscious psychic activity per se—that much has been definitively proven experimentally. The issue with contemporary theories is their reliance on a simplistic technological model that too often equates unconscious with *automatic*. The insights that one experiences in moments of discovery are not simply the product of an automated set of cognitive processes inherited from our evolutionary past or learned from our culture. The *creation* of automaticity in the brain is dependent on a prior indeterminacy, a plastic brain capable of being formed in response to its environment. Genuine insight arises from the interruption of these automatisms, from slippage, from productive deviation.[74]

This story suggests a new way of thinking about the relationship between conscious and unconscious cognition. Consciousness is not merely ephemeral, and neither is it just one specialized side of an unequal division of labor in thinking.[75] Instead, we might understand consciousness as the function of interruption. As Christof Koch writes: "Why aren't we just big bundles of unconscious zombie agents? Why bother with consciousness, which takes hundreds of milliseconds to set it? [Nature has] evolved a powerful and flexible system whose primary responsibility is to deal with the unexpected...to handle those special situations for which no automatic procedures are available."[76] Consciousness itself is not really the space for creative thinking. Creative thinking is *enabled* by the disruptive, roving attention of consciousness, which triggers but also interrupts the automatic responses of the unconscious mind. Human insight may no longer be the gift of the muse, but neither is it just the automatic production of an alien unconscious. Insight flows from the radical *indetermination* of human minds and brains, their susceptibility to being formed in new ways, and this is a plasticity that can never be entirely erased.

Notes

1. Malcolm Gladwell, *Blink: The Power of Thinking without Thinking* (New York: Little Brown, 2005).
2. Margaret A. Boden, *The Creative Mind: Myths and Mechanisms*, 2nd ed. (London: Routledge, 2004).
3. Nancy C. Andreasen, "A Journey into Chaos: Creativity and the Unconscious," *Mens Sana Monographs* 9 (2011): 42–53.
4. John Kounios and Mark Beerman, "The *Aha!* Moment: The Cognitive Neuroscience of Insight," *Current Directions in Psychological Science* 18 (2009): 210–16.
5. David Eagleman, *Incognito: The Secret Lives of the Brain* (New York: Pantheon, 2011), 4.
6. James S. Uleman, "Introduction: Becoming Aware of the New Unconscious," in *The New Unconscious*, ed. Ran R. Hassin, James S. Uleman, and John A. Bargh (Oxford: Oxford University Press, 2005), 4.

7. John F. Kihlstrom, "The Cognitive Unconscious," *Science* 237 (1987): 1447.
8. Eagleman, *Incognito*, 7.
9. Douglas Hofstadter, *Fluid Concepts and Creative Analogies* (New York: Basic Books, 1995), 97.
10. John A. Bargh and Tanya L. Chartrand, "The Unbearable Automaticity of Being," *American Psychologist* 54 (1999): 462–79.
11. George Miller, *The Psychology of Communication* (New York: Basic Books, 1967); Donald Broadbent, *Perception and Communication* (New York: Pergamon, 1958); Ulric Neisser, "The Multiplicity of Thought," *British Journal of Psychology* 54 (1963): 1–14.
12. Jan W. Wojcik, *Robert Boyle and the Limits of Reason* (Cambridge: Cambridge University Press, 1997).
13. Fernando Vidal, *The Sciences of the Soul: The Early Modern Origins of Psychology*, trans. Saskia Brown (Chicago: University of Chicago Press, 2011).
14. René Descartes, letter to Mersenne, in *Oeuvres de Descartes*, ed. Charles Adam and Paul Tannery (Paris: Vrin, 1973), 1: 263.
15. Descartes, *Traité de l'homme*, in *Oeuvres*, 11: 119–202.
16. Descartes, *Meditations on First Philosophy*, in *The Philosophical Writings of Descartes*, 3 vols., tr. John Cottingham, Robert Stoothoff, and Dugald Murdoch (Cambridge: Cambridge University Press, 1984–1991) 2: 21.
17. See Eugene Marshall, *The Spiritual Automaton: Spinoza's Science of the Mind* (Oxford: Oxford University Press, 2014.)
18. Leibniz, "Théodicée," in *Oeuvres Philosophiques de Leibniz*, ed. Paul Janet (Paris: Félix Alcan, 1900), §403.
19. John Locke, *An Essay on Human Understanding*, ed. Peter Nidditch (Oxford: Oxford University Press, 1979), Book 4, Ch. 17, §4.
20. David Hume, *Treatise of Human Nature* (Oxford: Oxford University Press, 1888), 179.
21. Gilles Deleuze, preface to English translation of *Empiricisme et subjectivité: Essai sur la nature humaine selon Hume* (New York: Columbia University Press, 2001), ix–x.
22. John Locke, "Examination of Malebranche," in *The Works of John Locke*, 10 vols. (London: Johnson, Robinson, and Richardson, 1801), 9: 217.
23. Hume, *Treatise*, 60.
24. Quoted in Herbert Dieckmann, "Diderot's Conception of Genius," *Journal of the History of Ideas* 2 (1941): 159.
25. Charles Bonnet, *Essai de psychologie; ou considerations sur les operations de l'âme sur l'habitude et sur l'éducation* (Paris: Samuel Fauche, 1783), 35, 124, 131.
26. David Hartley, *Observations on Man* (London: Leake and Frederick, 1749), 501.
27. Denis Diderot, "Eléments de physiologie," in *Œuvres complètes*, ed. H. Dieckmann, Jean Fabre, and Jacques Proust (Paris: Hermann, 1975) 12: 470.
28. Pierre Maine de Biran, *Influence de l'habitude sur la faculté de penser* (Paris: Presses universitaires de France, 1954), 42, 107.
29. Samuel Taylor Coleridge, *Lectures on Literature*, 2 vols., ed. R. A. Foakes (London: Routledge & Kegan Paul, 1987), 2: 221–22.
30. Arthur Schopenhauer, "The Art of Literature," in *The Essays of Arthur Schopenahuer*, trans. T. Bailey Saunders (New York: A. L. Burt, 1902).
31. Henri F. Ellenberger, *The Discovery of the Unconscious: The History and Evolution of Dynamic Psychiatry* (New York: Basic Books, 1970).
32. Herbert Spencer, *The Principles of Psychology* (London: Longman, 1855), 495.
33. Ibid., 566.
34. Eduard von Hartmann, *Philosophie des Unbewussten* (Berlin: C. Duncker, 1869).
35. William B. Carpenter, *Principles of Mental Physiology, with Their Applications to the Training and Discipline of the Mind, and the Study of Its Morbid Conditions* (London: Henry S. King, 1874), 515.
36. L. Dumont, "Une philosophie nouvelle en Allemagne,"(1872) in *Un débat sur l'inconscient avant Freud: La réception de Eduard von Hartmann chez les psychologues et philosophes français*, ed. Serge Nicolas and Laurent Fedi (Paris: L'Harmottan, 2008), 73.
37. Laura Otis, *Networking: Communicating with Bodies and Machines in the Nineteenth Century* (Ann Arbor: University of Michigan Press, 2001).

38. Charles Mercier, *The Nervous System and the Mind: A Treatise on the Dynamics of the Human Organism* (London: Macmillan, 1888), 190, 370.

39. Joseph John Murphy, *Habit and Intelligence, in Their Connexion with the Laws of Matter and Force: A Series of Scientific Essays*, 2 vols. (London: Macmillan, 1869) 2: 47.

40. Henry Maudsley, *On the Method of the Study of Mind: An Introductory Chapter to a Physiology and Pathology of the Mind* (London: John Churchill, 1865), 19.

41. Ibid., 30.

42. Francis Galton, "Psychometric Facts," *Popular Science Monthly* 14 (1879): 779–80.

43. Thomas Huxley, "On the Hypothesis That Animals Are Automata," *Fortnightly Review*, 95 (1874): 550–80.

44. Simon Schaffer, "Enlightened Automata," in *The Sciences in Enlightened Europe*, ed. William Clark, Jan Golinski, and Simon Schaffer (Chicago: University of Chicago Press, 1999), 126–65.

45. Charles S. Peirce, *Collected Papers of Charles Sanders Peirce*, 8 vols. (Cambridge, MA: Harvard University Press, 1931–1958) vol. 2, para. 59.

46. Charles S. Peirce, letter to A. Marquand, December 30, 1886, in C. Kloesel et al., eds., *Writings of Charles S. Peirce: A Chronological Edition* (Bloomington: Indiana University Press, 1993), 5: 421–22; original letter with the circuit design, 423.

47. Arthur Rothenberg, *The Emerging Goddess: The Creative Process in Art, Science, and Other Fields* (Chicago: University of Chicago Press, 1979), 395–96.

48. Herman Helmholtz, *Vorträge und Reden*, 4th ed. (Braunschweig: Druck und Verlag von Friedrich Vieweg und Sohn, 1896), 15.

49. Henri Poincaré, "L'invention mathématique," (1908) reprinted in Jacques Hadamard, *Essai sur la psychologie de l'invention dans la domaine mathématique* (Paris: Jacques Gabay, 2007), 144.

50. Graham Wallas, *The Art of Thought* (London: Jonathan Cape, 1931), 80-ff.

51. This research is summarized in Karl Lashley, *Brain Mechanisms and Intelligence* (Chicago: University of Chicago Press, 1930).

52. Wallas, *Art*, 36–45; quote 44–45.

53. William James, "Are We Automata?," *Mind* 4 (1879): 5.

54. William James, "Great Men, Great Thoughts, and the Environment," *Atlantic Monthly* 46 (1880): 457.

55. John Hughlings Jackson, *Selected Writings of Johns Hughlings Jackson*, vol. 2: *Evolution and Dissolution of the Nervous System* (London: Hodder and Stoughton, 1932) 2: 67.

56. William James, *Principles of Psychology*, 2 vols. (New York: Holt, 1890) 1: 105.

57. Wolfgang Köhler, *Intelligenzprüfungen an Menschenenaffen* (Berlin: Springer, 1917).

58. Karl Duncker, *Zur psychologie des produktiven denkens* (Berlin: Springer, 1935); Kurt Koffka, *The Growth of the Mind: An Introduction to Child Psychology* (New York: Harcourt Brace, 1925); Max Wertheimer, *Productive Thinking* (New York: Harper, 1945).

59. Alan Turing, "On Computable Numbers, with an Application to the Entscheidungsproblem," *Proceedings of the London Mathematical Society* 42 (1937): 230–65.

60. Alan Turing, "Computing Machinery and Intelligence," *Mind* 59 (1950): 433–60.

61. Ethel Dummer, "Introduction," in Dummer, ed., *The Unconscious: A Symposium* (Freeport, NY: Books for Libraries, 1928), 2.

62. Alan Turing, "Lecture on the Automatic Computing Engine," in *The Essential Turing*, ed. B. Jack Copeland (Oxford: Oxford University Press, 2004), 393.

63. R. W. Gerard, "The Biological Basis of Imagination," *The Scientific Monthly* 62 (1946): 496.

64. Alan Turing, "Intelligent Machinery," in *The Essential Turing*, 424.

65. Turing, "Computing Machinery," 459.

66. Allen Newell, J. C. Shaw, and Herbert Simon, *The Processes of Creative Thinking* (Santa Monica, CA: Rand Corporation, 1959), 2.

67. Herbert A. Simon, "Thinking by Computers," (1966) in Simon, *Models of Discovery, Boston Studies in the Philosophy of Science*, vol. 54 (Dordrecht: D. Reidel, 1977), 283.

68. David Rumelhart and James McElland, *Parallel Distributed Processing* (Cambridge, MA: MIT Press, 1986).

69. Rodney Brooks, "Intelligence without Representation," in Brooks, ed. *Cambrian Intelligence: The Early History of the New AI* (Cambridge, MA: MIT Press, 1999).

70. Douglas Hofstadter, "Variations on a Theme as the Crux of Creativity," in *Metamagical Themas: Questing for the Essence of Mind and Pattern* (New York: Basic Books, 1996), 252–53.

71. Ibid., 253.

72. Hofstadter, *Fluid Concepts*, Preface 5 and ch. 5.

73. Ibid., 237.

74. Catherine Malabou plays on the destructive meanings of the work plasticity in *The Ontology of the Accident: An Essay on Destructive Plasticity*, trans. Carolyn Shread (New York: Fordham University Press, 2012).

75. On this model of a "division of labor," see Daniel Kahneman, *Thinking, Fast and Slow* (New York: Macmillan, 2011).

76. Christof Koch, "On the Zombie Within," *Nature* 411 (2001): 893.

11
Genius and Evil
Darrin M. McMahon

"Genius. It is a word we use—rather mechanically—to describe a type appearing amongst us to rejoice the hearts of men; yet, seen and observed however closely, it remains an inscrutable, disturbing, even a painful puzzle."[1] The words are those of Thomas Mann, or rather of his character August von Goethe, the son of Johann Wolfgang von Goethe, as depicted in Mann's 1939 novel, *Lotte in Weimar.* The work is a fictional recreation of the actual, historical visit to Weimar in September of 1816 by Charlotte Kestner, the real-life model of the heroine "Lotte" of Goethe's 1774 novel, *Die Leiden des jungen Werthers* (*The Sorrows of Young Werther*). In art as in life, Lotte was a beautiful, though apparently happily married, woman, who drew the pining affections of young Werther, as she drew the affections of Goethe in his youth. The fictional Werther killed himself in despair, whereas Goethe transformed the experience into art, catapulting himself to the celebrity of genius in the process. Contemporaries wondered and whispered what the real Kestner might have done to encourage him, until in 1816 the beloved, recently widowed, returned.

Although comparatively little is known of Kestner's actual journey or of her documented meeting with the celebrated writer, Mann conceived the visit as a reckoning and calling to account of Goethe for having used, without Kestner's consent, their private experiences for artistic purposes. It was an expropriation that irrevocably changed Kestner's life, making her a public figure and causing her a good deal of suffering and shame. By what right, Charlotte demands, did Goethe take possession of and distort her story and life? By what right did artists claim the self-arrogated license to use others as a means to the allegedly higher ends of art?

An examination of the blurry lines between fact and fiction, private and public, *Lotte in Weimar* is an extended meditation on just this question. It is also an extended meditation on the question of genius, a question that occupied Mann in a number of his works, and that is bound up with a broad European rumination on the subject carried out since the eighteenth century. To what extent might geniuses be seen as exceptions to the normal laws and limitations that regulate human affairs? To what extent are geniuses exceptions, in Kantian terms, to the categorical imperative to treat all human beings as ends in themselves? As August von Goethe puts it in a conversation with Charlotte in Mann's novel, "Certain things are permissible and justifiable...only as a means to an end," stressing that "in the life of a dominating personality...there are many things which one must place in this debatable category."[2] *Lotte in Weimar* dramatizes the uncomfortable consequences of this maxim in both moral and psychological terms. Goethe himself, whom Mann admired greatly and with whom he identified personally, is presented, as Hayden White has observed, as a "petty social tyrant and egotistical windbag, manipulative of those over whom he has power and thoughtless of those who love and admire him."[3] Lotte suffers from anxiety and a nervous tick, acquired as a consequence of her fateful encounter, and August has been damaged much more severely, suffering from alcoholism, depression, and the long-term impact of emotional neglect. All those, in fact, who have come to know Goethe well are cognizant of the fact that something dark resides amidst the inner light of his genius. As Dr. Riemer, Goethe's assistant, explains to Lotte, a being such as Goethe—a genius—contains conflicting forces and contradictory powers.

> I am no theologian, my good friend, and no philosopher. But my experience has often led me to speculate upon the relation between, yes, the unity of the All and the Nothing, nihil...It follows that it is wrong to conceive of God and the Devil as opposed principles; more correctly, the diabolic is only one side—the wrong side, if you like—of the divine. If God is All, then He is also the Devil; and one cannot approach to the godlike without at the same time approaching to the diabolic—so that in a manner of speaking, heaven looks at you out of one eye, and the hell of the iciest negation and most destructive neutrality out of the other. But whether they lie close together or far apart, it is two eyes, my dear lady, that make up the gaze. So now I ask you: what sort of gaze is that wherein the horrifying contradiction of the two ideas is united? I will tell you, tell you and myself: it is the gaze of absolute art, which is at once absolute love and absolute nihilism and indifference and implies that horrifying approach to the godlike-diabolic which we call genius.[4]

The genius as godlike creator contains the capacity for both good and evil, and looks upon the world, accordingly, through a special moral gaze—one that is *beyond* good and evil, self-legislating and creative, creative ex-nihilo.

Where might Mann have found a basis for such frightening reflections? An imaginative artist of the very highest order, he was entirely capable of inventing them himself. Yet he was also a keen analyst and observer of major trends in European intellectual life, who had at his disposal a rich reflection on the varied capacities of geniuses that had accompanied those exalted beings since their birth and consecration in the eighteenth century.[5] Although it is not my intention here to chart an intellectual biography of Thomas Mann himself (a task beyond the scope of this chapter and one, in any case, that has been well performed already), I will seek to map a number of discourses linking genius to evil and moral exception that would have been available to him in 1939. As Mann well understood, these same discourses were available to other Europeans as well, above all in his native Germany, where, to his immense regret, they were put to use as far more than simply the raw material of literary and critical reflection.

Exception, good, and evil

Perhaps the most likely immediate source behind the dark reflections of Dr. Riemer's and Mann's rendering of the moral exception of the godlike-diabolic creator is Friedrich Nietzsche, or more precisely Nietzsche's widely resonant assertion that creation is amoral, beyond good and evil, and that morality itself is the product of visionary creators who alone see what lies on the human horizon. As Nietzsche put it in his most influential work, *Thus Spoke Zarathustra* (1885):

> What is good and evil, *no one knows yet*, unless it be he who creates. He however, [the creator] creates man's goal and gives the earth its meaning and its future. That anything at all is good and evil—that is his creation.[6]

The creative man is the maker of values. Self-legislating, he subscribes to a higher law of his own, one that might well look from the standpoint of the old law like "evil" in a more conventional sense. What would be the nature of a "genius of culture," Nietzsche asks in a revealing passage of his *Human, All Too Human* (1878). "He would manipulate falsehood, force, the most ruthless self-interest as his instruments so skillfully he could only be called an evil, demonic being," even though his ultimate goals would be "great and good."[7] Men of genius, he observes elsewhere, "are like explosives," the danger in them "extraordinary."[8]

Mann had certainly read Nietzsche closely and often engaged with him in his work, and so may well have had the philosopher in mind when considering the amoral and immoral tendencies of genius, along with the specific psychological dangers to which geniuses and their followers might succumb. Nietzsche was particularly insightful on the latter point, describing not only the "religious or semi-religious superstition" that frequently attended the genius cult with its belief in superior individuals of "supra-human origin" and "miraculous abilities," but also the corruption that resulted when "the sacrificial incense that is properly rendered only to a god penetrates the brain of the genius, so that his head begins to swim, and he regards himself as supra-human."[9] The consequences of this corruption included "the feeling of irresponsibility, of exceptional rights, the belief that [the genius] confers a favour by his mere presence, insane rage when anyone attempts even to compare him with others, let alone to rate him beneath them, or to draw attention to lapses in his work."[10] Mann's Goethe notably displays many of these same foibles in *Lotte in Weimar*. Nietzsche himself illustrated them with reference to the specific case of Julius Caesar, although he may well have had in mind the example of Richard Wagner (with whose work Mann was also intimately familiar), a man with whom Nietzsche had once been close and who drew the cult of genius in nineteenth-century Germany like few others, much to Nietzsche's later regret.[11]

Whether or not Nietzsche played a precise role behind the scenes in the orchestration of *Lotte in Weimar*, Mann was almost certainly picking up as well on a set of much older discussions that had accompanied talk of genius since the eighteenth century, and that continued to resound in Mann's own time. One such discussion traced to Goethe himself, who, as a lifelong expositor of the Faust legend, was highly sensitive to the moral temptations and transgressions that threatened individuals gifted with great intelligence and imagination. As Goethe is said to have mused, "There is no crime of which I cannot imagine myself the author."[12] Indeed, Goethe's description of the strange, intangible force that he believed could be detected in eminent individuals recalls the passage cited from Dr. Riemer above. As Goethe explained in his autobiography, this force was a liminal power that resides ambiguously between the sensible and the suprasensible,

> something which manifests itself only in contradictions, and which, therefore, could not be comprehended under any idea, still less under one word. It was not godlike, for it seemed unreasonable; not human, for it had no understanding; nor devilish, for it was beneficent; nor angelic, for it often betrayed a malicious pleasure. It resembled chance, for it evolved no consequences; it was like Providence, for it hinted at connection.[13]

Even a man whose powers of description were as finely honed as Goethe's found it difficult to describe this force, and yet he had no trouble naming it. "To this principle I gave the name of Daemonic (*Dämonisch*)," Goethe writes, "after the example of the ancients."[14] The "Daemonic," Goethe observes in his *Conversations with Eckermann*, "loves to throw itself into significant individuals," who possess and are possessed by this mysterious force. Goethe speaks of the Daemonic in both modes, emphasizing its "out of body origins" and its bodily presence—as in Byron's magnetic, sexual attraction or Napoleon's physical robustness, his ability to work at great length without food or sleep. "No productiveness of the highest kind," Goethe insists, "no remarkable discovery, no great thought that bears fruits and has results, is in the power of anyone; such things are above earthly control." Genius is "like the daemon," he adds, "which does with [an individual] what it pleases." "In such cases, man may often be considered an instrument in the higher government of the world—a vessel worthy to contain a divine influence."[15]

There is much that could be said about this daemonic force. Goethe described it at some length, and subsequent commentators have as well. But what is most relevant here is Goethe's self-conscious invocation of an ancient understanding of the daemonic (*daimonic*) forces that attend human beings, the Greek *daimon* being a tutelary spirit—the root of our modern term "demon"—and a rough equivalent to the Latin notion of a *genius*, the guardian and god of birth said to have watched over all men, leading them onward or astray. A *daimon* or a *genius* might be a good *daimon* (an *eu-daimon*) or an evil *daimon* (a *kakk-daimon* or *dys-daimon*), or mischievously a bit of both. In the opinion of the Latin writer Apuleius, active in the second century, and building on Greek precedents, all men are allotted not only a good *genius* but also an evil *genius*, an opinion that later commentators, pagan and Christian, would reaffirm.[16] Greek and Latin literature is replete with celebrated examples of the interventions of such beings. Plutarch, for example, memorably records the appearance of Brutus's evil *genius* on the eve of his death at the Battle of Philippi (an appearance that Shakespeare draws on in Act Four of *Julius Caesar*).[17] And there are many other such sightings and apparitions, though none as enduring as the long discussion of the divine sign said to have accompanied Socrates, his *daimonion*, the diminutive of *daimon*, the voice, the oracle that guided his way and prevented him, according to Plato and Xenophon, from making adverse decisions. The nature of Socrates's sign was a source of a great deal of speculation in the ancient world—Plutarch, Apuleius, and Maximus of Tyre, among others, wrote dialogues on the *genius* or *daimonion* of Socrates—and that discussion long endured. Christian authors, in this respect, not unlike Socrates's Athenian accusers, frequently charged that the philosopher's sign was a "false god," a strange demonic force that "turned his mind," as Tertullian observed, "from what was good."[18] Renaissance commentators, by contrast, armed with an arsenal of neo-Platonic and Hermetic learning on the subject of attendant spirits and angelic beings, were frequently more indulgent. But the point is that speculation about *daimones* or *genii*—evil or good—did not end with the ancient world, but long endured, often in a transmuted form in the Christian discussion of guardian angels and demons. If one looks up the word "genius" in European dictionaries well into the seventeenth century, it is perfectly common to come across definitions such as that contained in Henry Cockeram's *English Dictionarie* of 1623. "Genius," the lone entry reads, "A good angell, or a familiar evill spirit, the soule." It is worth recalling that what prompted Descartes's famous skeptical sally in the 1641 Latin edition of the *Meditations on First Philosophy* is a *genius malignus* (*un mauvais génie* in the French edition of 1647), an evil demon.[19] And while it is true that the great majority of enlightened authors in the eighteenth century joined with Descartes in discounting the existence of a demon deceiver, this only heightened the question of what might have occupied the place of the now dispelled apparition. Indeed, the subject of what the *daimonion* of Socrates might have been—and Socrates, after all, was a hero to the age of Enlightenment—was of great fascination to men and women in the eighteenth century. As J. G. A. Hamann complained in 1759, while himself adding to the cascade of words, "no cultivated reader of our day lacks talented friends" who could hold forth on the subject [of Socrates's famous *daimonion*] at length.[20] Hold forth they did, asking pointedly whether Socrates's "little demon" was simply a lie to deceive his followers, an invention of his admirers, the figment of a frenzied imagination, or a sign of something else that might accompany a powerful intellect.

These were hotly debated questions in the eighteenth century, and remained so in Goethe's time. A number of figures who exerted an early influence on him, including Hamann, Johann Gottfried von Herder, and Johann Caspar Lavater, frequently drew parallels between the ancient *genii* and modern geniuses, and contemporary novels like Carl Grosse's *Der Genius* (1790–1794)—similar in this respect to Mary Shelley's *Frankenstein*—played on the links between the ancient and modern forces of the occult.

To be sure, there is no indication that Goethe believed literally in the existence of demons, whether a Socratic *daimonion* or any other kind. But he did maintain that the *dämonische* could lead one into temptation or lead one astray like the evil *genii* of old. Something of the ancient spirit world continued to hover about exalted men.

There were other modern iterations of the long-standing association to transgression or evil as well, and the man who asserted the connection most boldly was Denis Diderot, a man, as it happens, who was also deeply interested in Socrates and his *daimonion*, and who developed the connection between modern genius and evil in his famous dialogue, *Le Neveu de Rameau* (*Rameau's Nephew*). Written in the 1760s, the work was never published in Diderot's lifetime, but only appeared in print in 1806 in a German translation carried out by none other than Goethe himself.

The text is set at the Palais Royal in Paris where the narrator, a *philosophe*, goes every day to people-watch and engage in idle reverie.[21] On this particular day, he encounters the nephew of the celebrated composer Jean-Philippe Rameau. The nephew is evidently a talented man—intelligent, provocative, with a gift for mime—but at the same time he is out of sorts, dissolute, frustrated, a chronic underachiever. He functions in the text as something like the narrator's alter ego, and the two—*lui* and the first-person *moi*—engage in speculation on a variety of subjects, the first of which is the subject of genius and the man of genius, and more specifically, that figure's apparent propensity for evil. "If I knew history," *lui* declares, "I would show you that evil always arrives on earth by means of some man of genius." "Men of genius are detestable," he adds, they are "bad citizens, bad fathers, mothers, brothers, parents, friends." And though Rameau acknowledges that it is men of genius who change the face of the globe ("ce sont eux qui changent la face du globe"), he would still be inclined to rid the world of their presence. If a child bore from birth the sign of this dangerous "gift of nature," Rameau reflects, "it would be advisable to smother him in bed, or to throw him to the dogs." Yet Rameau's own position is complicated by the fact that, despite his misgivings, he himself would like to be a genius, someone out of the ordinary, an original. "I admit it, I am jealous," he confesses, unable to stand what he describes as his own "mediocrity." Later, he points out chillingly, in the context of a discussion of great men, "that if it is important to be sublime in anything, it is above all the case with evil. One spits on a petty thief, but it is impossible to refuse a certain consideration to a great criminal." The *philosophe*, for his part, observes initially, in a typical Enlightenment refrain, that a "fool is more often an evil person than a man of intelligence," adding that those ages that have produced no geniuses are held in low esteem, and that often a genius who decries a general error or discovers a general truth is despised in his lifetime only to be appreciated later. Socrates is the consummate example. But even those who conducted themselves less virtuously than Socrates might be forgiven their shortcomings. The *philosophe* offers the example of the great dramatist Racine. Would *lui* prefer that Racine had been a good husband, a good father, a good uncle, neighbor, and businessman, but nothing more? Or rather that he was what he was—deceitful, treacherous, ambitious, envious, and nasty—yet the author of great works? Racine was like a tall tree who has caused other trees planted near him to wither and die, choking off their sunlight and nutrients. But he himself shot up high into the sky. The two continue in their banter like this for some time. And yet what becomes clear in the course of their conversation is that, despite different emphases, Rameau and the philosopher essentially agree about the nature of genius. As one critic rightly observes, "MOI and LUI see eye to eye on the concept of genius as a monstrous form of human species, differing in kind from the normal, and thus an anomaly and a deviant in its time."[22] Elsewhere, Diderot himself actually describes geniuses in this way, observing in his *Éleménts de physiologie* that they are "kinds of monsters."[23]

This hints at another form of explanation for the genius's alleged propensity to evil—a medical or biological one. Diderot himself did not develop this line of inquiry at any length, offering instead in *Rameau's Nephew* what was in effect a sociological explanation to account for the genius's apparent monstrosity and deviance. This explanation played on the genius's novelty and originality vis à vis the great mass of humanity, the majority of whom, as Diderot put it in his article "originality" in the *Encyclopedia*, were merely copies of copies. "La plupart des hommes ne sont en tous genres que des copies les uns des autres."[24] To be an original, by contrast, was exceedingly rare, and originality was already emerging as an essential property of genius in a new aesthetics that downplayed the importance of mimesis, the imitation of nature or established models or forms. As Kant put it in the *Critique of Judgment*, summarizing a century's aesthetic reflection on the subject, "everyone agrees that genius must be considered the very opposite of a spirit of imitation." From which it followed, naturally enough, that "originality must be its foremost property."[25] Geniuses provided the forms to be imitated by others. And given that, in Diderot's reckoning, imitation or mimesis was the living creed of most human beings, who tended simply to replicate the extant patterns laid out for them, it followed that the presence of a genius set up a necessary tension between the unique individual and the many who are the same. An original man like Socrates could be regarded as a hero by some, but it was not at all surprising that many others regarded him as a monster who was a threat to the society in which he lived.

Diderot thus offered a sociological account to explain the potential for conflict between the individual of genius and society. Yet his brief allusion to "monsters"—freaks or aberrations of nature—hinted at another explanation that would prove tremendously influential in the nineteenth century, the medical or physiological account associated with so-called "degeneration theory." And here there is a connection to Socrates as well, for one of the important early medical theorists of the theory of degeneration (*dégénéréscence*), the French clinician and psychologist Louis-Francisque Lélut, took up in the nineteenth century the question that had been posed repeatedly in the eighteenth: Just what, in the end, was the *daimonion* of Socrates? Lélut came to the conclusion in his *Du Démon de Socrates* (1836) that Socrates suffered from a form of aural hallucination induced by mental illness. His *"daimon"* or *"genius"* was simply the specter of a morbid imagination; the inner promptings of his "celestial voice" were voices in his head.[26]

Lélut's work was an early "pathography"—an account of the medical afflictions of geniuses and other eminent individuals—that would flourish as an independent genre in the nineteenth and early twentieth centuries. But it was also an early statement of the thesis that psychological illness or pathology might lead to what Jacques-Joseph Moreau described in his *La Psychologie morbide* (1859) as *"pathogénie,"* pathological genius that was understood as a kind of redeeming side effect of degenerative illness or madness. Socrates's demon—in other words, the source of his inspiration and genius—was his illness, for genius itself was what Moreau described as a "semi-morbid state of the brain."[27]

This language of degeneration, which had great resonance on the Continent beginning in the second half of the nineteenth century, provided a pseudoscientific packaging for a much older belief in the link between madness and human eminence. That belief had a long Platonic lineage in the idea of the *furor poeticus* or the *furor divinus*, the divine frenzy or madness that Plato had suggested overtook poets and prophets in the enthusiastic grip of inspiration. It also had a venerable Aristotelian or Pseudo-Aristotelian connection grounded in a theory of the humors, which posited a necessary link between mental prowess and the superabundance of black bile, the cause of melancholy and other nervous afflictions. Both the Platonic and Pseudo-Aristotelian accounts were reinvigorated in the Renaissance, and the long-standing link between illness and inspiration was reaffirmed in the early nineteenth century by the Romantics, who dramatized an alleged connection between creativity and madness. But it was the medical literature of degeneration that seemed to give that connection an apparent scientific legitimacy, while further positing a link between genius and aberration, evil, and crime ("moral insanity"). The physician Cesare Lombroso, for example, who was a criminologist as well as an important theorist of genius, made much of the connection to crime, observing in his 1889 *L'Uomo di genio*, a work that was quickly translated into a great many languages, including English as *The Man of Genius* in 1891, that "Everything is permitted to genius." Geniuses acted according to a "special morality," he claimed, at least if one were to judge by their demonstrated actions in the past.[28] The British criminologist H. T. F. Rhodes summarized this line of thought in his fittingly entitled study *Genius and Criminal: A Study in Rebellion* (1932), in which he argued that "it is the aim of the genius, to overthrow society and rebuild it upon lines that would bring it into harmony with *him*," citing Lenin and Napoleon as examples.[29] The wider Romantic contention that genius necessarily involved flouting or breaking established rules, laws or conventions—destroying in order to create anew—fed into this received notion. As Coleridge observed famously in the *Biographia Literaria*, in "times of tumult" men of "commanding genius" (the allusion is to Napoleon) are "destined to come forth as the shaping spirit of ruin, to destroy the wisdom of ages in order to substitute the fancies of a day, and to change kings and kingdoms."[30]

Thomas Mann was well familiar with this line of thinking—both with the Romantic exultation of rule-breaking and transgression, and with the medical literature of degeneration and pathological genius, which could claim important proponents in Germany, such Max Nordau and Wilhelm Lange-Eichbaum. The hero of Mann's great novel *Dr. Faustus*, Adrian Leverkühn, in fact sells his soul to the devil in exchange for creative musical genius, which he receives via a case of syphilis that degenerates and gives him, as a consequence, extraordinary creative powers. Leverkühn's genius is at once a special strain of illness, a form of madness, and a type of daemonic inspiration or possession.

Although by no means exhaustive, these are some of the principal ways in which the connections between genius and evil, immorality and amorality, were seized upon and articulated since the eighteenth century. They became particularly relevant in the modern period in the first half of the twentieth century in the context of what the Austrian scholar Edgar Zilsel called, in his 1918 book of the name, *Die Geniereligion*, the "religion of genius."[31] This was the widespread, and in Zilsel's view, deeply disturbing, cult of genius practiced across Europe, but particularly zealous in Austria and Germany, where, as early as the 1830s, David Friedrich Strauss was warning that it was the "only cult which is left over from the religious debris of the preceding cults for the educated of our time."[32] Kierkegaard, in the 1840s, wrote an essay, "On the Difference between the Genius and an Apostle," in which he attempted to stress that there *is* a difference between the genius and the apostle—a distinction that, in Kierkegaard's view, had been lost on too many of his contemporaries, who were all too ready to conflate the religious and secular types.[33] By the time Zilsel was writing in the early twentieth century, the distinction had been practically effaced. As the German psychiatrist and degeneration theorist Wilhelm Lange-Eichbaum explained in his 1931 *Das Genie-Problem* (The Problem of Genius), "Among modern civilized beings a reverence for genius has become a substitute for the lost dogmatic religions of the past."[34] It was that reverence, above all, as Lange-Eichbaum took pains to emphasize, that endowed the genius with dangerous force. Genius, he realized, was a social creation, mass adulation was the source of its power, and that was enough on its own—whatever genius's putative tendency to madness or evil—to make of it a combustible force in the hands of those who could claim, use, manipulate, or abuse it. As Zilsel and others feared, that is precisely what one former

Viennese art student and Munich bohemian did in the 1920s and 1930s. He laid claim to genius and proved tremendously successful in convincing others that genius is what moved him, so that they might be moved to grant him extraordinary privileges and power.

The way in which Adolf Hitler tapped into and made use of a discourse of genius to legitimate and further his rule is a subject in its own right, a subject that has been surprisingly overlooked.[35] But it is not at all surprising that perceptive analysts of genius such as Thomas Mann should have understood this at the time. In the very same year that he published *Lotte in Weimar*, Mann published an extraordinary essay in exile that lay bare the connection between Hitler and the genius cult. The essay is entitled *Bruder Hitler* in German, or "That Man Is My Brother" in the English translation that appeared simultaneously in *Esquire* magazine in March of 1939, with a subheading that reads, "And if genius is madness tempered with discretion, this sly sadist and plotter of revenge is a genius." What makes the essay extraordinary is that Mann acknowledged Hitler as what he called an "artist-phenomenon" and hence a brother of sorts, a relation, kin, an evil genius formed of a common (albeit degenerate) stock. There is now a considerable literature that understands Hitler's politics as a kind of "art by other means," and that seeks to draw links between his bohemian past and his political future.[36] But until relatively recently, that was a fairly controversial position. Yet Mann adopted it without flinching. "Our notion of genius," he writes, "has always been shrouded in a superstitious haze," but that haze is not thick enough today to obscure certain "painful truths," foremost of which was the realization that in Hitler one must confront debased genius and the debasement of the cult of genius in the extreme. "For today it is our fate to encounter genius in this one particular phase of all the phases possible to it."[37] Evil genius. Mann called it "distorted genius," genius that flaunted all standards of humanity, equality, and right. And yet by his own analysis—to say nothing of the far less critical view of many of his German contemporaries—there was something in the very thing genius that turned it in that direction. In his novel *Michael*, first published in the 1920s, Joseph Goebbels observed, "The people are for the statesman what stone is for the sculptor." He added shortly thereafter that *Genies verbrauchen Menschen. Das ist nun einmal so.* "Geniuses use up people, that is just the way it is."[38] The genius in the act of creation was beyond good and evil. Or as Adolf Hitler put it himself in *Mein Kampf*: "Geniuses of an extraordinary kind do not admit consideration of normal humanity."[39]

Notes

1. Thomas Mann, *The Beloved Returns: Lotte in Weimar*, trans. H. T. Lowe-Porter (New York: Alfred A. Knopf, 1940), 68. All subsequent citations from the text refer to this edition.
2. Ibid., 254.
3. Hayden White, "Introduction," *Lotte in Weimar: The Beloved Returns*, intro. Hayden White (Berkeley and Los Angeles: University of California Press, 1990), ix.
4. Mann, *Lotte in Weimar*, 82.

5. On the "birth" of genius in the eighteenth century, see my *Divine Fury: A History of Genius* (New York: Basic Books, 2013).

6. Friedrich Nietzsche, "On Old and New Tablets," paragraph 2, in *Thus Spoke Zarathustra*, trans. and intro. Walter Kauffman (New York: Penguin, 1978), 196.

7. Nietzsche, *Human, All Too Human: A Book for Free Spirits*, trans. R. J. Hollingdale; intro. Richard Schacht (Cambridge: Cambridge University Press, 1996), 115 (section 241).

8. Friedrich Nietzsche, "The Twilight of the Idols," in *The Portable Nietzsche*, ed. and trans. Walter Kaufmann (New York: Penguin, 1982), 547 (section 44).

9. Nietzsche, *Human, All Too Human*, 87–88 (section 164, "Peril and Prophet in the Cult of Genius"). See, as well, section 162 ("Cult of the Genius out of Vanity"), where Nietzsche very shrewdly describes how people's own high opinion of themselves "promotes the cult of the genius: for only if we think of him as being very remote from us, as a *miraculum*, does he not aggrieve us." (86).

10. Ibid., 88.

11. See Michael Tanner, "Nietzsche on Genius," in *Genius: The History of an Idea*, ed. Penelope Murray (London: Basil Blackwell, 1989), 128–40.

12. The citation from Goethe is often attributed to him, both in English and in German, including by reputable sources, but I have been unable to find its origin and suspect that it may be apocryphal.

13. Johann Wolfgang von Goethe, *The Autobiography of Goethe: Truth and Poetry from My Own Life*, 2 vols., trans. John Oxenford (London: George Bell, 1897–1900) 2: 157.

14. Ibid.

15. J. W. Goethe, *Conversations with Eckermann* (1823–1832), trans. John Oxenford (San Francisco: North Point Press, 1984), 199–205 (March 11, 1828). On Byron's attraction to women, see also the conversation of March 8, 1831.

16. See, for example, Apuleius, *On the God of Socrates* (*De Deo Socratis*), in Apuleius, *Rhetorical Works*, trans. Stephen Harrison, John Hilton, and Vincent Hunink, ed. Stephen Harrison (Oxford: Oxford University Press, 2001). On pagan demonology more generally in connection to the question of genius, see my *Divine Fury*, esp. ch. 1.

17. See Plutarch, "Marcus Brutus," in the Dryden translation of *Plutarch's Lives*, 2 vols., ed. Arthur Hugh Clough (New York: Modern Library, 2001) 2: 596–97.

18. For Tertullian's account of Socrates's "demon," and that of other early Christians, see my *Divine Fury*, 39–40.

19. See for example, the text of the 1641 Latin edition at http://www.thelatinlibrary.com/descartes/des.med1.shtml. Descartes invokes the *genius malignus* in Meditatio 1, paragraph 12.

20. J. G. A. Hamann, *Socratic Memorabilia*, trans. James C. O'Flaherty (Baltimore, MD: Johns Hopkins Press, 1967), 170–71.

21. All the following citations from *Rameau's Nephew* are taken from Denis Diderot, *Le neveu de Rameau*, ed. and intro. Jean-Claude Bonnet (Paris: Flammarion, 1983), 49–50, 101.

22. Otis Fellows, "The Theme of Genius in Diderot's *Neveu de Rameau*," *Diderot Studies* 2 (1952): 168–99 (citation on p. 189). See, as well, James Mall, "*Le Neveu de Rameau* and the Idea of Genius," *Eighteenth-Century Studies* 11 (1977): 26–39.

23. Diderot speaks of geniuses as monsters in his *Éléments de physiologie*, ed. J. Mayer (Paris: M. Didier, 1964), 296. He also refers to "le monstre appelé homme de génie" in his *Réfutation de l'ouvrage de Helvétius intitulé L'Homme* in *Oeuvres complètes*.

24. Denis Diderot, "Originalité," *Encyclopédie, ou Dictionnaire raisonné des sciences, des arts et des métiers*, accessed January 19, 2015, http://xn--encyclopdie-ibb.eu/index.php/logique/929124137-grammaire/1104404245-ORIGINALIT%C3%89.

25. Immanuel Kant, *Critique of Judgment*, intro. and trans. Werner S. Pluhar (Indianapolis: Hackett, 1987), 175–76.

26. L. F. Lélut, *Du démon de Socrates, spécimen d'une application de la science psychologique à celle de l'histoire* (Paris: Trinquart, 1836). On Lélut more generally, see my *Divine Fury*, 162–63.

27. Jacques-Joseph Moreau, *La psychologie morbide dans ses rapports avec la philosophie de l'histoire, ou De l'influence des névropathies sur le dynamisme intellectuel* (Paris: Victor Masson, 1859), 463.

28. Cesare Lombroso, *The Man of Genius*, rev. ed. (London: Walter Scott, 1917), 334.

29. Henry T. F. Rhodes, *Genius and Criminal: A Study in Rebellion* (London: John Murray, 1932), 59–61.

30. Samuel Taylor Coleridge, *Biographia Literaria, or Biographical Sketches of my Literary Life and Opinions*, ed. James Engell and W. Jackson Bates (Princeton, NJ: Princeton University Press, 1983), 32–33.

31. Edgar Zilsel, *Die Geniereligion: Ein kritischer Versuch über das moderne Persönlichkeitsideal*, intro. Johann Dvorak (Frankfurt: Suhrkamp, 1990 [1918]). On Zilsel and the "religion of genius," more generally, see McMahon, *Divine Fury*, ch. 6, as well as Julia Barbara Köhne, *Geniekult in Geisteswissenschaften und Literaturen um 1900 und seine filmischen Adaptionen* (Wien: Böhlau Verlag, 2014), esp. Part A.

32. David Friedrich Strauss, "Über Vergängliches und Bleibendes im Christentum" (1838), in *Zwei friedliche Blätter* (Altona, Germany: J. F. Hammerich, 1839), 101.

33. Søren Kierkegaard, *The Present Age and of the Difference between a Genius and an Apostle*, trans. Alexander Dru; intro. Walter Kaufmann (New York: Harper and Row, 1962), 89–90. "Of the Difference between a Genius and an Apostle" was written in 1847. It was first published in 1849, along with "The Present Age," in *Two Minor Ethical-Religious Essays*, under the pseudonym "H. H."

34. Wilhelm Lange-Eichbaum, *The Problem of Genius*, trans. Eden and Cedar Paul (New York: Macmillan, 1932), xvii.

35. I treat this subject at length in *Divine Fury*, 208–21.

36. The play on Clausewitz's famous observation that politics is "war by other means" is that of Hans Rudolf Vaget, whose article "Wagnerian Self-Fashioning: The Case of Adolf Hitler," *New German Critique* 101 (2007): 95–114, is itself an important contribution to the new literature recognizing the importance of aesthetic concerns to Hitler and the Nazis. In addition, see Richard A. Etlin, ed., *Art, Culture, and Media under the Third Reich* (Chicago: University of Chicago Press, 2002); Eric Michaud, *The Cult of Art in Nazi Germany*, trans. Janet Lloyd (Palo Alto, CA: Stanford University Press, 2004); Jonathan Petrapoulos, *Art as Politics in the Third Reich* (Chapel Hill: University of North Carolina Press, 1996); Frederick Spotts, *Hitler and the Power of Aesthetics* (New York: Overlook, 2003); Birgit Schwarz, *Geniewahn: Hitler und die Kunst* (Vienna: Bohlau, 2009); Otto W. Werckmeister, "Hitler the Artist," *Critical Inquiry* 23 (1997): 270–97. For all its richness, this body of work pays surprisingly little attention to the subject of genius.

37. Thomas Mann, "That Man Is My Brother," *Esquire* (March 1939): 31, 132–33.

38. Goebbels cited in Jochen Schmidt, *Die Geschichte des Genie-Gedankens in der deutschen Literatur, Philosophie und Politk 1750–1945*, 2 vols. (Heidelberg: Universitätsverlag, 2004) 2: 207.

39. Adolf Hitler, *Mein Kampf*, trans. Alvin Johnson; ed. John Chamberlain et al. (New York: Reynal and Hitchock, 1941), 669.

Contributors

David Bates is Professor and Chair of the Department of Rhetoric at the University of California, Berkeley, where he teaches Modern Intellectual History. The author of two books on Enlightenment thought, he is now completing a new work, *Thinking Technologies: An Artificial History of Natural Intelligence*, which traces the relations between technology, neurology, and cognition from Descartes to the Digital Epoch.

Janet Browne is Aramont Professor of the History of Science and chair of the Department of History of Science at Harvard University where she teaches history of biology. She was formerly an associate editor of the online Correspondence of Charles Darwin and taught at the Wellcome Institute for the History of Medicine at University College, London. She is the author of a two-volume biography on Charles Darwin.

John Carson is Associate Professor of History at the University of Michigan, where his research focuses on the history of the human sciences. In 2007, he published *The Measure of Merit: Talents, Intelligence, and Inequality in the French and American Republics, 1750–1940*, winner of the 2010 Cheiron Book Prize. Other publications include "Differentiating a Republican Citizenry: Talents, Human Science, and Enlightenment Theories of Governance" (2002).

Joyce E. Chaplin is the James Duncan Phillips Professor of Early American History and chair of American Studies at Harvard University. She is the editor of *Benjamin Franklin's Autobiography: A Norton Critical Edition* (2012) and author, most recently (with Alison Bashford), of *The New Worlds of Thomas Robert Malthus: Rereading the Principle of Population* (Princeton, 2016).

Lennard J. Davis is Distinguished Professor of Liberal Arts and Sciences at the University of Illinois at Chicago. He has written on the history and theory of the novel, as well as disability and biopolitics. He received a Guggenheim Fellowship for his book *Obsession: A History*. His most recent book, *Enabling Acts: The Hidden Story of How the Americans with Disabilities Act Gave the Largest US Minority Its Rights,* was published in July 2015.

Lucy Delap is a lecturer in Modern British History at the University of Cambridge, and fellow of Murray Edwards College. She works on the history of feminism, child sexual abuse, gender, labor and religion, and is currently working on men's encounters with women's liberation in the 1970s and 1980s. She published the prize-winning *The Feminist Avant-Garde: Transatlantic Encounters of the Early Twentieth Century* in 2007, and *Knowing Their Place: Domestic Service in Twentieth Century Britain* in 2011. She directed History & Policy between 2012 and 2015.

Nathalie Heinich, a sociologist, is a research director at the French National Center for Scientific Research (CNRS); she works within the Ecole des Hautes Etudes en Sciences Sociales (EHESS). Her publications have covered topics on the status of the artist and the notion of the author, the question of identity, and the history of sociology. She is the author, most recently, of *Le Paradigme de l'art contemporain* (Gallimard, 2014).

Julia Barbara Köhne is research associate at Humboldt University Berlin and senior lecturer ("Privatdozentin") at the University of Vienna. She is the author of *Geniekult in Geisteswissenschaften und Literaturen um 1900 und seine filmischen Adaptionen* (Vienna, 2014), *Kriegshysteriker: Strategische Bilder und mediale Techniken militärpsychiatrischen Wissens, 1914–1920* (Husum, 2009), and has edited, with Michael Elm and Kobi Kabalek, *The Horrors of Trauma in Cinema. Violence, Void, Visualization* (Cambridge Scholars Publishing, 2014).

Darrin M. McMahon is the Mary Brinsmead Wheelock professor of history at Dartmouth College and the author, most recently, of *Divine Fury: A History of Genius* (Basic Books, 2013), and editor, with Samuel Moyn, of *Rethinking Modern European Intellectual History* (Oxford, 2014).

Irina Sirotkina is a research fellow at the Institute for the History of Science and Technology, Russian Academy of Science (Moscow). A scholar of the human sciences, she is the author of *Diagnosing Literary Genius: A Cultural History of Psychiatry in Russia, 1880–1930* (2002) and has edited, with Jean-Gaël Barbara and Jean-Claude Dupont, *History of the Neurosciences in France and Russia: From Charcot and Sechenov to IBRO* (2011).

Index